Routledge Revivals

GREENE'S TU QUOQUE
OR,
THE CITTIE GALLANT

GREENE'S TU QUOQUE OR, THE CITTIE GALLANT

by J. Cooke

A critical edition
edited by
Alan J. Berman

The Renaissance Imagination
Volume 8

First published in 1984 by Garland Publishing, Inc.

This edition first published in 2018 by Routledge
2 Park Square, Milton Park, Abingdon, Oxon, OX14 4RN
and by Routledge
52 Vanderbilt Avenue, New York, NY 10017, USA

Routledge is an imprint of the Taylor & Francis Group, an informa business

© 1984 by Alan J. Berman

All rights reserved. No part of this book may be reprinted or reproduced or utilised in any form or by any electronic, mechanical, or other means, now known or hereafter invented, including photocopying and recording, or in any information storage or retrieval system, without permission in writing from the publishers.

Publisher's Note
The publisher has gone to great lengths to ensure the quality of this reprint but points out that some imperfections in the original copies may be apparent.

Disclaimer
The publisher has made every effort to trace copyright holders and welcomes correspondence from those they have been unable to contact.
A Library of Congress record exists under ISBN:

ISBN 13: 978-0-367-18250-2 (hbk)
ISBN 13: 978-0-367-18252-6 (pbk)
ISBN 13: 978-0-429-06032-8 (ebk)

The Renaissance Imagination
Important Literary and Theatrical Texts
from the Late Middle Ages
through the Seventeenth Century

Stephen Orgel
Editor

Greenes Tu quoque,
OR,
The Cittie Gallant.

As it hath beene diuers *nes acted by the Queenes Maiesties Seruants.*

Written by Io. COOKE Gent.

Reproduced by permission of The Houghton Library, Harvard University.

GREENE'S TU QUOQUE
OR,
THE CITTIE GALLANT

by J. Cooke

A critical edition
edited by
Alan J. Berman

The Renaissance Imagination
Volume 8

GARLAND PUBLISHING, INC.
NEW YORK & LONDON
1984

Copyright © 1984 by Alan J. Berman
All rights reserved

Library of Congress Cataloging in Publication Data

Cooke, Jo., fl. 1614–
Greene's Tu quoque.

(The Renaissance imagination ; v. 8)
Based on the 1614 quarto, this ed. is a revision of the editor's thesis (Ph.D.)—
Harvard University.
Bibliography: p.
I. Berman, Alan J. II. Title.
III. Title: Tu quoque. IV. Series.
PR2459.C6G7 1984   822'.3   83-49400
ISBN 0-8240-5456-3

Printed on acid-free, 250-year-life paper
Manufactured in the United States of America

CONTENTS

Introduction and Notes	vii
Critical Text	1
Press-Variants	107
Historical Collation	111
Critical Notes	123
Appendix	161
Bibliography	165

ACKNOWLEDGMENTS

This edition was first prepared as a doctoral dissertation, and I am deeply grateful for the generosity and patient counsel of my dissertation advisors: Professor G. Blakemore Evans, Cabot Professor of English Literature and Director of Graduate Studies Emeritus, Harvard University, and Dr. William Bond, Director of the Houghton Library. Dr. Katharine F. Pantzer of the Houghton Library graciously shared with me her observations on *Greene's Tu Quoque* that are included in her revision of Vol. I of Pollard and Redgrave's *Short-Title Catalogue*. Professor Stephen Orgel of The Johns Hopkins University helped me substantially with revising this edition for The Renaissance Imagination series. I appreciate the consistent professionalism and collegiality of Nina Kensharper of LaGuardia Community College of the City University of New York, the typist for this revised edition. Finally, I am indebted to the following libraries for providing reproductions of materials used in this edition: the Bodleian; the British Museum; the Henry E. Huntington Library; the Houghton Library, Harvard University; the Folger Shakespeare Library; and the Pierpont Morgan Library.

Alan J. Berman
Department of English
LaGuardia Community College,
City University of New York

A Critical Edition of

Greene's Tu Quoque, or The City Gallant

by Jo[hn] Cooke

INTRODUCTION

I

DATE AND AUTHORSHIP

The first recorded mention of *Greene's Tu Quoque* is an entry in the Revels Accounts which notes that "A Play called the City Gallant" was presented at Court on 9 and 19 November 1611 by the Queen's Players (i.e. Queen Anne's Men).[1] Subsequent entries in the Chamber and Revels Accounts indicate that Thomas Greene--the actor whose name ultimately became part of the title of the play when it was first published in 1614--received 20 pounds for the "Queene's players" for a play called "Tu Coque", which was again performed at Court on 27 December 1611 and on 2 February 1612.[2]

Further evidence for giving the *terminus a quo* of the play as 1611 is provided by a probable literary allusion in the text itself. Scene XVI, in which Staines disguises himself as an Italian gallant in order to gull Bubble and Scattergood, contains a passage that apparently satirizes *Coryate's Crudities*, published in two volumes in 1611:

> *Sta.* I am sir, a perfect Traveller, that have trampled over the face of this uneverss, and can speake *Greeke* and *Latine* as promptly as my owne naturall Language: I have composd a Booke, wherein I have set downe all the Wonders of the world that I have seene, and the whole scope of my Jornies, togeather with the miseries and lowsie fortunes I have endured therein.
> (XVI, 2204-10)[3]

Topical allusion in the text provides a basis for inferring the *terminus ad quem* of the play's composition as well. In Scene XII, several of the characters discuss going to see a play:

> *Scatt.* Yes fayth Brother: if it please you, let's goe see a Play at the Gloabe.
>
> *Bub.* I care not; any whither, so the Clowne have a part: For Ifayth I am no body without a Foole.

Ger. Why then wee'le goe to the Red Bull; they say *Green's* a good Clowne.

Bub. Greene? *Greene's* an Asse.

Scatt. Wherefore doe you say so?

Bub. Indeed I ha no reason: for they say, hee is as like mee as ever hee can looke. (XII, 1567-76)

The lines in the above passage that follow the reference to the Globe give solid evidence that *Tu Quoque* was performed at the Red Bull before August, 1612. As Thomas Greene was his company's clown and played the part of Bubble, the lines would have constituted a diverting *tour de force* for the audience.[4] In addition, it is apparent from the woodcut on the title page, representing Greene in the part of Bubble saying "Tu quoque, To you Sir", and from the final couplet of the text, spoken by Bubble (XIX, 2934-5), that the play was identified in the public mind with Greene's performance in this role. Thomas Greene died in 1612, a church register recording his burial on August 7 of that year.[5]

Finally, in his foreword to the text, Thomas Heywood indicates that both Greene and the author of the play were deceased by the time Q1 was published in 1614, and that he did not know whether or not the author had approved the publication (sig. A2, ll. 1-2, 7-8). There is reasonably strong evidence, then, for fixing the composition of the text on which Q1 is based at 1611-12. Although it is not certain whether the text of Q1 represents the earliest performances at Court in 1611, or was prepared from a later authorial MS intended for the stage production at the Red Bull, the discussion of the text will show that Q1 was almost certainly not printed from prompt-copy.

As for the author of the play, however, we cannot even be certain of his first name, and except for the title pages of the 1614, 1622, and undated editions of *Tu Quoque* (which give the author as IO. COOKE, IOHN COOKE, and JO. COOKE respectively), and the fact that in his foreword to the text, Heywood calls the author of *Tu Quoque* his "worthy friend" (sig. A2, ll. 1-2), there is no more known of this man, although there has been speculation that other works may have been written by him. E.K. Chambers notes that "I. Cooke" wrote commendatory verses to Drayton's *Legend of Cromwell* (1607), that "I. Cocke" contributed to Stephens' *Characters*, published in 1615, and that an entry in the Stationers' Register for 22 May 1604 mentions a book called "Fyftie epigrams written by J. Cooke Gent."[6] Chambers describes this work as lost, but it is still extant.[7] Although its title page gives the author only as "I.C. Gent.", the last epigram, which puns on the author's name, suggests that his name is "Cooke."[8] Since these *Epigrames* contain thumbnail "characters" of such types as gallants and spendthrift gamesters, it is certainly possible that the author of *Tu Quoque*--which contains characters like Bubble, Scattergood and Spendall--could have written them.

A much more doubtful attribution appears on the title page of the British Museum copy of the play *How a Man May Chuse a Good Wife from a Bad* (pub. 1602). This copy, which once belonged to David Garrick, has "Written By Ioshua Cooke" printed in ink on its title page, though there is no way of knowing when this inscription in pen was made, nor do there seem to be any other references to a "Ioshua Cooke."[9] A.E.H. Swaen, who edited this play, argues plausibly for Heywood's authorship,[10] as do Chambers, Fleay, and Adams.[11]

A bit more confusion is added by Dodsley, who, on the title page of his edition of *Tu Quoque*, ascribes the work to "Joseph COOKE."[12] This is easily explained, as Dodsley writes that the play was "printed originally without Date",[13] which means that Dodsley's copy-text was the Third Quarto (Q3), the only one of the three seventeenth-century quartos of the play that is undated. The title page of Q3 gives the author as "JO. COOKE", so that "Joseph" is obviously Dodsley's inferential lengthening of the abbreviated first name.

Dodsley was clearly unaware, then, of the Second Quarto (Q2), the title page of which gives the author as "IOHN COOKE." Q2 was published in 1622, only eight years after the printing of the first edition, and at least one man who knew the author, Thomas Heywood, was still alive. As Heywood's dedication indicates that the author was dead by 1614, one final piece of information may tell something about him. In his will, dated 3 January 1614, the actor Alexander Cooke speaks of a brother John, presumably as dead.[14] W.W. Greg reasonably speculates that this John Cooke may have been the author of *Greene's Tu Quoque*.[15]

II

COMPANY, PLAYHOUSE, AND STAGE HISTORY

Queen Anne's Men was formed late in 1603 or early in 1604 from the Earl of Worcester's Men.[16] Thomas Greene was apparently a member of the company at its formation, since his name appears in the undated draft license.[17] He was the leader and principal clown of the company until his death in 1612.[18] Thomas Heywood, formerly an actor and sharer in Worcester's Men,[19] became the most prolific and important playwright for the new company,[20] and William Rowley, who is conjectured to have written the memorial couplet on Thomas Greene, appearing just before Scene I of *Tu Quoque*,[21] also contributed to the company's repertoire.[22] When Thomas Greene died in 1612, Christopher Beeston became the leader of the company.[23] On the death of Queen Anne in 1619, the company lost its title,[24] and Robert Lee, who had been with Queen Anne's Men since 1604, succeeded as leader of the company, which then became known as the Red Bull Players or the Children of the

Revels until the company disbanded in 1623.[25]

In 1605, the Red Bull Theatre was built in St. James, Clerkenwell and served as the company's principal playhouse until 1617.[26] They also played at the Curtain and the Boar's Head between 1603 and 1606, at the Cockpit between 1617-19, and intermittently at the Red Bull until 1623.[27] The Red Bull may have been built to provide a better theatre than the Curtain in order to compete with their chief rivals, the King's Men at the Globe and Prince Henry's Men at the Fortune.[28] A license patent of April 15, 1609 authorized Queen Anne's Men to play "within their now usual homes, called the Red Bull in Clerkenwell and the Curtain in Hollywell." They were licensed to give "Comedies, Tragedies, histories, Enterludes, Moralles, Pastorelles, Stageplaies" in London and throughout the realm.[29] They played often at Court and toured annually in the country.[30] Yet, despite the company's apparent popularity and success, Thomas Greene's widow had to bring suit in 1623 to collect her share of 1s. 8d. per day for six days a week.[31] In fact, between 1619-23, the company was apparently broken up amid a good deal of litigation.[32]

From its inception, the Red Bull was, in Louis Wright's words, "frankly a plain man's playhouse, where clownery, clamor, and spectacle vied with subject matter flattering to the vanity of tradesmen."[33] An examination of the themes and characters of *Tu Quoque* in the following section shows that the play presents the citizen-tradesman as the Red Bull audience would want him portrayed on stage: one who values individual dignity, morality, courage, and industry, is rewarded for acting on these virtues, or is punished and then repentant for straying from them. The audience would not appreciate seeing these values treated with mockery or even levity, as they are in *Ram-Alley* (pub. 1611), *Tu Quoque*'s source.[34] *Ram-Alley* was a "coterie play" performed by the King's Revels at Whitefriars, and in *Tu Quoque*, as Alfred Harbage observes, the source materials "have received the customary cleansing" of the "popular playhouse."[35] Perhaps most of all, the Red Bull audience would have found any hint of cynicism or nihilism particularly unsettling. The best-known criticism of the Red Bull audience is probably related to this somewhat defensive self-conception of the citizen-tradesman and to his consequent negative reaction to a view of society or conventional values that he found threatening. John Webster's preface to *The White Devil* (pub. 1612) makes clear that the author regretted that his play was first performed at the Red Bull--according to Chambers, sometime between 1609 and 1612:[36]

> ... since it was acted in so dull a time of Winter, presented in so open and blacke [perhaps "bleake"] a Theater, that it wanted (that which is the only grace and setting out of a tragedy) a full and understanding Auditory: and that since that time I have noted, most of the people that come to that Playhouse, resemble those ignorant asses (who visiting Stationers shoppes their use is not to inquire for good bookes, but new bookes)....[37]

F.L. Lucas notes that Webster's indifference here to the feelings of Queen Anne's Men may be "because he had by now attached himself to the King's Men who produced his next play, *The Duchess of Malfi*, in 1613-4."[38] Their playhouse, the Blackfriars Theatre, was roofed and artificially lighted, unlike the Red Bull, which was still unroofed in 1609-14.[39] This was probably one reason for Webster's dissatisfaction.

G.F. Reynolds cites other items which "suggest that the reputation of the Red Bull was scarcely first class."[40] In 1610, certain citizens had to answer for "a notable outrage at the playhouse called the Red Bull", and in 1614, someone was bailed out for picking a pocket there. Several times between 1616 and 1622, the company was in trouble with the municipal authorities for not keeping the highways in the vicinity of the Red Bull in proper repair.[41]

As for the informing spirit of the Red Bull, Wright gives evidence that the theatre was thought of as offering manly and vigorous, rather than precious or effete, plays,[42] and C.R. Baskervill notes that the Red Bull, Curtain and Fortune were the only public theatres mentioned by name for frequently performing jigs.[43] This impression of down-to-earth heartiness is strengthened by the fact that bread, beer, ale, and fruit were sold at the Red Bull.[44]

Tu Quoque must have been very popular with the Red Bull audience as Greene's performance brought about the renaming of the play. Three quarto editions published between 1614 and 1628[45] suggest the play's ongoing popularity, as does a spiteful reaction against the play's success. In 1615, *Tu Quoque* was attacked by an I.H. in *This World's Folly*. Chambers reproduces the passage, an acrimonious tirade aimed as much against the stage generally as it is against this particular play. *Tu Quoque* is attacked for aping God's image with Greene's baboon antics.[46] Such language, reminiscent of Philip Stubbes' *The Anatomy of Abuses*, seems to be prompted by Puritan discontent rather than professional rivalry. The play was revived at Court by the Queen of Bohemia's Men on 6 January 1625 in place of *Twelfth Night*.[47] The durability of the play's appeal is suggested by G. Langbaine in *An Account of the English Dramatick Poets* (1691). Langbaine saw the play "acted since the King's Return" (i.e. after the Restoration), as he remembers, "in little *Lincolns-Inn-Fields* with good success: tho' the printed Copy be not divided into Acts" (p. 72). This comment suggests that the play was divided into acts in the performance that Langbaine saw. Finally, W.W. Greg notes that a droll called "The Bubble" was put together from passages culled from five different scenes of the play and included in *The Wits*, published in 1662 and 1672.[48]

III

PLAY, SOURCE, AND GENRE

Brian Gibbons gives a definition of City Comedy which, at first glance, would place both *Tu Quoque* and its source, *Ram-Alley*, somewhere within the bounds of the genre:

> We might define the genre City Comedy ... by the fact that the
> plays are all satiric and have urban settings, with characters
> and incident appropriate to such settings; they exclude mate-
> rial appropriate to romance, fairy tale, sentimental legend or
> patriotic chronicle.[49]

Yet when Gibbons distinguishes examples of "City Comedy" from London comedies that do not meet his criteria for inclusion in the genre, he lists *Ram-Alley* as a "City Comedy," but not *Tu Quoque*.[50] This is because Gibbons is really concerned with what he could have called "London Coterie Satire." In fact, his sub-title is, "A Study of Satiric Plays by Jonson, Marston and Middleton." But although Gibbons' exclusiveness in defining "City Comedy" is somewhat arbitrary, he is correct to see these comedies as distinctive from others contemporary with them. They are marked out, as he says, by a systematic and self-conscious critique of society, thereby constituting an art of critical realism, "expressing consciously satiric criticism but also suggesting deeper sources of conflict and change." Hence, these plays dramatize conflicting forces, rather than merely reflect manners.[51] Admittedly, *Tu Quoque*, and for that matter, Dekker's *The Shoemaker's Holiday*, are too sentimental on the one hand, and not rigorously satiric enough on the other, for Gibbons to call them "City Comedy." Alexander Leggatt sees these two plays as belonging to the tradition of the "moralizing comedy" of the public theatres.[52] Certainly, both plays, unlike *Ram-Alley*, are examples of what Leggatt calls "Citizen Comedy"--comedy about citizens and intended for the popular playhouse. At least, one can safely call both *Ram-Alley* and *Tu Quoque* "realistic London comedies," but to examine their most significant differences is to suggest some of the more general contrasts between the informing spirit of the coterie comedies and that of the popular comedies of the period.

Ram-Alley is a hearty and, by any standard, a bawdy play, dealing mainly with the rivalry between Sir Oliver Smallshanks and his son, William, for the hand of the rich widow Taffeta, a Ram-Alley whore. There is much intermittent satire, directed principally at the law and the court, and unlike *Tu Quoque*, the play observes the unities of time and place, with few gratuitous episodes that are not related to, or do not grow out of, the rivalry between father and son for the lusty widow.

In *Tu Quoque*, the main plot is concerned with the aspirations of the serving-man Bubble to act the gentleman befitting his new fortune. The play presents what must be one of the most good-natured spoofs on social climbing to be found in the drama of the period. The play is without malice because Bubble is totally without it himself, just as is the newly-knighted Sir Lionel Rash. Bubble is the epitome of the credulous gull, and Sir Lionel's hearty and unpretentious manner is reminiscent of Dekker's Simon Eyre. They are certainly no kin to characters such as Sir Giles

INTRODUCTION   xiii

Overreach, Massinger's crafty and cold-blooded entrepreneur
in *A New Way to Pay Old Debts*, or Quomodo in Middleton's
Michaelmas Term, who bend all their thoughts "to hook in
gentry." Like the citizen comedies of Dekker and Heywood,
Tu Quoque is naturally without scornful references to
citizens as a class, though such remarks occur in *Ram-Alley*
(e.g., 225-6). Bubble's good fortune is unpremeditated,
and the worst that he can be accused of is foolish affec-
tation. His invariable motto of *"tu quoque"* gives the
play its title, and some of the play's funniest episodes
result from Bubble being gulled by his former master,
Staines, his "tutor in behavior." *The Cambridge History
of English Literature*, for example, cites the satirizing
of the "affectations of the Italianate Englishman" in Scene
XVI as particularly effective.[53]

A sub-plot involving the fall and reclamation of the
profligate Spendall is the vehicle for the most earnest
didacticism of the play. When Spendall's recklessness
brings him to the paupers' hole of debtors' prison, he
addresses the audience directly:

> ... I could write my repentance to the world,
> And force th' impression of it in the hearts
> Of you, and my acquaintance, I might teach them
> By my example, to looke home to Thrift,
> And not to range abroad to seeke out Ruine.   (XV, 2152-6)

A moralizing passage such as this never appears in *Ram-
Alley*, any more than many of that play's observations on
human nature and society would be expressed in *Tu Quoque*,
such as Sir Oliver's casual judgment on man's essential
animalism ("Warme bloud the yong mans slaue, the ould mans
God", l. 2255), or Judge Tutchin's dictum on the law: "I
say as you say sister, but for the lawes, / There are so
many that men do stand in awe, / Of none at all...." (1971-3)

The tone of the gibes in *Ram-Alley* expresses amused
ridicule for the abuses of the law and the court, and for
the sexual misdemeanors, not only of its characters, but
of mankind generally. Sir Oliver speaks not only of his
own lust, but of a world where copulation thrives. Judge
Tutchin's view of the law is an indictment, not only of the
abuses of his own time, but of those inherent in human nature
and society. The following observation of the scapegrace
William expresses a point of view that is directly opposite
to the spirit of *Tu Quoque*:

> ... this is the difference,
> All great mens sinnes must still be humored,
> And poore mens vices largely punished,
> The priuiledge that great men haue in euill,
> Is this, they go vnpunisht to the Diuell[.]   (2114-18)

The general coarseness, matter-of-factness, and cynicism of *Ram-Alley* are presented by characters who have
gusto, and all, with the exception of the usurer Throate,

have what Fielding would call "good nature," so that only
the prudish would think it an unwholesome play. But it
does not maintain, as does *Tu Quoque*, the moral values of
self-respect, essential decency, brotherhood, modesty,
moderation, and conjugal fulfillment. Marriage represents
fulfillment in *Ram-Alley* as well, though William comes to
it despite his shoddy motivations, and Sir Oliver, despite
himself.
    The satire in *Tu Quoque* has a wider range and a more
genial tone than that of *Ram-Alley*. The personal and
social pretensions of its characters--the coyness of Gartred
and Joyce, the aping of foreign manners by Bubble and
Scattergood, the absurdity of the code of the duel as presented through Spendall and Staines--are shown as endearing
follies, or at the worst, as dangerous, but not malicious,
weaknesses. Examples of such hazardous flaws in the behavior of basically decent characters would be Spendall's
immoderate, indiscriminate generosity, his traffic with
and trust in whores and panders, and the prodigality that
is responsible for ruining Staines, Spendall, and Bubble
at one time or another. All these characters, however,
profit from experience and reform their lives. The moralizing in *Tu Quoque* advocates moderation and prudence, for
a return to the normal state of things which, without
pretensions or excesses, is naturally ordered and good,
just as normal life is naturally orderly and most people
are naturally good. In *Ram-Alley*, the characters are re-
deemed for the audience, not by their reconciliation with
conventional morality, but by the frankness and high spirits
which they exhibit in the pursuit of sex and money. *Tu
Quoque* treats prodigality and illicit sexual affairs as
aberrations which are best cured by hardship and an ensuing
change of heart. At the end of *Tu Quoque*, each of the
principal characters addresses an apologetic couplet to the
audience for his or her past errors. But *Ram-Alley* veers
away from moral judgments or apologies. Both Sir Oliver
and his son William are unscrupulous in their rivalry for
Taffeta. As Alfred Harbage points out, such a father-son
rivalry for the same woman would be unpalatable to the
audience of the popular theatre, and is accordingly expunged
from *Tu Quoque*.[54] In the end, William gets the better of
his father because, with Taffeta, whose values are not meant
to be thought of as wholly contemptible, sex and a sword
prove to be more persuasive than money. Clearly, the al-
ternative to William's successful suit--i.e., the success
of his father's, who also wants to marry Taffeta for her
money--would make for an unwholesome *dénouement*. We are
intended to admire William for his pluck and resourcefulness:
"The world shall praise my wit, admire my fate" (1704).
William is a younger son who has been "cashiered" by his
father. Luckily, his older brother is a fool: " ... If
God had not made / Some elder-brothers fooles, how should
witty / Yonger brothers be maintain'd"[?] (2627-9)
    In *Ram-Alley*, the world is inevitably the stage for
rivalry, double-dealing, and a scramble for self-interest,

where one who is without power or means must use wit, daring, and trickery, not virtue, forbearance, or moderation, to prevail.

At its worst, *Ram-Alley* lapses into gratuitous coarseness, though never into banality. *Tu Quoque* occasionally stumbles in this respect. It has more than a few vapid passages serving as "fill," as mechanical transitions between episodes. Yet its mood is more expansive, its characters more endearing and human than those of its source. Most of the characters in *Ram-Alley* are sketched instead of individualized, as most are representatives of the stock characters of Anglicized Plautine comedy. To be sure, *Tu Quoque* has correspondences to stock characters as well: a gull (Bubble), a shrewd servant (Staines), prodigals (Spendall and Scattergood), a shrewish-tongued woman (Joyce), a swaggerer (whom the infuriated Spendall beats off the stage). But just as we have more affection for the characters of *Tu Quoque*, we find, too, that its principals have more dimension and humanity than those of *Ram-Alley*. Both comedies are funny and effective. If *Tu Quoque* has fuller characterizations, the language of *Ram-Alley* is often wittier and generally more lively. We have here the characteristic strengths and weaknesses of two representative comedies, one coterie, one popular.

Except for scattered echoes, the indebtedness of *Tu Quoque* to its source is the scene in which a desperate young man successfully woos a rich widow (cf. *Tu Quoque*, XVII, 2500-2658 and Appendix, *Ram-Alley*, 2149-2253). Of course, the situation of the courtship has changed a good deal in *Tu Quoque*. In *Ram-Alley*, Smallshanks goes to woo a whore who is ambitious to become a lady, and he goes to woo her away from his father. Spendall goes to woo his benefactress, the chaste Widow Raysby, who has made possible his release from debtors' prison. There are recognizable similarities and some striking differences in the soliloquies wherein the two characters describe their motivations to marry. Smallshanks is simply down and out, and the widow is his only recourse. Besides, his father is too old to satisfy a wife. If he is cheating his father now, men will applaud his good fortune later: "all ends in this, / So they get gold, they care not whose it is" (2100-09). Besides, if he is unsuccessful, he must "turne Cittizen, / Be banckrout, and craue the Kings protection" (2147-8).

Spendall's soliloquy begins in Scene XVI, just after his friends "*looke strangely upon him, and Exeunt.*" "How ruthlesse men are to adversitie," he observes, resolving to act for himself without depending on his friends. Now, if only he could act as his spirit prompts him--more, as the widow has suggested to him:

> It was an argument of love in her
> To fetch mee out of Prison, and this night,
> She claspt my hand in hers, as who should say,
> Thou art my Purchase, and I hold thee thus.   (XVI, 2457-73)

Spendall is trying to raise his spirits with the thought that the widow might love him, but at least, unlike Smallshanks, he takes her feelings into account, and as Scene XVII is to show, he genuinely loves the widow (XV11, 2650-6). It is already being made apparent in Scene XVI that Spendall is a decent fellow. But the wooing scenes in both plays afford the most interesting contrasts between the two suitors.

With his sword at her throat, Smallshanks compels Taffeta to kiss him several times while he urges his suit. In most vivid, if unpleasant, language, he describes the odiousness of marrying his old father for money. The widow protests that William would prove unfaithful, and that he keeps a whore. It would probably occur to the audience that her scruples are somewhat inconsistent here, for she previously insisted on preserving her right to have lovers after her marriage to Sir Oliver. Smallshanks balks at the falsity of the charge. He keeps no whore: "She keepes her selfe and me, yet I protest, / Shees not dishonest." He assures the widow that he will now shake off all former ties and respect their bond of marriage. Suitably impressed with his daring, Taffeta accepts his suit, and both retire to the pleasures of love before their wedding, for "An honest contract is as good as marriadge" (2187-2253).

Spendall, too, must resort to the sword and to kisses under compulsion to woo his widow, and vows, like Smallshanks, that he would rather hang than starve. But as he has no older rival to denigrate, some of the graphic language with which Smallshanks renders his father grotesque is transferred in Spendall's speech to a description of the hypothetical rich old man she is likely to marry if she rejects his suit:

> And will you then, that have inough,
> Take to your Bed a bundle of diseases,
> Wrapt up in threescore yeares, to lie a hawking,
> Spitting, and coffing backwards and forwards
> That you shall not sleepe; but thrusting forth
> Your face out of the Bed, be glad to draw
> The Curtaines, such a steame shall reeke
> Out of this dunghill....

Spendall asks why the widow should not take compassion on a "reasonable handsome fellow," who will not only reawaken the widow to the pleasures of love, but will also give her a family--something that Smallshanks apparently did not think important enough to mention in his suit. The Widow Raysby protests that their union cannot be consummated until they are married. Then she binds him to the bedpost and destroys the contract he extorted from her by force. She lays before him the treasures he will never have. Did he think to squander her substance among his whores and panders? She encourages him to vent his rancor, now that he has no reason to dissemble. When he declines, asserting the sincerity of his affection, she accepts his suit. It was necessary that she make trial of him, "cause it shews / I give my selfe unto thee, am not forc'd." *Ram-Alley* does not pause over such scruples, nor does Smallshanks say, like Spendall, that "fore my dagger should ha drawne one droppe / Of thy chaste blood, it should have sluc'd out mine" (XVII, 2521-2653). Aside from the fact that the statement would have to be altered for Taffeta, it is not certain that Smallshanks does not mean what he says (i.e., that he would rather hang than starve). In *Tu Quoque*, then, self-interest is balanced against sincere affection, and the author takes care to underline Spendall's essential decency, whereas, in the rough-and-tumble world of *Ram-Alley*, the decency of Smallshanks is irrelevant, and its existence is somewhat doubtful.

Courtezans are important in both plays, representing the way of the world in *Ram-Alley* and the danger of imprudence and treachery in *Tu Quoque*. In *Ram-Alley* (800-24), we are given a *comédie humaine* from the courtezans' point of view, which reverses, and possibly parodies, the solemn "character" of a whore expressed in Dekker's *I Honest Whore*,[55] by having the whores give their own barbed "characters" of their clients. In *Tu Quoque*, Spendall's invective against Nan Tickleman (XIII, 1761-80), the ungrateful whore who betrays him when he is in need, may be said to contain a "character." Certainly, Nan and her pander and bawd have been treacherous, but they rationalize their behavior by affirming that: " ... tho wee somewhat / Impaire their Bodyes, yet wee doe good to their Soules; / For I am sure, wee still bring them to Repentance" (XIII, 1788-90). It is apparent that in *Tu Quoque*, even the whores and panders contribute to moralizing, if not to morality. When Pursenet goes on to swear by "Dis" (XIII, 1791), it merely reminds us that despite their betrayal of Spendall, they somehow do not seem very sinister.

The grimmest scene in the play, Scene XV, takes place in the paupers' ward of the debtors' prison, where the prisoners must scrounge for unsavory scraps from the almsbasket to stay alive. Even here, the jailer is not malevolent, showing an amused compassion for his charges, and in Scene XIX, when Bubble must beg for "some compassion" to save him from debtors' prison, it is given him, provided he will put on his old humility with his livery (XIX, 2891-2898). In *Tu Quoque*, then, we are presented with a world in which, though there are pitfalls resulting from financial recklessness, there are almost no damned souls on the pilgrimage.

Also there are, in Benavente's phrase, "bonds of interest" which draw the principals of the play together, so that it may be inaccurate to speak of a main plot and a sub-plot. Bubble and Staines, who are twice reversed as master and man, are also rivals for Joyce. Scattergood and Geraldine are rivals for her sister, Gartred, and Spendall and the Widow Raysby make up the third couple to be aided by Will Rash, who serves as a central force for harmony and finally brings all of them together. Though

Bubble loses his bride and his money to his old master, he is happy to get his old job back, and when Scattergood accepts his rival's triumph with resignation, it is time to "wind up all wrong" with a banquet (XIX, 2915).

The spirit of *Tu Quoque* is changed from that of its source by frequent expressions of love and sentiment. There is a clear distinction made between Spendall's affair with Nan Tickleman and the true love of Geraldine for Gartred, which is, like many fictional love affairs of the age, love at first sight. In *Ram-Alley*, except for Constantia, "love" means lust coupled with a *mariage de convenance*. But in *Tu Quoque*, Will Rash, the benign middleman for three couples, strikes the tone of sentimental comedy when summing up the situation in Middlesex:

> Well, this Love is a troublesome thing, *Jupiter* blesse mee out of his fingers: ther's no estate can rest for him: Hee runnes through all Countries, will travell through the *Ile of Man* in a minut; but never is quiet till hee come into *Middle-sex*, and there keepes his Christmas: Tis his habitation, his mantion; from whence, heele never out, till hee be fierd.(XIV, 1794-1800)

Love may be spoken of here as a "troublesome thing," but it is treated in the play as a force that naturally works for harmony, and as the play nears its conclusion, there is a warming of each character toward the rest, an upsurge of fellow-feeling, so that when the three couples, eloping by night, come upon each other in the street, Spendall identifies himself with: "Why we are honest folks," and they part from Will Rash with the salutation "Farewell brother." He addresses them with diminutive speech: " ... now farewell my little children of *Cupid*, that walke by two and two as if you went a feasting: let mee heare no more words, but be gone." (XVIII, 2687-2709)

The difference in spirit from *Ram-Alley* that is evidenced by such passages is a crucial one. The impetus of *Ram-Alley* arises, not only from the *élan* of its characters, but also from the heartiness with which the court, the law, and family and sexual relationships are held up to ridicule. The bonds of society are presented as merely official shams to be evaded as long as possible and accepted only when inevitable. Whether a character is motivated by sex or money, it is natural for him to strive greedily for himself. The attitude that is implicit in the play, however, never becomes sardonic, bitter, or grave. There is laughter from start to finish without sentimentalism or apology. But as we near the end of *Tu Quoque*, the laughter is hushed for brotherly acknowledgement and the recognition of man's more important business: marriage, responsibility, and good fellowship within society's bonds of interest.

In *The Knight of the Burning Pestle*, Beaumont and Fletcher wrote a parody on the sentimentality of London citizen comedy, and on the pride in being just "honest folks" that is expressed in *The Shoemaker's Holiday*. In places, citizen comedy has good material for parody, just as *Pamela* had for Fielding, but if its effusions are sometimes too saccharine, they often express sincerity and warmth, which make us care more about the characters than we often do with those in coterie satirical comedy. One of Will Rash's speeches is a good example of what is at once vulnerable to parody and characteristically ingratiating in the spirit of citizen comedy:

> I, you may crie farewell, but if my father should know of my villanie, how should I fare then? but all's one, I ha done my sisters good, my friends good, and my selfe good, and a generall good is alwaies to be respected before a particular: ther's eight score pounds a yeare saved, by the conveyance of this widdow.... (XVIII, 2712-17)

In one speech, then, we have the advocacy of loyalty, the beneficial effects of doing good, utilitarianism, and frugality. Similarly, when Sir Lionel Rash, who is outraged at Staines' elopement with Joyce, learns that Staines has recovered his mortgage, he bids him to "Stand up, the matter is well amended" (XIX, 2873). But citizens value more than financial solvency, as Old Geraldine indicates when he concurs in approving the marriage of his son to Gartred: " ... for since they love, / I'le not have the crime lie on my head, / To divide man and wife" (XIX, 2875-7). Though more than one character in *Ram-Alley* has no such scruples, we remember that in *The Shoemaker's Holiday*, the king himself shrinks from setting his authority over the bond of marriage.[56] Herein, the importance of social order and moral law is expressed from a characteristically middle-class point of view, by having a king, as Old Geraldine does here, respect a bond that is outside the reach of his power; for as one bows to a superior law, so will his own prerogatives be ensured and respected.

One would infer, from the comparison of *Tu Quoque* with its source, that the popular comedy has a much lower tolerance than the select comedy for the incorporation of forces, situations, or attitudes which are sinister or alienating enough to break the bonds of social and family order themselves. *Ram-Alley* is able to digest them into laughter. *Tu Quoque* steers clear of them.

IV

TEXT AND TEXTUAL HISTORY

The copy-text for this critical edition is the First Quarto (Q1), published in 1614.[57] Greg gives a description of its title page, along with a full descriptive collation.[58] An off-set print of the title page of Q1 is reproduced as the frontispiece of the book. It reads:

> Greene's Tu Quoque, | OR, | The Cittie Gallant. | *As it hath beene diuers times acted by the Queenes | Maiesties Seruants.* | Written by IO. COOKE Gent. | [woodcut: within a rule, of Thomas

Greene as Bubble, in doublet, hose, and two feathered hat, left hand clutching belt, right arm and forefinger raised in a beckoning gesture: a caption issuing from his mouth, cartoon-like, reads, "Tu quoque, To you Sir."] | Printed at London for *Iohn Trundle*. 1614.

The Second Quarto (Q2), was, as its title page indicates, printed in 1622 for Thomas Dewe,[59] who acquired the play in 1621, according to the Stationers' Register.[60] M. Flesher, the printer of the Third Quarto (Q3),[61] acquired the play in 1628.[62] Greg notes that the Stationers' Register entry, together with the state of the woodcut on the title page, place Q3 definitely later than Q2, though not earlier than 1628. He also observes that Q3 seems to have been printed from Q1, rather than from Q2.[63]

The historical collations bear out that Q1 was the copy-text for the two subsequent quartos. The speech-prefixes "*Francis.*" and "*Fran.*" rather than "*Spend.*" for Spendall, which appear on sig. B1 (I, 1, 3), never to recur in Q1, are retained in Q2-3, as are examples of obvious misprints or compositorial error first appearing in Q1. One example on sig. C1 (III, 294) occurs where "We" in Q1-3 is clearly a misprint for "Why", as emended by Dodsley and subsequent editors. Similarly, Dodsley and the later editors correctly emend six erroneous speech-prefixes which first appear on sig. M1 of Q1 that are retained in Q2-3 (XIX, 2850, 2852, 2854, 2858, 2862, 2873): the lines here given to Scattergood in the quartos ("*Scat.*") are certainly intended for Staines ("*Sta.*").

Substantive or semi-substantive emendations made by Dodsley and subsequent editors--i.e., their alterations of Q1 readings that are followed in Q2-3, excluding their additional emendations--number 192; readings later emended that first appear in Q1 and that are retained in Q2 number 69; those given in Q1 that are retained in Q3, though altered in Q2, number 18 (e.g., see Historical Collation: II, 162; VI, 607; VII, 750; XII, 1548). Moreover, Q1 and Q3 have nearly the same number of unambiguous accidentals, 16 and 17 respectively, though Q2 has a significantly higher number, 45. There are 23 unique accidentals in Q2, and Q1 and Q3 share a noteworthy accidental in XVI, 2198 ("Hee-lip") that is corrected in Q2 ("Her-lip").

Dodsley's preface indicates that Q3 was his copy-text,[64] and the number of substantive and semi-substantive readings that originate in Q3 and that are adopted by Dodsley, Reed, Scott [?], Collier and Hazlitt--66--gives evidence that Q3 was almost certainly the copy-text for all five editors. Hazlitt was the first editor to note the existence of Q2.[65]

The present edition is the first to divide the play into scenes and to number lines. Of the previous emendations made by Dodsley or later editors, 37 are accepted in the present text; 42 emendations are initiated in this edition. However, 131 readings, originating in Q1 and followed in Q2-3, emended by later editors, are retained in this text. The five previous editions of *Tu Quoque* beginning with Dodsley's are listed in the headnote to the Historical Collation of this edition.

Greg notes that the printer of Q1 appears, from the ornament used on the title page and on sig. A2, to have been Edward Allde.[66] It is true that Allde used this ornament. R.B. McKerrow reproduces it in an article on Allde, and his description and illustration of it are identical to the ornament in *Tu Quoque*.[67] However, none of the ornamental initials that McKerrow exhibits as having been used by Allde exactly matches those appearing on sigs. A2 and B1 of Q1.[68]

A later article by C. William Miller contains stronger evidence to suggest that the printer of Q1 was Nicholas Okes.[69] Firstly, Okes, like Allde, was actively printing when Q1 was published.[70] Then, the identical ornament that appears in Q1 was used by Okes in at least seven works published between 1607-15.[71] Miller notes that Okes had a full stock of ornaments, partly because he purchased and received many from his predecessors.[72] More conclusive evidence for connecting Q1 with Okes is revealed when one notes that the ornamental initial "T" appearing on sig. A2 of Q1 is used in two works printed by Okes in 1616 and 1622, and that the ornamental initial "W" on sig. B1 is employed in two other of Okes' productions, one published in 1611, the other in 1616.[73] Okes printed a great many books important to English drama, including play quartos of Heywood.[74] In fact, an example of the same ornament that appears on sigs. A2 and B1 of Q1 of *Tu Quoque* is used by Okes in his edition of Heywood's *An Apology for Actors* (1612).[75] In the "Epistle" to that work, Heywood praises Okes as an honest and careful workman.[76]

It may be that Q1 was printed in two sections; as Greg points out, this is suggested by the differences in the running-title.[77] There are four sets of running-titles in Q1. Set # 1 is identical to the head-title, and appears on sigs. A-F4^v, L1-M2. It contains three swash letters: capitals "G" and "Q" and a terminal swash "e." Set # 2 contains the swash "G," but a lower-case "q," and the final "e" is not a swash letter; this same terminal "e" is what distinguishes set # 4. Set # 3, however, has neither the swash "G," nor the terminal swash "e." Set # 2 occurs on sigs. G1, G2, H1, H2, I1, I2 and K1. Set # 3 appears on sigs. G1^v, G2^v, H1^v, H2^v, I1^v, I2^v, K1^v and K2^v. Finally, set # 4 is found on numerous signatures: G3-G4^v, H3-H4^v, I3-I4^v, K2, and K3-K4^v. All four sets of running-titles, then, appear on both inner and outer formes.

An intriguing pattern emerges when correlating the seven signature notations that are printed with periods with their corresponding running-titles: sigs. G. [G1], H. [H1], I. [I1], I2., and K. [K1] are printed with RT set # 2; sigs. G3. and K2. appear with RT set # 4. Periods occur, then, on signature notations in both outer and inner formes; moreover, all four sets of running-titles are used on both the outer and inner formes of the same sheets.

However, the differences in the running-titles between G-K and B-F, L-M, together with the fact that only the signature-marks on gatherings G-K include a full stop, suggest the work of two presses, and possibly, of two compositors.[78] Still, no meaningful pattern seems to emerge by comparing orthographic variations of the same words, variations in stage directions, speech-prefixes or catchword patterns appearing in quires G-K with those in B-F, L-M. Similar variations, including the use of two distinct letters for "E," "s" and "W" occur on both outer and inner formes throughout the text. In addition, the compositor was not necessarily involved in transferring the skeletons, which included the headlines, from forme to forme. Hence, although the running-titles suggest the use of two presses, it is possible that formes exhibiting several different sets of skeletons were worked off on the same press; similarly, though the signature-marks and running-titles suggest the possibility of two compositors, there is no additional clear pattern of evidence for inferring more than one compositor for Q1.

Six copies of Q1 were collated for press-variants, which appear in sheets B (outer forme), C (inner), D (outer), E (outer and inner), G (outer), H (outer, three states, and inner), I (inner), K (outer and inner), L (outer and inner), and M (inner). None suggests authorial correction, and, as Heywood's foreword makes clear, the author was deceased when Q1 was being printed.

There is, however, good evidence to infer authorial provenance for the MS from which Q1 was printed. In Scene I, the speech-prefixes *"Francis."* and *"Fran."* for Spendall are never repeated (I, 1, 3), though he is frequently called *"Frank"* and once called *"Francis"* (XII, 1524) by other characters. Similarly, the opening stage direction of Scene XV introduces a *"Lock-fast,"* and a later stage direction indicates that a *"Lock."* exits (XV, SD, 2089), though the character is consistently designated as *"Hold."* (i.e. *"Holdfast"*) in the speech-prefixes (2040-89). In the same scene, the stage directions have *"Prisoners"* enter and exit (XV, SD, 2112, 2137), though, apparently, only one prisoner speaks (XV, 2111-36). Another ambiguity occurs in Scene XIX, in which a stage direction reads *"Enter a Sergeant"* (XIX, SD, 2850). Subsequently, the character is twice addressed as "Sergeant" (XIX, 2858, 2883), but several lines afterward, Staines calls on two "Sergeants" to return with Bubble (XIX, 2892). In addition, there are two permissive forms appearing in stage directions which are characteristic of foul papers. In Scene VIII, the scrivener Blank enters with *"another"* (VIII, SD, 811), and a stage direction in Scene XIV reads, *"Heere they two talke and rayle what they list"* (XIV, SD, 2014).[79] In Scene IX, Ambush the broker speaks three lines (IX, 1070, 1072, 1076), though neither an entrance nor an exit is given for this character. Further suggestions of authorial provenance are the fourteen stage directions in Latin contained in Q1, as well as seven clearly anticipatory stage directions (see Historical Collation: I, 42; VI, 645; VII, 716; IX, 1148; XVI, 2398; XVII, 2555; XIX, 2773). Q1, then, is apparently printed from foul papers, or from a scribal copy of the author's MS. Certainly, the Q1 text does not suggest the kind of provenance associated with prompt-copy that had served for performances at the Red Bull.

V

NOTE ON THE APPARATUS OF THE CRITICAL TEXT

Bracketed material in the Critical Text denotes an emendation to Q1, the copy-text. All emendations to the copy-text, including corrections of accidentals, are given at the bottom of the page on which they occur. Following the lemma giving the Critical Text reading, set off by a bracket, is the source of the accepted reading--either the previous edition or editor, or "ed.", denoting that the emendation originates with the present editor. The original Q1 reading follows a semi-colon. Double-slashes or virgules (//) signal another emendation that occurs in the same line. The Historical Collation appearing after the Critical Text lists only substantive and semi-substantive readings.

This edition retains the spelling, punctuation, lineation and italics of Q1 whenever possible. A slash at the right-hand margin indicates the end of a page in Q1; the beginning of a new page is indicated within brackets at the right-hand margin. Full references for all previous editions cited in the textual notes are given in the Bibliography. The textual notes include the following abbreviations: OSD (opening stage direction), SD (stage direction), and SP (speech-prefix). $Q1(c)$ indicates a corrected reading in the 1614 quarto; $Q1(u)$ signals the reading that appears in uncorrected copies of Q1.

NOTES TO INTRODUCTION

1. E.K. Chambers, *The Elizabethan Stage* (1923), IV, 178. Also see G.F. Reynolds, *The Staging of Elizabethan Plays at the Red Bull Theater, 1605-1625* (1940), p. 19.
2. Chambers, IV, 178; Reynolds, p. 19.
3. All scene and line numbers refer to the present text.
4. Reynolds, p. 7.
5. E. Nungezer, *A Dictionary of Actors and Other Persons Associated with the Public Representation of Plays in England before 1642* (1929), p. 161.
6. Chambers, III, 269.
7. Chambers, III, 269; *Epigrames. Served Out in 52. Severall Dishes for Every Man To Tast without Surfeiting* (1604). See A.W. Pollard and G.R. Redgrave, *A Short-Title Catalogue of Books*

Printed in England, Scotland, and Ireland, and of English Books Printed Abroad, 1475-1640 (1926), # 5672. Hereafter cited as STC.
8. Sig. E2^v:

> Reader I know not how I haue pleas'd thy mind,
> With these rude Epigrams harsh vnrefind,
> But if they be not drest vnto thy taste,
> Then blame the Cooke for making too much hast,
> Ile ner'e make promise to remaine thy debter,
> But if thou likst them not, would thou hadst better.

9. J. Cooke, *How a Man May Chuse a Good Wife from a Bad,* ed. A.E.H. Swaen, in Materialien zur Kunde des älteren englischen Dramas (1912), XXXV, vi. Hereafter cited as Swaen.
10. Swaen, pp. vii-xiii.
11. Chambers, IV, 20.
12. R. Dodsley, *A Select Collection of Old Plays* (1744), III, 1.
13. Dodsley, III, 2.
14. Chambers, III, 269.
15. W.W. Greg, *Dramatic Documents from the Elizabethan Playhouses* (1931), I, 49.
16. Nungezer, p. 161.
17. Nungezer, p. 161.
18. Reynolds, pp. 7-8. Also see F.E. Schelling, *Elizabethan Playwrights* (1925), p. 194.
19. Nungezer, p. 190.
20. Reynolds, p. 7; Schelling, p. 194.
21. The couplet appears on sig. A4^v. I. Reed was the first to conjecture that the couplet was probably by William Rowley in his ed. of *Tu Quoque* (*A Select Collection of Old Plays*, 2nd. ed. [1780], VII, 539).
22. For the five plays written or co-authored by William Rowley that were performed at the Red Bull, see Reynolds, pp. 18-25.
23. Reynolds, p. 8.
24. Reynolds, p. 9.
25. Greg, *Dramatic Documents*, I, 47.
26. Reynolds, pp. 6-7.
27. B. Gibbons, *Jacobean City Comedy* (1968), p. 222; Reynolds, p. 25.
28. Reynolds, p. 6.
29. Reynolds, pp. 6-7.
30. Reynolds, p. 7; Chambers, II, 230-40.
31. Reynolds, p. 7.
32. Schelling, p. 194.
33. L.B. Wright, *Middle-Class Culture in Elizabethan England* (1935), p. 609.
34. Cf. *Tu Quoque*, Sc. XVII, 11. 2500-2658 and L. Barry's *Ram-Alley*, 2149-2253 (see Appendix). All references to *Ram-Alley* are to the ed. of C.E. Jones in Materials for the Study of the Old English Drama, new series, gen. ed. H. De Vocht (1952), Vol. XXIII.
35. A. Harbage, *Shakespeare and the Rival Traditions* (1952), p. 177.
36. Chambers, III, 509.
37. In *The Complete Works of John Webster*, ed. F.L. Lucas (1928), I, 107. Hereafter cited as Lucas.
38. Lucas, I, 195.

INTRODUCTION   xxv

39. Reynolds, p. 30; Lucas, I, 195.
40. Reynolds, p. 7.
41. Reynolds, p. 8.
42. Wright, p. 612.
43. Charles R. Baskervill, *The Elizabethan Jig and Related Song Drama* (1929), p. 115.
44. Reynolds, p. 9.
45. The First and Second Quartos were published in 1614 and 1622 respectively. W.W. Greg infers that the Third Quarto was not printed before 1628, both from an entry in the Stationers' Register and from the state of the woodcut on the title page (in W.W. Greg, *A Bibliography of the English Printed Drama to the Restoration* [1939], I, 464-5).
46. Chambers, IV, 254.
47. Chambers, III, 270.
48. Greg, *Bibliography of the English Printed Drama*, I, 465.
49. Gibbons, p. 24.
50. Gibbons, pp. 219-20. In fact, pp. 218, 220 reveal that to Gibbons' mind, Queen Anne's Men did not put on one play that he would designate as "City Comedy."
51. Gibbons, p. 17.
52. Alexander Leggatt, *Citizen Comedy in the Age of Shakespeare* (1973), p. 101.
53. A.W. Ward and A.R. Waller, eds., *The Drama to 1642: Part Two*, Vol. VI of *The Cambridge History of English Literature* (1917), p. 246.
54. A. Harbage, *Shakespeare and the Rival Traditions*, p. 209.
55. Thomas Dekker (with Thomas Middleton), *The Honest Whore, Part I*, II.i.319-97, 400-23, in Vol. II of *The Dramatic Works of Thomas Dekker*, ed. F. Bowers, rev. ed. (1964). All references to Dekker are from the Bowers edition.
56. Thomas Dekker, *The Shoemaker's Holiday*, V.v.61-5, 102-04.
57. *STC*, # 5673.
58. Greg, *Bibliography of the English Printed Drama*, I, 463-4.
59. *STC*, # 5674.
60. The SR entry reads: "1621 Sept. 2. Tr. J. Trundle to T. Dewe: a play booke, Greenes Tu Quoque." (Greg, *Bibliography of the English Printed Drama*, I, 464.)
61. *STC*, # 5675. The imprint on the title page of Q3 reads: "Printed at London by M. Flesher."
62. The SR entries tracing *Tu Quoque* from Thomas Dewe, for whom Q2 was printed, to M. Flesher, the printer of Q3, read as follows: "1627 Dec. 3. Tr. Anne Helme to W. Washington, as a copy of J. Helme or T. Dewe: Greenes Tu Quoque.... 1628 May 21. Tr. W. Washington to (M.) Flesher: Greenes Tu Quoque." (Greg, *Bibliography of the English Printed Drama*, I, 464.)
63. Greg, *Bibliography of the English Printed Drama*, I, 464.
64. Dodsley, III, 2, speaks of the play as "being printed originally without Date" and Q3 is the only undated quarto.
65. W.C. Hazlitt, *A Select Collection of Old English Plays*, 4th. ed. (1875), XI, 174.
66. Greg, *Bibliography of the English Printed Drama*, I, 464.
67. R.B. McKerrow, "Edward Allde as a Typical Trade Printer," *The Library*, 4th. ser., *Transactions of the Bibliographical Society*, X, No. 2 (Sept. 1929), 121-62. See pp. 153-4.
68. McKerrow, "Edward Allde as a Typical Trade Printer," pp. 149-62.

69. C. William Miller, "A London Ornament Stock: 1598-1683," *Studies in Bibliography: Papers of the Bibliographical Society of the University of Virginia*, ed. F. Bowers, VII (1955), 125-51.
70. See Miller, p. 129, and McKerrow, "Edward Allde as a Typical Trade Printer," p. 136.
71. Cf. Miller, pp. 136-7, 142, ornament # 22, and *STC*, # 16623a, # 19567, # 24064, # 13776, # 13309, # 24578, and # 18514.
72. Miller, pp. 129-30.
73. Cf. Miller, pp. 136-7, 142, figures # T(5), W(9), and *STC*, # 15711, # 22305, # 13783, and # 19090.
74. Miller, p. 129.
75. Cf. Miller, pp. 136-7, 142, ornament # 22, and *STC*, # 13309.
76. Thomas Heywood, *An Apology for Actors* (1612), sigs. G4-G4^v; headed on sig. G4, "To my approued good Friend, Mr. *Nicholas Okes*."
77. Greg, *Bibliography of the English Printed Drama*, I, 464.
78. Dr. Katharine F. Pantzer of the Houghton Library, Harvard University, notes in her forthcoming revision of Vol. I of Pollard and Redgrave's *STC*, that quires G.-K. may be by a different compositor or printer, possibly William White.
79. Another permissive form which follows this stage direction, the speech-prefix "*All speake.*" instead of "*Rash.*", may probably be explained as compositorial error rather than as an authorial lapse of concentration. This is even more likely for the six clearly erroneous speech-prefixes in Scene XIX, which give six of Staines' speeches to Scattergood (XIX, 2850 ff.): "*Sc.*" and "*St.*" could easily be confused in secretary hand.

Greene's Tu Quoque
or,
The Cittie Gallant

[DRAMATIS PERSONAE

SIR LIONEL RASH
WILL RASH, *his son*
OLD GERALDINE
GERALDINE, *his son*
SPENDALL
STAINES
BUBBLE
LONGFIELD
BALLANCE
SCATTERGOOD
NINNIHAMMER, *his servant*
BLANK, *a scrivener*
PURSENET, *a pander*
LODGE, *a prison warden*
HOLDFAST, *his assistant*
FOX, *a jailer*

GATHERSCRAP, *a jailhouse feeder*
BASKETHILT, *Sir Lionel's servant*
SPRINKLE, *Bubble's servant*
SWAGGERER
AMBUSH, *a broker*
PRISONERS
GARTRED, *Sir Lionel's daughter*
JOYCE, *her sister*
WIDOW RAYSBY
PHYLLIS, *her servant*
SWEATMAN, *a bawd*
NAN TICKLEMAN, *a whore*
A LINEN SELLER
MESSENGERS, DRAWERS, BOYS,
  SERGEANTS, SERVANTS]

DRAMATIS PERSONAE] *heading and list first supplied by Dodsley* 2 *his son*] *ed.* 3 OLD GERALDINE] *Collier* 4 *his son*] *ed.* 11 *his servant*] *ed.* 12 *a scrivener*] *ed.* 13 *a pander*] *ed.* 14 *a ... warden*] *ed.* 15 *his assistant*] *ed.* 16 *a jailer*] *ed.* 17 *a ... feeder*] *ed.* 18 *Sir ... servant*] *ed.* 19 *Bubble's servant*] *ed.* 21 AMBUSH, *a broker*] *ed.* 23 *Sir ... daughter*] *ed.* 24 *her sister*] *ed.* 25 RAYSBY] *ed.* 26 *her servant*] *ed.* 29-31 A ... SERVANTS] *ed.*; DRAWERS &c. *Dodsley*

To the Reader. [A2]

TO gratulate the love and memory of my worthy friend the
Author, and my entirely beloved Fellow, the Actor, I
could not chuse being in the way just when this Play was
to be published in Print, but to prefixe some token of
my affection to either in the frontispice of the Booke. 5
For the Gentleman that wrote it, his Poem it selfe can better
speake his praise, then any Oratory from me. Nor can I tell
whether this worke was divulged with his consent or no: but
howsoever, since it hath past the Test of the stage with so
generall and applause, pitty it were but it should   10
likewise have the honour of the Presse. As for Maister
Greene, all that I will speake of him (and that without
flattery) is this (if I were worthy to censure) there was not
an Actor of his nature in his time of better ability in
performance of what he undertooke; more applaudent by 15
the Audience, of greater grace at the Court, or of more generall love in the Citty, and so with this briefe character of
his memory, I commit him to rest,

              Thomas Heywood.

4 Print] *Q2*; Priut 5 frontispice] *Q2* (Frontispice); frontispire

Upon the death of Thomas Greene. [A4ᵛ]

How fast bleake Autumne changeth Floraes dye,
What yesterday was **(Greene)** *now's seare and dry.*
                                        W.R.

But her innocent manner obviously appeared
      Full of distress.
And on the other side, a little distance from me,
A knight of very noble array   50
Came right toward her down the path
      Without company;
And so it seemed they might be lover and beloved.
Then I pushed myself inside the leaves,
So hidden I was that they could not see me at all.   55
      But when that lover,
To whom Nature had granted her considerable gifts,
Had approached that lady of worth,
Like a gracious gentleman, wise and well-mannered,
      He greeted her.   60
And the lady who was oppressed by thought,
Without responding to him, passed him by.
And he turned back at once,
      And then took her
By the robe, and softly said to her: 65
"My sweet lady, have you scorn
For my greeting?" And when she saw him,
      She answered
Sighing, that she'd not attended to it:
"To be sure, sir, I heard you not at all   70
Because my thoughts prevented it;
      But if I've done
Anything ignoble or impolite,
Please pardon me for it, if you would."
The knight, without more argument,   75
      Said softly:
"Lady, no pardon here is needed,
For there has been no misdeed or wrong intention;
But I beg you please tell me
      Your thoughts."   80
Then the lady deeply sighed
And said: "For the sake of God, leave me in peace, fair sir,
For I don't need you to increase the anxiety
      Or the frustration
That I receive from them." At this he began to move   85
Closer to her, to draw out her thoughts,
And said to her: "Very sweet and noble one
      I see you're sad.
But I swear to you and promise by my faith
That, if you'd reveal your troubles to me,   90
I would do everything in my power
      To put them right."
And the lady undertook to thank him for this
And said: "Sir, no one can help me in this,

```
Ne nuls fors Dieus ne porroit alegier                95
      La grief dolour
Qui fait palir et teindre ma coulour,
Qui tient mon cuer en tristesse et en plour,
Et qui me met en si dure langour
      Qu'a dire voir                                100
Nuls cuer qui soit n'en porroit plus avoir."
"Dame, et quels mauls vos fait si fort doloir?
Dites le moy; que je cuit recevoir
      Si tres grief peinne,
Si dolereuse, si dure, si greveinne,             105
Si amere, que soiez bien certeinne,
Il n'est dame, ne creature humeinne,
      Ne n'iert jamais,
Qui tele peinne endurast onques mais."
"Certes, sire, je croy bien que tel fais          110
Ne portez pas a vo cuer que je fais.
      Pour ce sarez
Ma pensée qu'a savoir desirez.
Mais tout avant, vos me prometterez
Que sans mentir la vostre me direz."              115
      "Tenez, ma dame.
Je vous promet par may foy et par m'ame
Que le penser qui m'esprent et enflame
Et qui souvent mon cuer mort et entame
      Vous gehiray                                120
De chief en chief, ne ja n'en mentiray."
"Certes, sire, et je le vous diray."
"Or dites donc; je vous escouteray
      Moult volentiers."

"Sire, il a bien .vij. ans ou .viij. entiers      125
Que mes cuers a esté sers et rentiers
A Bonne Amour, si qu'apris ses sentiers
      Ay tres m'enfance.
Car dès premiers que j'eus sa congnoissance,
Cuer, corps, povoir, vie, avoir, et puissance     130
Et quanqu'il fu de moy, mis par plaisance
      En son servage.
Et elle me retint en son hommage
Et me donna de tres loial corage                  [10v]
A bel et bon, dous, gracieus, et sage,            135
      Qui de valour,
De courtoisie et de parfaite honnour,
Et de plaisant maintient avoit la flour,
Et des tres bons estoit tout le millour.
      Et s'ot en li                               140
```

126. A renties--131. A plaisence

Nor none save God could alleviate 95
        The terrible grief
Which taints and pales my complexion,
Which holds fast my heart in sorrow and in tears,
Which leaves me in such hard languor
        That, to tell the truth, 100
No heart that exists could ever have more."
"Lady, what misfortune makes your pain so great?
Tell it to me; for I think to have received
        A hurt so very painful
So sorrowful, so strong, so heavy, 105
So bitter that, of this you may be sure,
There is no woman, no human being,
        And never was,
Who has ever endured this kind of pain."
"Surely, sir, I firmly believe that you 110
Bear not the same burden in your heart that I do.
        Therefore you'll know
My thoughts as you have wished.
But, before all this, you will promise me
To tell me yours without any lies." 115
        "Agreed, my lady.
I promise you by my faith and by my soul
That the thought which inflames and burns me
And which often eats at my heart and rends it
        I will confess to you 120
Completely, and in nothing will I lie."
"So be it, sir, and now I'll tell you mine."
"Speak then, and I will listen to you
        Most willingly."

"Sir, altogether now it's seven years or eight 125
That my heart's been serf and vassal
To Good Love, whose ways I have come to learn
        Since my childhood.
For when I encountered Love the first time
I gladly placed heart, body, strength, life, 130
My goods and power, whatever there was of me,
        At her disposal.
As her vassal she retained me
And entrusted to me the loyal heart
Of one who was handsome and good, sweet, wise, and gracious,
        Who in valor,
In courtesy, in perfect honor,
In his pleasant demeanor was the very flower,
And of the very good was indeed the best.
        And he had 140

Gent corps faitis, cointe, apert, et joli,
Juene, gentil, de maniere garni,
Plein de tout ce qu'il faut a vray ami.
   Et d'estre amez
Par dessus tous estoit dignes clamez,   145
Car il estoit vrais, loiaus, et secrez,
Et en trestous fais amoureus discrez;*
   Et je l'amoie
Si loiaument que tout mon cuer mettoie
En li amer, n'autre entente n'avoie;   150
Qu'en li estoit m'esperence, ma joie,
   Et mon plaisir,
Mon cuer, m'amor, mon penser, mon desir.
De tous les biens pooit mes cuers joïr
Par li veoïr seulement et oïr.   155
   Tous mes confors
Estoit en li; c'estoit tous mes depors,
Tous mes solas, mes deduis, mes tresors.
C'estoit mes murs, mes chastiaus, mes ressors.
   Et il m'amoit;   160
Par dessus tout me servoit et cremoit;
Son cuer, s'amour, sa dame me clamoit.
Tous estoit miens; mes cuers bien le savoit;
   Ne riens desplaire
Ne li peüst qui a moy deüst plaire   165
De nos .ij. cuers estoit si juste paire
Qu'onques ne fu l'un a l'autre contraire;
   Einsois estoient
Tuit d'un acort; une pensée avoient.
De volenté, de desir se sambloient;   170
Un bien, un mal, une joie sentoient
   Conjointement,
N'onques ne fu entre eaus .ij. autrement;
Mais c'a esté toudis si loyaument
Qu'il n'ot onques un villain pensement   175
   En nos amours.
Lasse, dolente! Or est bien a rebours.
Car mes douceurs sont dolereus labours,
Et mes joies sont ameres dolours,
   Et mi penser,   180
En qui mes cuers se soloit deliter
Et doucement de tous maus conforter,
Sont et seront dolent, triste, et amer.
   En obscurté
Seront mi jour, plein de maleürté,   185
Et mi espoir sans nulle seürté,
Et ma douceur sera dure durté

147. AFMB et discrez--174. F toudis este

just nothing: where's the wench?
Gerald. [*Points to his heart.*] Shee's heere sir, heere.
Long. Uds pitty! unbutton man, thou'lt stifle her else.
Ger. Nay good sir, will you goe?
Long. With all my heart, I stay but for you. 115
Spen. Doe you heare sir?
Long. What say?
Spend. Will you take it for thirteene?
Long. Not a penny more then I bid. *Ex. Ger. and Long.*
Spend. Why then say you might have had a good 120
bargaine. Where's this boy to make up the wares? heere's
some tenne peeces opened, and all to no purpose.

Enter Boy.

Boy. O *Franke*! shut up shop, shut up shop.
Spend. Shut up shop, boy, why?
Boy. My Master is come from the Court knighted, and 125
bid / us, for he sayes he will have the first yeare of [B3]
the reigne of his Knighthood kept holiday; here he comes.

Enter Sir Lionell.

Spend. God give your worship joy, sir.
Sir Lion. O *Francke*! I have the worship now in the 129
right kinde: the sword of Knighthood sticks stil upon my
shoulders, and I feele the blow in my purse, it has cut
two leather bagges asunder; but all's one, honour must be
purchac'd: I will give over my Citty coate, and betake my
selfe to the Court jacket; as for trade, I will deale in't
no longer: I will seate thee in my shop, and it shall be
thy care to aske men what they lacke; my stocke shall be
summed up, and I will call thee to an account for it. 137
Spend. My service sir, never deserv'd so much,
Nor could I ever hope so large a bounty
Could spring out of your love.
Sir Lion. That's all one, 140

112 SD [*Points to his heart.*]] *Hazlitt* 121 bargaine.] *Dodsley*;
bargaine; 128 SD *Sir*] *Dodsley*; *sir* 130 kinde:] *ed.*; kinde,
135 longer:] *ed.*; longer, 136 lacke;] *ed.*; lacke,

I do love to do things beyond mens hopes.
To morrow I remoove into the Strand,
There for this quarter dwell, the next at *Fulham*:
He that hath choice, may shift, the whilst shalt thou
Be maister of this house, and rent it free.   145
Spend. I thanke you sir.
Sir Lion. To day Ile go dine with my Lord Maior: to
morrow with the Sherifes, and next day with the Aldermen.
I will spread the Ensigne of my knighthood over the face
of the Citty, which shall strike as great a terrour to my
enemies, as ever *Tamberlaine* to the Turkes.   151
Come *Franke*, come in with me, and see the meate,
Upon the which my knighthood first shall eate. *Ex: omnes.*

[SCENE II]

Enter Staines.

Staines. There is a divell has haunted me these three
yeares, in likenesse of an Usurer, a fellow that in all
his life never eat three groat loaves out of his owne purse,
nor never warmed him but at other mens fires, never saw a
joynt of mutton in his owne house these foure and twenty
yeares, but alwayes cosoned the poore prisoners, for he
alwayes bought his victualls / out of the almes-[B3^V] 160
basket, and yet this rogue now feedes upon capons which my
tenants sent him out of the Countrey; he is Landlord forsooth
over all my possessions: well, I am spent, and this rogue
has consumed me; I dare not walke abroade to see my friends,
for feare the Serjeants should take acquaintance of me:
my refuge is *Ireland*, or *Virginia*; necessitie cries out,
and I will presently to *Westchester*.   167

Enter Bubble.

How now! *Bubble* hast thou pack'd up all thy things? our
parting time is come: nay pre thee doe not weepe.

141 hopes.] *Dodsley*; hopes,   148 Aldermen.] *Collier*; Aldermen,

Bub. Affection sir will burst out. 170
Staines. Thou hast beene a faithfull servant to me,
go to thy uncle, hee'l give thee entertainement: tell him
upon the stonie rocke of his mercilesse hart my fortunes
suffer shipwracke.
Bub. I will tell him he is an usuring rascall, and 175
one that would do the Common-wealth good, if he were hanged.
Staines. Which thou hast cause to wish for, thou arte
his heire, my affectionate *Bubble*.
Bub. But Master, wherefore should we be parted?
Staines. Because my fortunes are desperate, thine 180
are hopefull.
Bub. Why but whither doe you meane to goe Maister?
Staines. Why to Sea.
Bub. To sea! Lord blesse us, me thinks I heare of a
tempest already, but what will you doe at Sea? 185
Staines. Why as other Gallants doe that are spent,
turne pyrate.
Bub. O Maister! have the grace of Wapping before your
eyes, remember a high tide, give not your friends cause to
wet their hankerchers: nay Maister, Ile tell you a 190
better course then so, you and I will goe and robbe mine
uncle; if we scape, wee'le dominiere together, if we be
taken, wee'le be hanged together at Tyburne, that's the
warmer gallowes of the two.

Enter a Messenger.

Mes. By your leave sir, whereabouts dwels one Master 195
Bubble?
Bub. Doe you heare, my friend, doe you know Master
Bubble if you doe see him?
Mes. No in truth doe I not.
Bub. What is your businesse with Maister *Bubble*? / 200
Mes. Marry sir, I come with welcome newes to him. [B4]
Bub. Tell it, my friend, I am the man.

172 entertainement:] *Reed*; entertainement, 195, 197 Master] *Hazlitt*;
M. 201 SP *Mes.*] *Q1* (catchword / *Mess.* / B3^v)

Mes. May I be assured sir, that your name is master
Bubble?
Bub. I tell thee, honest friend, my name is master   205
Bubble, Master *Bartholomew Bubble.*
Mes. Why then sir, you are heire to a million, for
your uncle the rich usurer is dead.
Bub. Pray thee honest friend, goe to the next   209
Haberdashers, and bid him send me a new melancholy hat,
and take thou that for thy labour.
Mes. I will sir.   *Exit.*

    Enter another Messenger hastily, and knockes.

Bub. Umh, umh, umh.
Sta. [*Aside.*] I would the newes were true; see how
my little *Bubble* is blowne up with't!   215
Bub. Doe you heare, my friend, for what doe you
knocke there?
2. Mes. Marry sir, I would speake with the worshipfull
Master *Bubble.*
Bub. The worshipfull! and what would you doe with   220
the worshipfull Master *Bubble?* I am the man.
2. Mes. I cry your worship mercy then, Master Thong
the Belt-maker sent me to your worship, to give you notice,
that your uncle is dead, and that you are his onely heire.
                   Exit.
Bub. [*Aside.*] Thy newes is good, and I have look'd
    for't long: 225
Thankes unto thee, my friend, and goodman Thong.

           Enter Maister Blancke.

Staines. Certainely, this newes is true: for see
another, by this light, his Scrivener! now Master *Blancke,*
whither away so fast?
Bla. Maister *Staines*, God save you, where is your   230
man?

214 SD [*Aside.*]] *ed.*   225 SD [*Aside.*]] *ed.*   228 Master] *Hazlitt;* M.

SC. II]   GREENE'S TU QUOQUE   13

Staines. Why looke you sir, doe you not see him?
Bla. God save the right worshipfull master *Bubble*; I
bring you heavy newes with a light heart.
Bub. What are you?   235
Bla. I am your worships poore Scrivener.
Bub. He is an honest man it seems, for he has both
his eares.
Bla. I am one that your worships uncle committed some /
trust in for the putting out of his mony, and I [B4^v] 240
hope I shall have the putting out of yours.
Bub. The putting out of mine! would you have the
putting out of money?
Bla. Yea sir.
Bub. No sir, I am olde enough to put out my owne   245
mony.
Bla. I have writings of your worships.
Sta. [*Aside to Blank.*] As thou lov'st thy profite,
hold thy tongue: thou and I will conferre.
Bub. Do you heare, my friend, can you tell me when, 250
and how my uncle died?
Bla. Yes sir, he died this morning, and hee was
kill'd by a Butcher.
Bub. How! by a Butcher?
Bla. Yes indeed sir, for going this morning into the 255
Market, to cheapen meate, hee fell downe starke dead,
because a Butcher ask'd him foure shillings for a shoulder
of Mutton.
Bu. How, stark dead? and could not *aqua vitae* fetch
him again?   260
Bla. No sir, nor *Rosa solis* neither, and yet there
was triall made of both.
Bu. [*Aside.*] I shall love *aqua vitae* and *rosa solis*
the better while I live.
Sta. Will it please your worship to accept of my   265

248 S D [*Aside to Blank.*]] ed.; [*Aside.*]] *Hazlitt* 249 tongue:]
Q1(c); tongue, *Q1(u)* 253 Butcher.] *Q3*; Butcher? 259 How,]
Q2; How 263 SD [*Aside.*]] *Hazlitt*

poore service? you know my case is desperate; I beseech
you that I may feed upon your bread, tho it be of the
brownest, and drinke of your drinke tho it be of the
smallest, for I am humble in body, and dejected in minde,
and will do your worship as good service for forty   270
shillings a yeare, as another shall for 3. pounds.
Bub. I wil not stand with you for such a matter,
because you have beene my master, but otherwise, I will
entertaine no man without some Knights or Ladies Letter
for their behaviour. *Gervase* I take it is your christen
name.   276
Sta. Yes if it please your worship.
Bub. Well *Gervase*, be a good servant, and you shall
finde me a dutifull master: and because you have beene a
Gentleman, I will entertaine you for my Tutor in   280
behaviour; Conduct me to my pallace.   *Exeunt omnes.*

[SCENE III]

Enter Geraldine as in his study, reading.

Ger. As little children love to play with fire, /
And will not leave till they themselves doe burne,   [Cl]
So did I fondly dally with Desire:
Untill Loves flames grew hote, I could not turne,   285
Nor well avoyde; but sigh and sob, and mourne
As children doe, whenas they feele the paine,
Till tender mother kisse them whole againe.
Fie, what unsavery stuffe is this? but shee,
Whose mature judgement can distinguish things,   290
Will thus conceit; tales that are harshest told,
Have smoothest meanings, and to speake are bold:
It is the first-borne Sonet of my braine:
Why suck'd a white leafe from my blacke-lipp'd penne
So sad employment?   295

266 service?] *Dodsley*; ser- / uice, // desperate;] *Dodsley*;
desperate, 275 behaviour.] *Hazlitt*; behauiour,
Sc. III OSD *study,*] *Reed*; *study* 293 braine:] *ed.*; braine,
294 Why] *Dodsley*; We 295 employment?] *Dodsley*; employment,

[SC. III] GREENE'S TU QUOQUE

Enter Will Rash and Longfield.

Yet the dry paper drinkes it up as deep,
As if it flowed from *Petrarkes* cunning Quill.
Rash. How now! what have we heere? a Sonet and a
Satire coupled together like my Ladies Dogge and her
Munkie; *As little children &c.* 300
Ger. Pre thee away, by the deepest oath that can be
sworne, thou shalt not reade it; by our friendship I conjure
thee, pre thee let goe.
Rash. Now in the name of *Cupid*, what want'st thou, a
pigeon, a dove, a mate, a turtle, dost love fowle, ha?
O no, shee's fairer thrice then is the Queene, 306
Whom beauteous *Venus* called is by name.
Pre thee let mee know what she is thou lovest, that I may
shunne her, if I should chance to meete her.
Long. Why Ile tell you sir what she is, if you do 310
not know.
Rash. No not I, I protest.
Long. Why t'is your sister.
Rash. How! my sister?
Long. Yes, your eldest sister. 315
Rash. Now God blesse the man, he had better chuse a
wench that has been borne and bred in an alley, her tongue
is a perpetual motion. Thought is not so swift as it is;
and for pride, the woman that had her Ruffe poak'd by the
divell, is but a Puritan to her; thou could'st never 320
have fastned thy affection on a worse subject: shee'l
flowt faster then a court-waiting woman / in [Cl^V]
progresse; any man that comes in the way of honesty does she
set her marke upon, that is, a villainous Jeast; for she is
a kinde of Poetesse, and will make Ballads upon the 325
calves of your legges: I pre thee let her alone, shee'l
never make a good wife for any man unlesse it be a Leather
dresser; for perhaps he, in time, may turne her.

298 heere?] *Reed*; heere, 302 it;] *Reed*; it, 307-8 name. / Pre thee]
Hazlitt; name, pre thee 314 SP *Rash.*] *Q2*; *no period, Q1* 318 motion.]
ed.; motion, 320 her;] *ed.*; her, 321 subject:] *ed.*; subiect,
323 progresse;] *Dodsley*; progresse,

Ger. Thou hast a Priviledge to utter this,
But by my life my owne bloud could not scape   330
A chasticement for thus prophaning her,
Whose vertues sits above mens calumnies.
Had mine owne brother spoke thus liberally,
My fury should have taught him better manners.
Long. No more words as you feare a challenge.   335
Rash. [*Aside to Longfield.*] I may tell thee in thine
eare, I am glad to heare what I do; I pray God send her no
worse husband, nor he no worse wife: [*To Geraldine.*] do
you heare love, will you take your Cloak and Rapier, and
walke abroad into some wholesome aire? I do much feare
thy infection, good councell I see will do no good on   341
thee: But pursue the end,
And to thy thoughts, Ile prove a faithfull friend. *Exeunt.*

[SCENE IV]

*Enter Spendall, Nan Tickleman, Sweatman,
Pursenet, and a Drawer.*

Spend. Here's a spacious roome to walke in: sirra set
downe the candle, and fetch us up a quart of Ipocras, and
so wee'l part.   346
Sweat. Nay faith Sonne, wee'l have a pottle, let's
ne'r be covetous in our yong dayes.
Spend. A pottle sirra, doe you heare?
Dra. Yes sir, you shall.   [*Exit.*]   350
Spend. How now wench! how dost?
Tickle. Faith I am somewhat sicke, yet I should be well
enough if I had a new gowne.
Spend. Why heere's my hand, within these three dayes
thou shalt have one.   355

---

332 calumnies.] *Q2*; calumnies,   336 SD [*Aside to Longfield.*]] *ed.*
338 SD [*To Geraldine.*]] *ed.*   342 But ... end, /] *ed.*; but /
343 And ... friend.] *Collier*; *as prose, Q1* (but / pursue ... friend)
// SD *Exeunt.*] *Reed*; *Exit.*   344 in:] *Reed*; in,   350 SD [*Exit.*]] *ed.*

Sweat. And will you (sonne) remember me for a new
fore-part? by my troth, my old one is worne so bare, I am
asham'd any body should see't.
Spend. Why, did I ever faile of my promise? /
Sweat. No in sinceritie didst thou not. [C2] 360

Enter Drawer.

Dra. Heere's a cup of rich Ipocras.
Spend. Here sister, mother, and master Pursnet; nay
good sir, be not so dejected, for by this wine, to morrow
I will send you stuffe for a new suite, and as much as
shall line you a cloake cleane through. 365
Purs. I thanke you, and shall study to deserve.
Spend. Heere boy, fill, and hang that curmogin that's
good for no body but himselfe. [*Exit Drawer.*]
Purs. Heroickly spoken by this Candle, t'is pity thou
wert not made a Lord. 370
Spend. A Lord! by this Light I doe not thinke but to
bee Lord Maior of London before I die, and have three
Pageants carried before me, besides a Shippe and an
Unicorne; prentices may pray for that time, for whensoever
it happens, I will make another Shrovetuesday for them.

Enter Drawer.

Dra. Yong master *Rash* has sent you a quart of Maligoe.
Spend. Master *Rash*! zownds! how does he know I am here?
Dra. Nay, I know not sir. 378
Spend. Know not! it comes through you and your rascally
glib-tongu'd companions; t'is my Masters sonne, a fine
gentleman he is, and a boon companion, I must go see him.

Exit Spend.

Sweat. Boy, fill us a cup of your maligo, wee'l drinke
to Master *Spendall* in his absence, there's not a finer
spirit of a Cittizen within the walles: here master

357 fore-part?] *Reed*; fore-part,   368 SD [*Exit Drawer.*]] *ed.*
377 Master] *Collier*; M. // zownds!] *Dodsley*; zownds   380 companions;]
Dodsley; companions,   383 Master] *Collier*; M.   384 walles:] *Dodsley*;
walles,

Pursnet you shall pledge him.   385
Purs. Ile not refuse it were it puddle: by *Stix* he is
a bountifull Gentleman, and I shall report him so: heere
Mistris *Tickleman*, shall I charge you?
Tickle. Doe your worst Sergeant, Ile pledge my yoong 389
Spendall a whole sea, as they say; fa la la la la, would
the Musicke were heere againe, I doe beginne to be wanton.
Ipocras sirra, and a drie bisket; here bawd, a carowse.
Sweat. Bawd! I faith you beginne to grow light ith
head; I pray, no more such words, for if you doe, I shall
grow into distempers.   395
Tickle. Distempers! hang your distempers, be angry
with / me and thou dar'st! I pray, who feedes you, [C2^v]
but I? who keepes the feather-beddes from the Brokers, but
I? tis not your sawsege face, thicke clowted creame
rampallion at home, that snuffles in the nose like a   400
decayed Bagge-pipe.
Purs. Nay, sweete Mistris *Tickle-man*, be concordant,
reverence Antiquitie.

        Enter Rash, Longfield, and Spendal.

Rash. Save you, sweete creatures of beauty, save you:
How now olde *Belzebub*, how dost thou?   405
Sweat. Belzebub! Belzebub in thy face!
Spend. Nay, good words Mistris Sweatman, hee's a young
Gallant, you must not weigh what he sayes.   408
Rash. I would my lamentable complayning Lover had beene
heere, heere had beene a Supersedeas for his melancholy,
and yfaith *Francke* I am glad my father has turn'd over his
shop to thee, I hope I, or any friend of mine, shall have so
much credite with thee, as to stand in thy bookes for a
suite of Sattin.
Spend. For a whole peece, if you please: any friend   415
of yours shall command me to the last remnant.

---

386 he] *Q2*; hs   388 Mistris] *Q2*; M   390 say;] *ed.*; say,   391 wanton.]
Dodsley; wanton,   394 head;] *ed.*; head,   397 dar'st!] *ed.*; dar'st,
406 face!] *Hazlitt*; face.   415 please:] *ed.*; please,

Rash. Why God a mercy *Francke*! what, shall's to dice?
Spend. Dice or drincke, heere's forty crownes: as long
as that will last, any thing.
Rash. Why there spoke a gingling Boy. 420
Spend. A pox of money, t'is but rubbish, and he that
hoord's it up, is but a Scavenger: if there be cardes ith
house, let's goe to Primero.
Rash. Primero! why I thought thou hadst not been so
much gamster as to play at it. 425
Spend. Gamster (to say truth) I am none, but what is
it I will not be in good company? I will fit my selfe to
all humors, I will game with a Gamster, drinke with a
drunkard, be civill with a cittizen, fight with a swaggerer,
and drabbe with a whoore-master. 430

Enter a Swaggerer puffing. /

Rash. An excellent humour yfaith. [C3]
Long. Zownds! what have we heere?
Spend. A land Porpoise, I thinke.
Rash. This is no angry, nor no roaring boy, but a
blustering boy; now *Eolus* defend us, what puffes are 435
these?
Swag. I doe smell a whoore.
Dra. O Gentlemen, give him good words, hee's one of the
roaring boyes.
Swag. Rogue! 440
Dra. Heere sir.
Swag. Take my cloake, I must unbuckle, my pickled
oysters worke; puffe, puffe.
Spend. Puffe, puffe.
Swag. Dost thou retort? in opposition stand. 445
Spend. Out you swaggering Rogue! Zownds, Ile kicke
him out of the roome! *Beates him away.*

---

417 Francke!] *ed.*; Francke, 418 crownes:] *Collier*; crownes, 432
Zownds!] *Reed*; Zownds 440 Rogue!] *Reed*; Rogue. 445 retort?]
Dodsley; retort, 446 Rogue!] *Collier*; Rogue, // Zownds,] *Dodsley*;
Zownds 447 roome!] *Hazlitt*; roome.

20   GREENE'S TU QUOQUE   [SC. IV

Tickle. Out, alas! their naked tooles are out!
Spend. Feare not (sweet heart;) come along with me. 449

                              Exeunt omnes.

                    [SCENE V]

                Enter Gartred sola.

Gart. Thrice happy dayes they were, and too soone gone,
When as the heart was coupled with the tongue,
And no deceitfull flattery or guile
Hung on the Lovers teare-commixed smile:
Could women learne but that imperiousnesse,
By which men use to stint our happinesse,   455
When they have purchast us for to be theirs,
By customarie sighs and forced teares;
To give us bittes of kindnesse lest we faint,
But no aboundance, that we ever want,
And still are begging; which too well they know   460
Endeeres affection, and doth make it grow:
Had we these sleights, how happy were we then,
That we might glory over love-sicke men?
But Arts we know not, nor have any skill,
To faine a sowre looke to a pleasing will,   465
                    Enter Joyce.
Nor cowch a secret love in shew of hate, /
But if we like, must be compassionate;   [C3^V]
Yet I will strive to bridle and conceale
The hid affection which my heart doth feele.
Joyce. Now the boy with the Bird-bolt be praisde: 470
nay faith sister forward, t'was an excellent passion, come
let's heare, what is hee? if hee be a proper man, and have
a blacke eye, a smooth chinne, and a curld pate, take him

448 Out,] *Dodsley*; Out // are out!] *ed.*; are out,   452 guile] *Q3*;
guile: 457 teares;] *Dodsley*; teares,   466 hate,] *ed.*; hate:
468 conceale] *Dodsley*; conceale,   470 SP *Joyce.*] *Dodsley*; no
period, *Q1*

wench; if my father will not consent, runne away with him,
I'le helpe to convey you.   475
Gart. You talke strangely sister.
Joyce. Sister, sister, dissemble not with me, though
you doe meane to dissemble with your lover, though you have
protested to conceale your affection; by this tongue you
shall not, for I'le discover all as soone as I know the
Gentleman.   481
Gart. Discover, what will you discover?
Joyce. Mary, enough Ile warrant thee: first and
formost, Ile tell him thou readst love-passions in print,
and speakest everie morning without booke to thy looking-
glasse; next, that thou never sleep'st till an houre after
the Bell-man; that as soone as thou art asleepe, thou art
in a dreame, and in a dreame thou art the kindest and
comfortablest bed-fellow for kissings and embracings; by
this hand, I can not rest for thee; but our father--   490

                    Enter Sir Lyonell.

Lyonell. How now! what are you two consulting on, on
husbands? you thinke you loose time I am sure, but holde
your owne a little Girles, it shall not be long ere I'le
provide for you: and for you *Gartred*, I have bethought my
selfe already: 495
Whirle-pit the usurer is late deceast,
A man of unknowne wealth, which he has left
Unto a provident kinsman as I heare,
That was once servant to that unthrift *Staines*.
A prudent Gentleman they say he is,   500
And (as I take it) called maister *Bubble*.
Joyce. Bubble!
Lyonell. Yes nimble-chappes, what say you to that? /
Joyce. Nothing, but that I wish his Christen name   [C4]

---

474 wench;] *Dodsley*; wench, 477, 483 SP *Joyce.*] *Dodsley*; *no period,
Q1* 483 thee:] *ed.*; thee, 486 sleep'st] *ed.*; sleep'st, 490 thee:]
Hazlitt; thee, // father--] *Q3*; father.-- // SD *Sir*] *Q2*; *sir*
493 a little] *Q3*; alittle 495 already:] *ed.*; already, 503 SP
Lyonell.] *Q2*; *no period, Q1*

                     were *Water*.   505
Gart. Sir, I'm at your disposing, but my minde
Stands not as yet towards marriage:
Were you so pleasde I would a little longer
Enjoy the quiet of a single bed.   509
Lyonell. Heere's the right tricke of them all: let a man
Be motion'd to um, they could be content
To leade a single life forsooth, when the harlotries
Doe pine and runne into diseases,
Eate chalke and oate-meale, cry and creep in corners,
Which are manifest tokens of their longings,   515
And yet they will dissemble. But *Gartred*,
As you doe owe me reverence, and will pay it,
Prepare your selfe to like this Gentleman,
Who can maintaine thee in thy choice of Gownes,
Of tyres, of servants, and of costly Jewells;   520
Nay for a neede, out of his easie nature,
Mai'st draw him to the keeping of a Coach
For Countrey, and Carroach for *London*,
Indeed what mightst thou not?

                     Enter a Servant.

Servant. Sir, here's one come from Master *Bubble*, to   525
invite you to the funerall of his uncle.
Lyonell. Thanke the Messenger, and make him drinke;
Tell him I will not faile to wait the coarse.
Yet stay, I will goe talke with him my selfe:
Gartred, thinke upon what I have tolde you,   530
And let me er't be long receive your answere.

                     Exeunt Lyonell & Ser.

Joyce. Sister, sister.
Gart. What say you sister?
Joyce. Shall I provide a Cord?

---

507 marriage:] *ed*.; marriage,   510 SP *Lyonell*.] *Q2*; *no period*, *Q1* //
all:] *Collier*; all,   524 not?] *Q3*; not.   526 invite] *Q1(c)*; inuĭte
Q1(u)   527 SP *Lyonell*.] *Q2*; *no period*, *Q1* // drinke;] *ed*.; drinke,
528 coarse.] *ed*.; coarse,   532, 534 SP *Joyce*.] *Q3*; *no period*, *Q1*

Gart. A Cord! what to doe?   535
Joyce. Why to let thee out at the window; doe not I know
that thou wilt runne away with the Gentleman, for whom you
made the passion, rather then indure this same *Bubble* [C4^v]
that my father talkes of, t'were good you would let mee bee
of your councell, lest I breake the necke of your plot.
Gart. Sister, know I love thee,   541
And I'le not thinke a thought thou shalt not know;
I love a Gentleman that answeres me,
In all the rites of love as faithfully,
Has woo'd me oft with Sonets, and with teares,   545
Yet I seeme still to slight him: Experience tells,
The Jewell that's enjoy'd is not esteem'd,
Things hardly got, are alwayes highest deem'd.
Joyce. You say wel sister, but it is not good to linger
out too long, continuance of time will take away any mans
stomacke i'th world; I hope the next time that he comes to
you, I shall see him.   552
Gart. You shall.
Joyce. Why goe to then, you shall have my opinion of him;
if he deserve thee, thou shalt delay him no longer; for
if you can not finde in your heart to tell him you love him,
I'le sigh it out for you; come, we little creatures must
helpe one another.   558

                        Exeunt.

                        [SCENE VI]

                    Enter Geraldine.

Ger. How cheerefully things looke in this place:
Tis alwayes Spring-time heere, such is the grace   560
And potencie of her who has the blisse,
To make it still *Elizeum* where she is:
Nor doth the King of flames in's golden fires,

536, 549, 554 SP *Joyce.*] *Q3; no period, Q1*   538 Bubble] *Dodsley*;
Bubble,   554 him;] *Dodsley*; him,   559 place:] *ed.*; place,

After a tempest answer mens desires,
When as he casts his comfortable beames,   565
Over the flowrie fields and silver streames,
As her illustrate Beautie strikes in me,
And wrappes my soule up to felicitie.

Enter Gartred and Joyce aloft.

Joyce. Doe you heare sir?
Gart. Why sister, what will you doe?   570
Joyce. By my mayden-head, an oath which I ne'r tooke
in vaine, either goe downe and comfort him, or I'le call him
up, / and disclose all: What, will you have no mercie? [Dl]
but let a proper man, that might spend the spirit of his
youth upon your selfe, fall into a consumption, for shame
sister.   576
Gart. Y'are the strangest creature, what would you have
me doe?
Joy. Marry, I would have you goe to him, take him by   579
the hand, and grype him, say y'are welcome, I love you
with all my heart, you are the man must doe the feat, and
take him about the necke, and kisse upon the bargaine.
Gart. Fie how you talke, 'tis meere immodestie,
The common'st strumpet would not doe so much.
Joy. Mary the better, for such as are honest, should   585
still doe what the common strumpet will not: Speake, will
you doe it?
Gart. Ile loose his company forever first.
Joyce. Doe you heare sir? heere's a Gentlewoman would
speake with you.   590
Gart. Why sister, pray sister.
Joyce. One that loves you with all her heart, yet is
asham'd to confesse it.
Gart. Good sister hold your tongue, I will goe downe
to him.   595
Joyce. Doe not jeast with me, for by this hand I'le

569, 571 SP *Joyce.*] *Q3*; *no period, Q1* 585-7 Mary ... should ... it?]
as prose, ed.; Mary ... honest, / Should ... not: / Speake ... it?

eyther get him up, or goe downe my selfe, and reade the
whole History of your love to him.
Gart. If youle forbeare to call, I will goe downe.
Joyce. Let me see your backe then, and heare you? 600
doe not use him scurvily you were best; unset all your
tyrannical looks, and bid him lovingly welcome, or as I live,
I'le stretch out my voice againe; [*Exit Gartred.*] uds foot,
I must take some paines I see, or wee shall never have this
geare cotton: but to say truth, the fault is in my 605
melancholy Monsieur, for if hee had but halfe so much
spirit, as he has flesh, hee might ha boorded her by this.
Enter Gart. [*below*]. But see, yonder she marches; now a
passion of his side of halfe an houre long: his hatte is
off already, as if he were begging one poore penny-worth
of kindnesse. / 611
Ger. Shall I presume (faire Mistris) on your hand [D1^v]
to lay my unworthy lip?
Joyce. Fie upon him, I am asham'd to heare him, you 614
shall have a Country fellow at a Maie-pole go better to
his worke: he had neede to be constant, for hee is able
to spoile as many Maides as he shall fall in love withall.
Gart. Sir, you professe love unto me, let me intreate
you it may appeare but in some small request.
Ger. Let me know it (Lady) and I shall soone effect 620
it.
Gart. But for this present to forbeare this place,
Because my father is expected heere.
Ger. I am gone Lady.
Joyce. Doe you heare sir? 625
Ger. Did you call?
Joyce. Looke up to the window.
Ger. What say you Gentlewoman?
Gart. Nay pray sir goe, it is my sister call's to
hasten you. 630

603 SD [*Exit Gartred.*]] ed. 608 SD *Enter* ... [*below*].] ed.; after l.
611, Q1 // [*below*]] Hazlitt 609 long:] Hazlitt; long, 615 Maie-pole]
Dodsley; Maie-pole, 621 it.] Q2; *possible colon,* Q1

Joyce. I call to speake with you, pray stay a little.
Ger. The Gentlewoman has something to say to me.
Gart. She has nothing, I doe conjure you, as you love
me, stay not. *Exit Joyce.*
Ger. The power of Magicke can not fasten me, I am 635
gone.
Gart. Good sir, looke backe no more, what voice ere call
 you:
Imagine, going from me, you were comming,
And use the same speede, as you love my safety. *Exit Ger.*
Wilde-witted sister, I have prevented you: 640
I will not have my love yet open'd to him;
By how much longer 'tis ere it be knowne,
By so much dearer 'twill be when 'tis purchast:
But I must use my strength to stop her journey,
For she will after him: *Enter Joyce [below].* and see,
she comes; 645
Nay sister, you are at furdest.
Joyce.   Let me goe you were best.
For if you wrastle with me I shall throw you:
Passion, come backe, foole, lover,
Turne againe, and kisse your belly full, /
For heere she is will stand you, doe your worst: [D2] 650
Will you let me goe?
Gart.   Yes, if youle stay.
Joyce. If I stirre a foote, hang me: you shall come
together of your selves and be naught; doe what you will,
for if 'ere I trouble my selfe againe, let me want help in
such a case when I need. 655
Gart. Nay but pre thee sister be not angry.

631 a little] *Q2*; alittle   637 you:] *ed.*; you,   640 Wilde-witted] *Dodsley*; Wilde witted // you:] *Reed*; you,   641 him;] *ed.*; him, 645 SD [below]] *Hazlitt*; SD after 1. 645, *Dodsley*; after 1. 642, *Q1* 646-9 Let ... belly full] *as verse, Hazlitt*; *as prose, Q1* (Let ... for ... passion ... turne)   647 you:] *ed.*; you,   648-9 Passion ... lover, / Turne ... belly full] *ed.*; Passion ... again, / And ... bellyful *Hazlitt*   652 me:] *ed.*; me,   653 selues] *Q2*; selues, // naught;] *Dodsley*; naught,   654-5 trouble ... need.] *as prose, Reed*; trouble ... help / In ... need.

SC. VII]   GREENE'S TU QUOQUE   27

Joyce. I will be angry: udsfoot, I cannot indure such
foolerie, I: two bashful fooles that would couple together,
and yet ha not the faces.
Gart. Nay pre thee sweete sister.   660
Joyce. Come, come, let me goe, birds that want the
use of reason and speach can couple together in one day,
and yet you that have both cannot conclude in twenty.
Gart. Why what good would it doe you to tell him?
Joyce. Doe not talke to me, for I am deafe to any   665
thing you say, goe weepe and crie.
Gart. Nay but sister.   *Exeunt ambo.*

[SCENE VII]

Enter Staines, and a Drawer with wine.

Sta. Drawer, bid them make haste at home, tell them
they are comming from church.
Dra. I will sir.   *Exit Drawer.*   670
Sta. That I should live to be a serving-man, a
fellow which scalds his mouth with another mans porredge,
brings up meat for other mens bellies, and carries away the
bones for his own, changes his cleane trencher for a fowle
one, and is glad of it, and yet did I never live so merry
a life, when I was my masters master, as now I doe, being
man to my man, and I will stand too't for all my former
speeches, a serving-man lives a better life then his Master,
and thus I proove it; the saying is, The nearer the bone
the sweeter the flesh: then must the serving-man needes
eate the sweeter flesh, for hee alwayes pickes the bones.
And againe the Proverb sayes, The deeper the sweeter: 682
There has the serving-man the vantage againe, for he drinks
still in the bottome of the pot; hee filles his belly, and
never / askes what's to pay? weares broad-cloth,[D2^V]685
and yet dares walke Watling-streete, without any feare of

657 angry:] *ed.*; angry, 658 I:] *ed.*; I, 662 speach] *ed.*; speach,
668-9 Drawer ... tell ... church.] *as prose, ed.*; Drawer ... home, /
Tell ... church. 684 pot;] *Dodsley*; pot,

his Draper: and for his colours, they are according to the
season: in the Summer hee is apparrelled (for the most part)
like the heavens, in blew, in the winter, like the earth,
in freeze.   690

Enter Bubble, Sir Lionell, and Long-field and Sprinckle.

But see, I am prevented in my Encomium, I could have
maintain'd this theame these two houres.
Lyon. Well, God rest his soule, hee's gone, and we
must all follow him.
Bub. I, I, hee's gone Sir *Lionell*, hee's gone.   695
Lyonell. Why tho he be gone, what then? 'tis not you
that can fetch him againe, with all your cunning; it must
bee your comfort, that he died well.
Bub. Truly and so it is, I would to God I had eene   699
another unckle that would die no worse; surely I shall
weepe againe, if I should find my hankercher.
Long. How now! what, are these onions?
Bub. I, I Sir *Lyonell*, they are my onions, I thought to
have had them roasted this morning for my cold: *Gervase* you
have not wept to day; pray take your onions Gentlemen,
the remembrance of death is sharpe, therefore there is a
banquet within to sweeten your conceits: I pray walke in
Gentlemen, walke you in; you know I must needes be
melancholie, and keepe my Chamber. *Gervase*, usher them
into the banquet.   710
Sta. I shall sir, please you Sir *Lyonell*.
Lyonell. Well Master *Bubble*, wee'le goe in and taste
of your bountie. In the meane time, you must be of good
cheere.
Bub. If griefe take not away my stomacke, I will   715

688 season:] *ed.*; season, 690 SD *Sir*] *Q2*; *sir* 691-2 But ... houres.]
as prose, Collier; But ... Encomium, / I ... houres. 694 him.] *Q1(c)*;
him *Q1(u)* 695 Sir] *Dodsley*; sir 696 SP *Lyonell.*] *Q2*; *no period, Q1*
697 cunning;] *Dodsley*; cunning, 703 Sir] *Q2*; sir 705 to day;]
Hazlitt; to day, 708 you in;] *Dodsley*; you in, 709 Chamber.] *Dodsley*;
Chamber, 711 Sir] *Dodsley*; sir 712 SP *Lyonell.*] *Q2*; *no period, Q1*
712-14 Well ... cheere.] *as prose, ed.*; Well ... bountie. / In ...
cheere. 715-17 If ... *Sprinckle.*] *as prose, ed.*; If ... stomacke, /
I ... *Sprinckle.*

have good cheere I warrant you.

                          Gentlemen and Gervase goe out.
Sprinckle.
Sprin. Sir.
Bub. Had the women puddings to their dole?
Sprin. Yes sir.   720
Bub. And how did they take them? /
Sprin. Why with their hands, how should they take   [D3]
um?
Bub. O thou *Hercules* of ignorance! I mean, how were
they satisfied?   725
Sprin. By my troth sir, but so so, and yet some of
them had two.
Bub. O insatiable women! whom two puddings would not
satisfie, but vanish *Sprinckle*; bidde your fellow *Gervase*
come hither: *Exit Sprinckle.*   730
And off my mourning roabes, griefe to the grave,
For I have golde, and therefore will be brave:
In silkes I'le rattle it of every colour,
And when I goe by water scorne a Sculler;
In blacke carnation velvet I will cloake me,   735

                    Enter Staines.

And when men bid God save mee, Cry *Tu quoque*:
It is needefull a Gentleman should speake Latine sometimes,
is it not *Gervase*?
Sta. O very gracefull sir, your most accomplish't
Gentlemen are knowne by it.   740
Bub. Why then will I make use of that little I have
upon times and occasions; heere *Gervase*, take this bag, and
runne presently to the Mercers: buy me seven ells of horse
flesh colour'd taffata, nine yards of yellow sattin, and
eight yards of orenge tawney velvet; then runne to the
Tailers, the Haberdashers, the Sempsters, the Cutlers, the

---

716 you.] *Dodsley*; you // SD Gentlemen ... out.] *ed.*; *after l. 711*,
Q1   734 Sculler;] *ed.*; Sculler,   741-3 Why ... Mercers] *as prose*,
Dodsley; Why ... haue, / Vpon ... bag, / And ... Mercers   743
Mercers:] *ed.*; Mercers,

Perfumers, and to all trades whatsoe'r that belong to the
making up of a Gentleman; and amongst the rest, let not the
Barber bee forgotten: and looke that hee be an excellent
fellow, and one that can snacke his fingers with   750
dexteritie.
Sta.   I shall fit you sir.
Bub.   Doe so good *Gervase*; it is time my beard were
corrected, for it is growne so sawsie, as it beginnes to
play with my nose.   755
Staines.   Your nose sir must indure it, for it is in
part the fashion.
Bub.   Is it in fashion? why then my nose shall indure
it, let it tickle his worst. /
Sta.   Why now y'are ith right sir, if you will [D3^v]   760
be a true Gallant, you must beare things resolute, as this
sir: if you be at an Ordinary, and chance to loose your
money at play, you must not fret and fume, teare cardes,
and fling away dice, as your ignorant gamster, or country-
Gentleman does, but you must put on a calme temperate 765
action, with a kind of carelesse smile, in contempt of
Fortune, as not being able with all her engins to batter down
one peece of your estate, that your means may be thought
invincible; never tell your money, nor what you have wonne,
nor what you have lost: if a question be made, your   770
answer must be, what I have lost, I have lost, what I have
wonne, I have wonne: a close heart and free hand, makes a
man admired: a testerne or a shilling to a servant that
brings you a glasse of beere, bindes his hands to his
lippes; you shall have more service of him then his   775
Master; hee will be more humble to you, then a Cheater
before a Magistrate.
Bub.   *Gervase*, give mee thy hand: I thinke thou hast
more wit then I that am thy Master, and for this Speech

---

753 *Gervase*;] *Dodsley*; Geruase, 762 sir:] *ed.*; sir, 769 invincible;]
ed.; inuincible, 770 made,] *Dodsley*; made: 772 wonne:] *ed.*; wonne,
773 admired:] *Collier*; admired, 775 lippes;] *Dodsley*; lippes,
776 Master;] *Dodsley*; Master, 777 Magistrate.] *Q2*; Magistrate:
778 hand:] *Dodsley*; hand,

onely, I doe here create thee my steward: I do long me
thinkes to be at an Ordinary, to smile at Fortune, and to
be bountifull: *Gervase*, about your businesse good *Gervase*,
whilest I goe and meditate upon a Gentleman-like behaviour:
I have an excellent gate already *Gervase*, have I not?
Sta. *Hercules* himselfe sir, had never a better gate.   785
Bub. But dispatch *Gervase*, the sattin and the velvet
must be thought upon, and the *Tu quoque* must not bee
forgotten: for whensoever I give Armes, that shall be my
Motto.   *Exit Bub.*
Sta. What a fortune had I throwne upon me when I   790
preferred my selfe into this fellowes service! indeede I
serve my selfe, and not him, for this Golde heere is mine
owne truely purchased: he has credite, and shall run ith
bookes for't. I'le carry things so cunningly, that he shall
not be able to looke into my actions; my morgage I have
already got into my hands: the rent hee shall enjoy a while,
till his riot constraine him to sell it, which I will purchase with his owne money. I must cheate a little, I have
beene cheated upon, therefore I hope / the world will a [D4]
little the better excuse mee: what his unckle craftily
got from me, I will knavishly recover of him: to come by
it, I must vary shapes, and my first shift shall be in
sattin: 803
Proteus propitious be to my disguise,
And I shall prosper in my enterprise.   *Exit.*   805

[SCENE VIII]

Enter Spendall, Pursenet, and a boy with Rackets.

Spend. A Rubber sirra.
Boy. You shall sir.
Spend. And bid those two men you said would speak with

---

782 Gervase, about] *Q2*; Geruase about   783 behaviour:] *ed.*; behauiour,
790 me] *Hazlitt*; me,   794 for't.] *Dodsley*; for't,   795 actions;]
ed.; actions,   798 money.] *Dodsley*; money,   800 mee:] *ed.*; mee,
801 him:] *ed.*; him,

me, come in.
Boy. I will sir. *Exit Boy.* 810
Spend. Did I not play this Sett well?

Enter Blancke and another.

Purs. Excellent well by *Phaeton*, by *Erebus*, it went as if it had cut the Line.
Bla. God blesse you sir.
Spend. Master *Blanke*! welcome. 815
Bla. Here's the Gentlemans man, sir, has brought the mony.
Ser. Wilt please you tell sir?
Spend. Have you the Bond ready master *Blanke*?
Bla. Yes sir. 820
Spend. Tis well: *Pursenet*, help to tell——10. 11. 12. What time have you given?
Bla. The thirteenth of the next Month.
Spend. Tis well, here's light golde.
Ser. T'will be the lesse troublesome to carry. 825
Spend. You say well sir, how much hast thou tolde?
Purs. In golde and silver here is twenty pounds.
Bla. Tis right Master *Spendall*, I'le warrant you.
Spend. I'le take your warrant sir, and tell no further: come let me see the Condition of this Obligation. 830
Purs. [*Aside.*] A man may winne from him that cares not
   for't.
This royall *Caesar* doth regard no Cash,
Has throwne away as much in Duckes and Drakes,
As would have bought some 50000. Capons.
Spend. Tis very well; so: lend me your penne. / 835
Purs. This is the Captaine of brave Citizens, [D4^V]
The *Agamemnon* of all merry Greekes,
A *Stukely* or a *Sherley* for his spirit,
Bounty and Royalty to men at armes.

---

816 man, sir,] *Dodsley*; man sir   821 well:] *Reed*; well,   829 further:] *ed.*; further,   831 SD [*Aside.*]] *Hazlitt* // for't] *Dodsley*; for't, 834 50000.] *Q2*; *possible comma, Q1*   835 so:] *ed.*; so,

SC. VIII]   GREENE'S TU QUOQUE   33

Bla. You give this as your deed?   840
Spend. Marry do I sir.
Bla. Pleaseth this Gentleman to be a witnesse?
Spend. Yes Mary shall he: *Pursenet*, your hand.
Purs. My hand is at thy service, Noble *Brutus*.
Spend. There's for your kindnesse master *Blanke*.   845
Bla. I thanke you sir.
Spend. [*Gives money to servant.*] For your paines.
Ser. I'le take my leave of you.
Spend. What, must you be gone too, maister *Blancke*?
Bla. Yes indeede sir, I must to the Exchange.   850
Spend. Farewell to both. [*Exeunt Blank and Servant.*]
              Pursenet,
Take that twenty pounds, and give it mistris *Sweatman*:
Bid her pay her Landlord and Apothecarie,
And let her Butcher and her Baker stay;
They're honest men, and I'le take order with them.   855
Purs. The Butcher and the Baker then shall stay.
Spend. They must till I am somewhat stronger purst.
Purs. If this be all, I have my errand perfect.
                                          Exit Purs.
Spend. Heere sirra, heere's for balls, there's for
your selfe.   860
Boy. I thanke your worship.
Spend. Commend me to your mistris.   *Exit Spend.*
Boy. I will sir; in good faith 'tis the liberall'st
Gentleman that comes into our Court: why he cares no more
for a shilling then I doe for a box o'th eare, God blesse
him.   *Exit.*   866

840 deed?] *Dodsley*; deed. 842 witnesse?] *Dodsley*; witnesse. 843 he:]
ed.; he, 847 SD [*Gives ... servant.*]] *ed.* 851 both.] *Dodsley*; both,
// SD [*Exeunt ... Servant.*]] *ed.* 861, 863 SP Boy.] *Q2; no period, Q1*
864 Court:] *Collier*; Court, 866 Exit] *Q2;* Exis

[SCENE IX]

Enter Staines Gallant, Long-field and a Servant.

Sta. Sirra, what a clocke i'st?
Ser. Past tenne sir.
Sta. Heere will not be a Gallant seene this houre.
Ser. Within this quarter sir, and lesse, they meete   870
heere as soone as at any Ordinary i'th towne. /
Sta. Hast any Tobacco?   [E1]
Ser. Yes sir.
Sta. Fill.
Long. Why thou report'st miracles, things not to be   875
beleeved: I protest to thee, had'st thou not unrip't thy
selfe to me, I should never have knowne thee.
Sta. I tell you true sir, I was so farre gone, that
desperation knocked at mine elbow, and whispered newes to
mee out of Barbarie.   880
Lon. Well, I'm glad so good an occasion staid thee at
home, and mai'st thou prosper in thy project, and goe on,
with best successe of thy invention.
Sta. False dice say Amen, for that's my induction: I
do meane to cheat to day without respect of persons: 885
When sawest thou *Will Rash*?
Long. This morning at his Chamber, heele be heere.
Sta. Why then doe thou give him my name and character,
for my aime is wholy at my worshipfull Master.
Lon. Nay thou shalt take another into him, one that   890
laughs out his life in this Ordinary, thankes any man that
winnes his money; all the while his money is loosing, he
sweares by the crosse of this silver, and when it is gone,
hee changeth it to the hilts of his sword.   894

Enter Scatter-good and Ninnie-hammer.

---

868 SP *Ser.*] *Q1(c); Ser Q1(u)*   881-3 Well ... invention.] *as prose,
ed.*; Well ... home, / And ... on, / With ... inuention.   884-6 False
... *Rash*?] *as prose, ed.*; False ... induction, / I ... persons: /
When ... *Rash*?   887 Chamber,] *Q2; comma uncertain, Q1*

Sta. Hee'le be an excellent coach-horse for my captaine.
Scat. Save you Gallants, save you.
Lon. How think ye now? have I not carv'd him out to you?
Sta. Th'ast lighted me into his heart, I see him throughly. 900
Scat. *Ninni-hammer.*
Nin. Sir.
Scat. Take my cloake and rapier also: I thinke it be early Gentlemen, what time doe you take it to be?
Sta. Inclining to eleven sir. 905
Scat. Inclining! a good word; I would it were inclining to twelve, for by my stomacke it should be high Noone: but what shall we doe Gallants? shall we to cardes, till our Company come?
Long. Please you sir. / 910
Scat. *Harry*, fetch, sir, Cardes, me thinkes 'tis [El^V] an unseemely sight to see Gentlemen stand idle: please you to impart your smoake?
Long. Very willingly sir.
Scat. In good faith a pipe of excellent vapour. 915
Long. The best the house yeeldes.
Scat. Had you it in the house? I had thought it had beene your owne: 'tis not so good now as I tooke it to be: Come Gentlemen, what's your game?
Sta. Why Gleeke, that's your onely game. 920
Scat. Gleeke let it be, for I am perswaded I shall gleeke some of you; cut sir.
Long. What play we, twelve pence gleeke?
Scat. Twelve pence? a crowne; uds foote I will not spoile my memory for twelve pence. 925
Long. With all my heart.
Sta. Honnor.
Scat. What ist, Harts?

911 fetch, sir,] *ed.*; fetch sir 912 idle:] *Q3*; idle, 913 smoake?] *Dodsley*; smoake. 923 gleeke?] *Q3*; gleeke. 924 pence?] *Q3*; pence,

Sta. The King, what say you?
Scat. Why I bid thirteene.   930
Sta. Foureteene.
Scat. Fifteene.
Sta. Sixteene.
Long. Sixteene, seventeene.
Sta. You shal ha't for me.   935
Scat. Eighteene.
Long. Take it to you sir.
Scat. Udslid I'le not be out-brav'd.
Sta. I vie it.
Long. I'le none of it.   940
Scat. Nor I.
Sta. Give me a mournavall of aces, and a gleek of
queenes.
Long. And me a gleeke of knaves.
Scat. Udslid, I am gleek't this time.   945

                    Enter Will Rash.
Stay. Play.
Rash. Equall fortunes befall you Gallants.
Scat. *Will Rash,* well, I pray see what a vile game I
have.
Rash. What's your game, Gleeke?   950
Scat. Yes faith, Gleek, and I have not one Courtcarde,
but the knave of Clubbes. /
Rash. Thou hast a wilde hand indeed: thy small   [E2]
cardes shew like a troupe of rebelles, and the knave of
Clubbes their chiefe Leader.   955
Scat. And so they doe as God save me, by the crosse of
this silver he sayes true.

                    Enter Spendall.
Sta. Pray, play sir.
Long. Honnor.
Rash. How goe the stockes Gentlemen, what's won or   960
lost?

930 I] *Q1(c);* I' *Q1(u)*   949 have.] *Q2;* haue   958 sir.] *Dodsley;* sir:

SC. IX]   GREENE'S TU QUOQUE   37

Sta.   This is the first game.
Scat. Yes this is the first game, but by the crosse of
this silver heere's all of five pounds.
Spend. Good day to you Gentlemen.   965
Rash. Francke, welcome by this hand, how dost lad?
Spend. And how does thy wench yfaith?
Rash. Why fat and plump like thy geldings: thou giv'st
them both good provender it seemes: go to, thou art one of
the madd'st wagges, of a Cittizen i'th towne, the whole
company talkes of thee already.   971
Spend. Talke, why let um talke, udsfoot I pay scot and
lot, and all manner of dueties else, as well as the best of
um: it may be they understand I keepe a whoore, a horse,
and a kennell of hownds, what's that to them? no mans
purse opens for't but mine owne; and so long, my hownds
shall eate flesh, my horse bread, and my whoore weare velvet.
Rash. Why there spoke a courageous Boy.   978
Spend. Udsfoote, shall I be confin'd all the dayes of
my life to walke under a pent-house? no, I'le take my
pleasure whiles my youth affoords it.   981
Scat. By the crosse of these hilts, I'le never play at
Gleeke againe, whilst I have a nose on my face: I smell the
knavery of the game.
Spend. Why what's the matter? who has lost?   985
Scat. Mary, that have I, by the hiltes of my sword, I
have lost forty crowns, in as small time almost, as while a
man might tell it. /
Spend. Change your Game for dice, we are a full   [E2^v]
number for *Novum.*   990
Scatt. With all my heart, where's Master *Ambush* the

965 SP *Spend.*] *Q2*; *Spend,*   967 yfaith?] *Dodsley*; yfaith. 968-71 Why
... already.] *as prose, Reed;* Why ... plump / Like ... prouender /
It ... wagges, / Of ... thee / already.   969 seemes:] *Dodsley;* seemes,
970 i'th] *Dodsley;* 'ith   978 SP *Rash.*] *Q3;* no period, *Q1*   982-4 By ...
game.] *as prose, An. Brit. Dr.;* By ... Gleeke / againe ... face, /
I ... game.   983 face:] *ed.;* face,   989-90 Change ... *Novum.*]
as prose, Collier; Change ... dice, / We ... *Nouum.*   991, 994 Master]
Hazlitt; M.

Broaker, *Ninni-hammer*?
Nin. Sir.
Scat. Go to Master *Ambush*, and bid him send me twenty
marks upon this Diamond. 995

Enter Bubble.

Nin. I will sir. [*Exit Ninnihammer.*]
Long. Looke you (to make us the merrier) who comes here.
Rash. A fresh Gamster: Master *Bubble*, God save you.
Bub. Tu quoque sir.
Spend. God save you Maister *Bubble*. 1000
Bub. Tu quoque.
Sta. Save you sir.
Bub. Et tu quoque.
Long. Good maister *Bubble*.
Bub. Et tu quoque. 1005
Scatt. Is your name Master *Bubble*?
Bub. Maister *Bubble* is my name, sir.
Scat. God save you sir.
Bub. Et tu quoque.
Scat. I would be better acquainted with you. 1010
Bub. And I with you.
Scat. Pray let us salute againe.
Bub. With all my heart sir.
Lon. Behold yonder the oke and the Ivy how they imbrace.
Rash. Excellent acquaintance, they shall be the 1015
Gemini.
Bub. Shall I desire your name sir?
Scat. Maister *Scattergood*.
Bub. Of the *Scattergoods* of *London*? 1019
Scat. No indeed sir, of the *Scattergoods* of Hampshire.
Bub. Good Maister *Scattergood*.
Sta. Come Gentlemen, heere's dice.
Scat. Please you advance to the Table?

---

992 Broaker, *Ninni-hammer*?] *Q3*; Broaker *Ninni-hammer*? 996 SD [*Exit
Ninnihammer.*]] *ed.* 998 Gamster:] *ed.*; Gamster, 998, 1004 *Bubble*]
Q1(c); *Bubleb Q1(u)*

Bub. No indeede sir.
Scatt. Pray will you goe? / 1025
Bub. I will goe sir over the whole world for your [E3] sake, but in curtesie I will not budge a foote.

Enter Ninnihammer [with Ambush the Broker].

Nin. Heere is the Cash you sent me for, and master *Rash*, heere is a Letter from one of your sisters.
Spend. I have the dice, set Gentlemen. 1030
Long. From which sister?
Rash. From the mad-cap, I know by the hand.
Spend. For me, fix.
Omnes. And fix that.
Sta. Nine; 1, 2, 3, 4, 5, 6, 7, and 8: eighteene 1035 shillings.
Spend. What's yours sir?
Scat. Mine's a Bakers dozen: master *Bubble* tel your mony.
Bub. In good faith I am but a simple Gamster, and 1040 doe not know what to doe.
Scat. Why you must tell your money, and hee'le pay you.
Bub. My mony! I do know how much my mony is, but he shall not pay me, I have a better conscience then so: what, for throwing the dice twice? yfaith he should have but a hard bargaine of it. 1046
Rash. Witty rascall, I must needes away.
Long. Why what's the matter?
Rash. Why the lovers can not agree: thou shalt along with me, and know all. 1050
Long. But first let mee instruct thee in the condition of this Gentleman: whom dost thou take him to be?
Rash. Nay, hee's a stranger, I know him not.

1026-7 I ... foote.] *as prose, Hazlitt*; I ... sake, / But ... foote.
1027 curtesie] *Q2*; curtesie   1027 SD [*with* ... *Broker*]] *ed.*   1028-9 Heere ... sisters.] *as prose, Collier*; Heere ... *Rash*, / Heere ... sisters,   1029 sisters.] *Q2*; sisters,   1044 what,] *Reed*; what   1045 twice?] *Dodsley*; twice,   1049 agree:] *Dodsley*; agree,   1052 Gentleman:] *Dodsley*; Gentleman,

Long. By this light but you doe, if his beard were off:
'tis *Staines*. 1055
Rash. The divell it is as soone: and what's his purpose
in this disguise?
Long. Why cheating: doe you not see how he playes upon
his worshipfull Maister, and the rest?
Rash. By my faith he drawes apace. 1060
Spend. A pox upon these dice, give's a fresh bale.
Bubb. Ha ha, the dice are not to be blamed, a man may
per- / ceive this is no Gentlemanly gamster, by his [E3^V]
chafing: do you heare, my friend, fill me a glasse of
beere, and ther's a shilling for your paines. 1065
Dra. Your worship shall sir.
Rash. Why how now *Franke*, what hast lost?
Spend. Fifteene pounds and upwards: is there never an
honest fellow?
Amb. What, doe you lacke money sir? 1070
Spend. Yes, canst furnish me?
Amb. Upon a sufficient pawne sir.
Spend. You know my shop; bid my man deliver you a piece
of three pile velvet, and let me have as much money as you
dare adventure upon't. 1075
Amb. You shall sir. [*Exit Ambush.*]
Spend. A pox of this lucke, it will not last ever:
Play sir, I'le set you.
Rash. *Franke*, better fortune befall thee: and 1079
Gentlemen, I must take my leave, for I must leave you.
Scat. Must you needes be gone?
Rash. Indeede I must.
Bub. Et tu quoque?
Long. Yes truely.
Scat. At your discretions Gentlemen. 1085
Rash. Farewell. *Exeunt Rash & Long.*

1054 off:] *Dodsley*; off, 1058 cheating:] *ed.*; cheating, 1059 rest?]
Dodsley; rest. 1069 fellow?] *Dodsley*; fellow. 1073 shop;] *Dodsley*;
possible comma, *Q1* 1076 SD [*Exit Ambush.*]] *ed.* 1077-8 A ... you.]
as prose, *Hazlitt*; A ... euer: / Play ... you.

Sta. Cry you mercy sir, I am chanc'd with you all
Gentlemen: heere I have 7, heere 7, and heere 10.
Spend. T'is right sir, and ten that.
Bub. And nine that. 1090
Sta. Two fives at all.   *Drawes all.*
Bub. One and five that.
Spend. [*Aside.*] Umh, and can a suite of Sattin cheate
so grossely? By this light there's nought on one die but
fives and sixes; I must not be thus gull'd. 1095
Bub. Come Maister *Spendall*, set.
Spend. No sir, I have done.
Scatt. Why then let us all leave, for I thinke dinner's
neare ready. /
Dra. Your meat's upon the Table.   [E4] 1100
Scat. On the Table! come Gentlemen, we do our
stomackes wrong: Master *Bubble*, what have you lost?
Bub. That's no matter, what I have lost, I have lost;
nor can I chuse but smile at the foolishnes of the dice.
Sta. I am but your steward Gentlemen, for after 1105
dinner I may rsstore it againe.
Bub. Master *Scatter-good*, will you walke in?
Scat. I'le wait upon you sir, come Gentlemen, will you
follow?

          Exeunt: manent Spendall & Staines.

Sta. Yes sir, I'le follow you. 1110
Spen. Heare you sir, a word.
Sta. Ten if you please.
Spend. I have lost fifteene pounds.
Sta. And I have found it.
Spend. You say right, found it you have indeed, 1115
But never wonne it: doe you know this die?
Sta. Not I sir.
Spend. You seeme a Gentleman, and you may perceive

1093 SD [*Aside.*]] Hazlitt   1094-5 but fives] *Q2*; butfiues   1095 sixes;]
Q2; sixes,   1099 ready.] *Q2*; *possible comma, Q1*   1102, 1107 Master]
Hazlitt; M.   1109 SD *Exeunt*] Reed; *Exit*   1114 SP *Sta.*] *Q2*; *no period, Q1*

I have some respect unto your credite,
To take you thus aside: will you restore   1120
What you ha drawne from me unlawfully?
Sta. Sirra, by your out-side you seeme a cittizen,
Whose Cockes-comb, I were apt enough to breake,
But for the Lawe; goe y'are a prating Jacke,
Nor is't your hopes, of crying out for clubbes,   1125
Can save you from my chasticement, if once
You shall but dare to utter this againe.
Spend. You lie, you dare not.
Sta. Lie! nay villaine, now thou temptst me to thy
  death.
Spend. Soft, you must buy it dearer,   1130
The best bloud flowes within you is the price.
Sta. Darst thou resist, thou art no Cittizen.
Spend. I am a Cittizen.
Sta. Say thou arte a Gentleman, and I am satisfied,
For then I know thou'lt answer me in field.   1135
Spend. Ile say directly what I am, a Citizen, /
And I will meete thee in the field as fairely   [E4^v]
As the best Gentleman that weares a sword.
Sta. I accept it, the meeting place?
Spend. Beyond the Maze in Tuttle.   1140
Sta. What weapon?
Spend. Single rapier.
Sta. The time?
Spend. To morrow.
Sta. The houre?   1145
Spend. Twixt nine and ten.
Sta. Tis good, I shall expect you, farewell.
Spend. Farewell sir.   *Ex. omnes.*

1120 aside:] *ed.*; aside, 1125 is't] *Dodsley*; 'ist 1139 place?] *Q3*;
place. 1143 time?] *Q3*; time. 1145 houre?] *Q3*; houre. 1148 SD *Ex.
omnes.*] *Dodsley*; after l. 1147, *Q1*

[SCENE X]

Enter Will Rash, Long-field, and Joyce.

Rash. Why I commend thee Gerle, thou speak'st as thou thinkst, thy tongue and thy heart are Relatives, and 1150 thou wert not my sister, I should at this time fall in love with thee.
Joyce. You should not need, for and you were not my brother, I should fall in love with you, for I love a proper man with my heart, and so does all the Sex of us, let my sister dissemble never so much: I am out of charity with these nice and squemish tricks, we were borne for men, and men for us, and wee must together.
Rash. This same plaine dealing is a Jewell in thee.
Joyce. And let mee enjoy that Jewell, for I love   1160
plaine dealing with my heart.
Rash. Th'art a good wench yfaith: I should never be ashamed to call thee sister, though thou shouldst marry a Broomeman: but your lover me thinkes is over tedious.

Enter Geraldine.

Joyce. No, looke ye sir, could you wish a man to   1165
come better upon his q? let us withdraw.
Rash. Close, close, for the prosecution of the plot, wench: See he prepares.
Joyce. Silence.
Gerald. The Sunne is yet wrapt in *Auroraes* armes,   1170
And lull'd with her delight, forgets his creatures: /
Awake thou god of heate,   [F1]
I call thee up, and taske thee for thy slownesse;
Poynt all thy beames through yonder flaring glasse,
And raise a beauty brighter then thy selfe; *Musicke.*1175
Musitions, give to each Instrument a tongue,
To breathe sweete musicke in the eares of her

1156 much:] *ed.*; much, 1162 Th'art] *Q2*; Tha'rt // yfaith:] *ed.*; yfaith, 1164 Broomeman:] *Q2*; Broome- / man: 1165 SP *Joyce.*] *Q2*; *no period*, *Q1* 1166 q?] *Dodsley*; q, 1168 wench:] *ed.*; wench,

To whom I sent it as a messenger.

Enter Gartred aloft.

Gart. Sir, your musicke is so good, that I must say I
like it; but the Bringer so ill welcome, that I could be
content to loose it: if you plaid for mony, there 'tis; if
for love, heere's none; if for goodwill, I thanke you, and
when you will you may be gone.
Ger. Leave me not intranc'd: sing not my death,
Thy voyce is able to make Satires tame,   1185
And call rough windes to her obedience.
Gart. Sir, sir, our eares itch not for flattery:
Heere you besiege my window, that I dare not
Put forth my selfe to take the gentle Ayre,
But you are in the fieldes, and volley out   1190
Your woes, your plaints, your loves, your injuries.
Ger. Since you have heard, and know them, give redresse,
True beauty never yet was mercilesse.
Gart. Sir, rest thus satisfied, my minde was never
    woman,
Never alter'd, nor shall it now beginne: 1195
So fare you well.   *Exit Gart.*
Rash. Sfoot, she playes the terrible tyrannizing
Tamberlaine over him: this it is to turne Turke, from a most
absolute compleate Gentleman, to a most absurd ridiculous
and fond lover.   1200
Long. Oh, when a woman knowes the power and authoritie
of her eie.
Joyce. Fie upon her, shee's good for nothing then, no
more then a jade that knowes his owne strength: The windowe
is clasped: now brother, pursue your project, and   1205
deliver your friend from the tyranny of my domineering
sister.

1183 gone.] *Q2*; gone, 1187-91 Sir ... injuries.] *as verse, ed.; as
prose, Q1* (Sir ... heere ... be- / siege ... put ... the / gentle
... but ... your / woes ... iniuries.) 1187 flattery:] *ed.*; flattery,
1195 Never] *ed.*; neuer 1198 him:] *ed.*; him, 1205 clasped:] *ed.*;
clasped,

SC. X]   GREENE'S TU QUOQUE   45

Rash. Doe you heare, you drunkard in love, come in to /
us and be ruled: you would little thinke, that the   [F1^v]
wench that talked so scurvily out of the window there,
is more inamored on thee then thou on her: nay, looke you
now, see if hee turne not away slighting our good councell:
I am no Christian if shee doe not sigh, whine, and grow sicke
for thee: looke you sir, I will bring you in good witnesse
against her.   1215
Joyce. Sir, y'are
My brothers friend, and I'le be plaine with you:
You doe not take the course to winne my sister,
But indirectly goe about the bush: you come
And fiddle heere, and keepe a coile in verse: 1220
Holde off your hatte, and beg to kisse her hand,
Which makes her prowd.
But to bee short, in two lines thus it is:
Who most doth love, must seeme most to neglect it,
For those that shew most love, are least respected.   1225
Long. A good observation by my faith.
Rash. Well this instruction comes too late now:
Stand you close, and let me prosecute my invention:
Sister, O sister, wake, arise sister.   1229

                    Enter Gartred above.

Gart. How now brother, why call you with such terrour?
Rash. How can you sleepe so sound, and heare such
         groanes,
So horride and so tedious to the eare,
That I was frighted hither by the sound?
O sister, heere lies a Gentleman that lov'd you too deerely,
And himselfe too ill, as by his death appeares,   1235
I can report no further without teares;
Assist me now.

1209 ruled:] *ed.*; ruled, 1216-23 Sir ... is:] *as verse, Collier; as
prose, Q1* (Sir ... with / you, you ... but indi- / rectly ... and ...
and / keepe ... holde ... kisse / her ... which ... two / lines ...
is:) 1227 now:] *Dodsley*; now, 1228 invention:] *ed.*; inuention,

Long. When he came first, death startled in his eyes,
His hand had not forsooke the dagger hilt,
But still he gave it strength, as if he feard   1240
He had not sent it home unto his heart.
Gart. Enough, enough,
If you will have me live, give him no name,
Suspition tells me 'tis my *Geraldine*:
But be it whom it will, I'le come to him, /   1245
To suffer death as resolute as he.   *Exit Gart.*   [F2]
Rash. Did not I tell you 'twould take? downe sir downe.
Ger. I ghesse what y'ould have me doe.
Long. O for a little bloud to besprinckle him.
Rash. No matter for blood, I'le not suffer her to   1250
come neare him, till the plot have tane his full height.
Ger. A scarffe ore my face, lest I betray my selfe.

                    Enter Gartred belowe.

Rash. Heere, heere, lie still, she comes: Now *Mercurie*,
Be propitious.
Gart. Where lies this spectacle of blood?
This tragicke Sceane?
Rash.   Yonder lies *Geraldine*.   1255
Gart. O let me see him with his face of death!
Why doe you stay me from my *Geraldine*?
Rash. Because, unworthy as thou art, thou shalt not see
The man now dead, whom living thou didst scorne:
The worst part that he had, deserv'd thy best,   1260
But yet contemn'd, deluded, mock'd, despisde by you,
Unfit for aught but for the generall marke
Which you were made for, mans creation.
Gart. Burst not my heart before I see my Love:
Brother, upon my knees I begge your leave,   1265
That I may see the wound of *Geraldine*:
I will embalme his body with my teares,

1247 take?] *Dodsley*; take, 1253-4 Heere ... *Mercurie*, / Be propitious.] *ed.*; Heere ... comes, / Now ... be propitious. 1253 comes:] *Dodsley*; comes, 1255 Sceane?] *Dodsley*; Sceane. 1259 scorne:] *ed.*; scorne, 1264 Love:] *Dodsley*; Loue, 1266 *Geraldine*:] *Reed*; *Geraldine*,

And carry him unto his sepulcher,
From whence I'le never rise, but be interr'd
In the same dust he shall be buried in.   1270
Long. I doe protest shee drawes sad teares from me,
I pre thee let her see her *Geraldine*.
Gart. Brother, if e'er you lov'd me as a sister,
Deprive me not the sight of *Geraldine*.   1274
Rash. Well, I am contented you shall touch his lippes,
But neither see his face nor yet his wound.
Gart. Not see his face? /
Rash. Nay, I have sworne it to the contrary: [F2^V]
Nay, harke you further yet.
Gart. What now?   1280
Rash. But one kisse, no more.
Gart. Why then no more.
Rash. Marry this liberty I'le give you:
If you intend to make any speach of repentance
Over him, I am content, so it be short.   1285
Gart. What you command is Law, and I obey.
Joyce. Peace, give eare to the passion.
Gart. Before I touch thy body, I implore
Thy discontented ghost to be appeasde:
Send not unto me till I come my selfe: 1290
Then shalt thou know how much I honor'd thee.
O see the colour of his corall lippe!
Which in despight of death lives full and fresh,
As when he was the beauty of his Sex: 1294
T'were sinne worthy the worst of plagues to leave thee:
Not all the strength and pollicie of man
Shall snatch me from thy bosome.
Long.   Looke, looke,
I think shee'l ravish him.
Rash.   Why how now sister?
Gart. Shall we have both one grave? here I am chain'd,
Thunder nor Earthquakes shall shake me off.   1300

1276 wound.] *Q2*; wound, 1283 you:] *Dodsley*; you, 1285 it] *Q2*; it
1297-8 Looke, looke, / I ... him.] *ed.*; *as one line, Q1*

Rash. No? I'le try that: come dead man, awake,
Up with your bag and baggage, and let's have
No more fooling.
Gart. And live's my *Geraldine*?
Rash. Live? faith I,
Why should he not? he was never dead, 1305
That I know on.
Ger. It is no wonder *Geraldine* should live,
Tho he had emptied all his vitall spirites:
The Lute of *Orpheus* spake not halfe so sweete,
When he descended to th' infernall vaults, 1310
To fetch againe his faire *Euridice*,
As did thy sweete voyce to *Geraldine*. /
Gart. I'le exercise that voyce, since it doth please [F3]
My better selfe, my constant *Geraldine*.
Joyce. Why so la, heere's an end of an old Song, 1315
Why could not this have beene done before I pray?
Gart. O y'are a goodly sister, this is your plot:
Well, I shall live one day to requite you.
Joyce. Spare me not, for wheresoever I set my affection,
although it be upon a Colliar, if I fall backe, unlesse
it bee in the right kinde, binde mee to a stake, and let
mee be burned to death with char-coale. 1322
Rash. Well, thou art a mad wench, and there's no more
to be done at this time, but as wee brought you together,
so to part you, you must not lie at racke and manger:
there be those within, that will forbid the banes: Time
must shake good Fortune by the hand, before you two must be
great, specially you sister; come leave swearing. 1328
Gart. Must we then part?
Rash. Must you part? why how thinke you? udsfoote,
I do thinke we shall have as much to do to get her from him,
as we had to bring her to him: this love of women is of a

1301 that:] *ed.*; that, 1301-3 No? ... fooling.] *as verse, ed.*; *as
prose, Q1* (No? ... vp ... no) 1308 spirites:] *ed.*; spirites, 1316
Why ... pray?] *as one line, ed.*; Why ... before / I pray? 1326
banes:] *Collier;* banes,

SC. XI] GREENE'S TU QUOQUE 49

strange qualitie, and has more trickes then a Juggler.
Gart. But this, [*Kisses him.*] and then farewell.
Ger. Thy company is heaven, thy absence hell. 1335
Rash. Lord who'ld thinke it?
Joyce. Come wench. *Exeunt omnes.*

[SCENE XI]

Enter Spendall, and Staines.

Spend. This ground is firme and even, I'le goe no
 further.
Sta. This be the place then, and prepare you sir,
You shall have faire play for your life of me, 1340
For looke sir, I'le be open breasted to you.
Spend. Shame light on him that thinkes his safety lieth
 in a French doublet.
Nay I would strippe my selfe, would comelinesse /
Give sufferance to the deed, and fight with thee, [F3^V]
As naked as a Mauritanian Moore. 1345
Sta. Give me thy hand, by my heart I love thee:
Thou art the highest spirited Cittizen,
That ever Guild-hall tooke notice of.
Spend. Talke not what I am, untill you have tried me.
Sta. Come on sir. *They fight.* 1350
Spend. Now sir, your life is mine.
Sta. Why then take it, for I'le not begge it of thee.
Spend. Nobly resolv'd, I love thee for those words.
Heere take thy armes againe, and if thy malice
Have spent it selfe like mine, then let us part 1355
More friendly then we met at first incounter.
Sta. Sir, I accept this gift of you, but not your
 friendship,
Untill I shall recover't with my honour.
Spend. Will you fight againe then?

1334 SD [*Kisses him.*]] *ed.* 1346 thee:] *ed.*; thee, 1353 words.]
Dodsley; words,

Sta. Yes. 1360
Spend. Faith thou dost well then, justly to whip my
 folly.
But come sir.
Sta. Hold, y'are hurt I take it.
Spend. Hurt! where? zownds I feele it not.
Sta. You bleed I am sure.
Spend. Sblood, I thinke you weare
A cattes claw upon your Rapiers point: 1365
I am scratcht indeed, but small as 'tis, I must
Have blood for blood.
Sta. Y'are bent to kill I see.
Spend. No by my hopes, if I can scape that sinne,
And keepe my good name, I'le never offer't. 1369
Sta. Well sir, your worst.
Spend. We both bleed now I take it,
And if the motion may be equall thought,
To part with clasp'd hands, I shall first subscribe.
Sta. It were unmanlinesse in me to refuse
The safety of us both, my hand shall never
Fall from such a charitable motion. / 1375
Spend. Then joyne we both, and heere our malice [F4]
 ends:
Tho foes we came to th' field, wee'l depart frends. *Exeunt.*

[SCENE XII]

 Enter Sir Lyonell, and a Servant.

Lyon. Come, come, follow me knave, follow me, I have the
best nose i'th house, I thinke: either wee shall have rainie
weather, or the vaults unstop'd: sirra, goe see, I 1380
would not have my guesse smell out any such inconvenience:

1364-67 Sblood ... weare / A ... point: / I ... must / Have ...
blood.] *ed.*; Sblood ... point, / I ... 'tis, / I ... blood. 1365
point:] *Collier*; point, 1372 hands,] *Dodsley*; hands:
Sc. XII OSD *Sir*] *Dodsley*; sir 1379 i'th] *ed.*; 'ith // thinke:]
ed.; thinke,

SC. XII]   GREENE'S TU QUOQUE   51

Doe you heare sirra, *Symon*?
Ser. Sir.
Lyon. Bid the Kitchin-maide skowre the sincke, and make
cleane her backe-side, for the wind lies just upon't.
Ser. I will sir.   1386
Lyon. And bid *Anthonie* put on his white fustian doublet,
for hee must wait to day: *Exit Servant.* It doth mee so
much good to stirre and talke, to place this, and displace
that, that I shall neede no Apothecaries prescriptions.
I have sent my daughter this morning as farre as Pimliko to
fetch a draught of Derby ale, that it may fetch a colour in
her cheekes, the puling harlotrie looks so pale, and it is
all for want of a man, for so their mother would say, God
rest her soule, before she died.   1395

Enter Bubble, Scattergood, Staines, [and Servant].

Ser. Sir, the Gentlemen are come already.
Lyon. How knave, the Gentlemen?
Ser. Yes sir, yonder they are.
Lyonell. Gods pretious, we are too tardie: let one be
sent presently to meete the gerles, and hasten their   1400
comming home quickely: how, dost thou stand dreaming? [*Exit
Servant.*] Gentlemen, I see you love me, you are carefull of
your houre; you may be deceived in your cheare, but not in
your welcome.
Bub. Thankes, and *Tu quoque* is a word for all.   1405
Scatterg. A pretty concise roome: Sir *Lyonell*, where
are your daughters?
Lyon. They are at your service sir, and forth comming.
Bub. Gods will *Gervase*! how shall I behave my selfe to
the Gentlewomen? /   1410
Sta. Why advance your selfe toward them, with a   [F4ᵛ]

1388 SD Exit Servant.] *Reed; after l. 1395, Q1* 1390 prescriptions.]
Dodsley; prescriptions, 1395 SD Scattergood, Staines, [and Servant].]
Reed; Scattergood, and Staines. 1397 Gentlemen?] *Hazlitt;* Gentlemen!
1399 tardie:] *Dodsley;* tardie, 1401 how,] *Dodsley;* how 1401-2 SD
[Exit Servant.]] *Reed* 1406 Sir] *Dodsley;* sir 1407 daughters] *Q2;*
danghters

comely steppe, and in your salute, be carefull you strike not
too high, nor too lowe, and afterward for your discourse,
your *Tu quoque* will beare you out.
Bub. Nay, and that be all, I care not, for I'le set   1415
a good face on't, that's flat: and for my neather parts,
let them speake for themselves: here's a legge, and ever a
Baker in England shew me a better, I'le give him mine for
nothing.
Sta. O that's a speciall thing that I must caution   1420
you of.
Bub. What sweete *Gervase*?
Sta. Why for commending your selfe; never whilest you
live commend your selfe: and then you shall have the
Ladies themselves commend you.   1425
Bub. I would they would else.
Sta. Why they will I'le assure you sir, and the more
vilely you speake of your selfe, the more will they strive
to collaud you.

Enter Gartred and Joyce.

Bub. Let me alone to dispraise my selfe, I'le make   1430
my selfe the arrantest Cockes-combe within a whole Countrey.
Lyonell. Heere come the Gipsies, the Sunne-burn'd
    gerles,
Whose beauties will not utter them alone,
They must have bagges although my credite cracke for't.
Bub. Is this the eldest sir?   1435
Lyonell. Yes marry is she sir.
Bub. I'le kisse the yongest first, because she likes me
    best.
Scat. Marry sir, and whilest you are there, I'le be
    heere:
O delicious touch! I thinke in conscience   1439
Her lippes are lined quite through with Orenge Tawny velvet.
Bub. [*Aside.*] They kisse exceeding well, I doe not

1430-1 Let ... Countrey.] *as prose, Collier*; Let ... my selfe, /
I'le ... whole / Countrey. 1441 SD [*Aside.*]] *ed.*

thinke but they have beene brought up too't: I will beginne
to her like a Gentleman in a set speech: Faire Ladie, shall
I speake a word with you?
Joyce. With me sir? / 1445
Bub. With you Lady,--this way,--a litle more,--   [G1]
So now tis well, umh--
Even as a Drummer,--or a Pewterer--
Joy. Which of the two no matter,
For one beates on a Drumme, tother a Platter.   1450
Bub. In good fayth sweet Lady you say true:
But pray marke me further, I will begin againe.
Joy. I pray Sir doe.
Bub. Even as a Drummer, as I sayd before,--
Or as a Pewterer--   1455
Joy. Very good Sir.
Bub. Doo--doo--doo--
Joy. What doe they doo?
Bub. By my troth Lady, I doe not know, for to say
truth, I am a kind of an Asse.   1460
Joy. How Sir, an Asse?
Bub. Yes indeed Lady.
Joy. Nay that you are not.
Bub. So God ha mee, I am Lady: you never saw an
arranter Asse in your life.   1465
Joy. Why heer's a Gentleman, your friend, will not
say so.
Bub. Yfayth but he shall: How say you sir, am not I an
Asse?
Scatt. Yes by my troth Lady is he: Why Ile say any   1470
thing my brother *Bubble* sayes.
Gart. [*Aside.*] Is this the man my Father chose for mee
To make a Husband of? O God, how blind

1442 too't:] *ed.*; too't, 1448, 1455 Pewterer--] *Reed*; Pewterer.
1457 doo--doo--] *ed.*; doo--doo. 1459 know,] *ed.*; know: 1468-9
Yfaith ... am ... Asse?] *as prose, ed.*; Yfayth ... sir, / Am ...
Asse? 1472 SD [*Aside.*]] *ed.* // chose] *Dodsley*; choose // mee]
Dodsley; mee, 1473 To] *Dodsley*; to

              Are parents in our loves: so they have wealth,
              They care not to what thinges they marry us.   1475
      Bub. Pray looke upon mee Lady.
      Joy. So I doe sir.
      Bub. I, but looke upon mee well, and tell mee if you
      ever saw any man looke so scurvily, as I doe.
      Joy. [*Aside.*] The fellow sure is frantique.   1480
      Bub. You doe not marke mee?
      Joy. Yes indeed sir. /
      Bub. I, but looke upon mee well: Did you ever see   [G1^v]
      a worse timberd Legge?
      Joy. By my fayth tis a pretty foure square Legge.   1485
      Bub. I but your foure square Legges are none of the
      best. Oh! *Jarvis, Jarvis.*
      Sta. Excellent well sir.
      Bub. What say you now to mee Lady, can you find ere a
      good inch about mee?   1490
      Joy. Yes that I can sir.
      Bub. Find it, and take it sweete Lady: There I thinke
      I bobd her, *Jarvis?*
      Joy. Well sir, disparadge not your selfe so: for if you
      were the man you'd make your selfe, yet out of your   1495
      behaviour and discourse, I could find cause enough to love
      you.
      Bub. Augh! now shee comes to mee: My behaviour? alas,
      alas, tis clownicall; and my discourse is very bald, bald:
      You shall not heare mee breake a good Jeast in a twelve
      month.   1501
      Joy. No sir? why now you breake a good Jeast.

1474 Are] *Dodsley*; are // wealth] *Q1(c)*; weath *Q1(u)*   1475 They]
Dodsley; they   1479 doe.] *ed.*; doe?   1480 SD [*Aside.*]] *Hazlitt*
1483-4 I ... Legge?] *as prose, ed.*; I ... well: / Did ... Legge?
1487 *Jarvis,*] *Q2*; Iarnis,   1492-3 Find ... *Jarvis?*] *as prose, Collier*;
Find ... Lady: / There ... *Iaruis?*   1494-1497 Well ... you.] *as prose,
ed.*; Well ... were / The ... your / Behauiour ... enough / To ... you.
1495 your selfe,] *Reed*; your selfe;   1498-1501 Augh ... month.]
as prose, Collier; Augh ... alas, / alas ... bald: / You ... Ieast /
in ... month.

SC. XII]   GREENE'S TU QUOQUE   55

Bub. No, I want the *Boone Joure*, and the *Tu quoques*,
which yonder Gentleman has: Ther's a bob for him too:
There's a Gentleman, and you talke of a Gentleman.   1505
Joy. Who hee? hee's a Coxcombe indeed.
Bub. We are sworne Brothers in good fayth Lady.

                    Enter Servant.

Scatt. Yes in truth wee are sworne Brothers, and do
meane to goe both alike, and to have Horses alike.
Joy. And they shall be sworne Brothers too?   1510
Scatt. If it please them, Lady.
Ser. Master *Ballance*, the Goldsmith, desires to speake
with you.
Lyo. Bid him come, knave.   [*Exit Servant.*]
Scatt. I woonder (Sir *Lyonell*) your sonne *Will Rash* 1515
is not heere.
Lyo. Is hee of your aquaintance, sir?
Scatt. O very familiar: hee strooke mee a boxe on the
eare / once, and from thence grew my love to him.   [G2]

                    Enter Ballance.

Lyo. It was a signe of vertue in you sir;   1520
But heele be heere at dinner. Maister *Ballance*,
What makes you so strange? Come, you're welcome:
What's the Newes?
Balla.   Why sir, the old Newes:
Your man *Francis* royots still,
And little hope of thrift there is in him;   1525
Therefore I come to advise your Worship,
To take some order whilst there's something left.
The better part of his best Ware's consumd.
Lyo. Speake softly Maister *Ballance*.

1503-05 No ... Gentleman.] *as prose, Collier*; No ... *quoques*, / Which
... too: / There's ... Gentleman? 1505 Gentleman.] *Q3*; Gentleman?
1512 Master] *Hazlitt*; M. // Goldsmith,] *Reed*; Goldsmith 1514 SD
[*Exit Servant.*]] *ed.* 1516 heere.] *Reed*; heere? 1520-3 It ... Newes?]
as verse, ed.; *as prose, Q1* (It ... but ... what ... what's) 1523-4
Why ... Newes: / Your ... still,] *ed.*; *as one line, Q1* (your) 1527
left.] *Q3*; left,

But is there no hope of his recoverie?   1530
Ball. None at all sir, for hees already layd to be
arested by some that I know.
Lyo. Well, I doe suffer for him, and am loath
Indeed to doe, what I am constraind to doe:
Well sir, I meane to ceaze on what is left.   1535
And harke you one word more.
Joy. What haynous sinne has yonder man committed,
To have so great a punishment as waite
Upon the humors of an idle Foole:
A very proper Fellow, good Legge, good Face,   1540
A Body well proportiond: but his minde
Bewrayes he never came of Generous kinde.

     Enter Will Rash and Geraldine.

Lyo. Goe to, no more of this at this time.
What sir, are you come?
Rash. Yes sir, and have made bold to bring a Guist
  along.   1545
Lyo. Maister *Geraldines* sonne of *Essex*?
Ger. The same sir.
Lyo. Ye're welcom sir, when wil your Father be in towne?
Ger. T'will not be long, sir.
Lyo. I shall be glad to see him when he coms.   1550
Ger. I thanke you sir. /
Lyo. In the meane time you're welcome; pray be not [G2^V]
  strange.
Ile leave my Sonne amongst you Gentlemen,
I have some busines: harke you Master *Ballance*,
Dinner will soone be readie; one word more.   1555

       Exeunt Lyo. & Bal.

Rash. And how does my little *Asinus* and his *Tu quoque*
here? Oh you pretty sweet-fac'd rogues, that for your

1538 punishment] *ed.*; punishment, 1539 Upon] *Q2*; vpon 1552
strange.] *Dodsley*; strange, 1554 Master] *Hazlitt*; M. 1555 SD
Exeunt] *Dodsley*; Exit

SC. XII]   GREENE'S TU QUOQUE   57

countenances might be *Alexander* and *Lodwicke*: What sayes the
old man to you? wil't be a match? shall wee call Brothers?
Scatt. Ifayth with all my heart; if Mistris *Gartred*   1560
will, wee will be married to morrow.
Bub. S'fott, if Mistris *Joyce* will, wee'le be married
to night.
Rash. Why you couragious Boyes, and worthy Wenches, made
out of Waxe. But what shall's doe when wee have dinde,
shall's goe see a Play?   1566
Scatt. Yes fayth Brother: if it please you, let's goe
see a Play at the Gloabe.
Bub. I care not; any whither, so the Clowne have a part:
For Ifayth I am no body without a Foole.   1570
Ger. Why then wee'le goe to the Red Bull; they say
Green's a good Clowne.
Bub. Greene? Greene's an Asse.
Scatt. Wherefore doe you say so?
Bub. Indeed I ha no reason: for they say, hee is   1575
as like mee as ever hee can looke.
Scatt. Well then, to the Bull.
Rash. A good resolution, continue it: nay on.
Bub. Not before the Gentlewomen; not I never.
Rash. O while you live, men before women: Custome   1580
hath plac'd it so.
Bub. Why then Custome is not so mannerly, as I would be.

        [*Exeunt Bubble and Scattergood.*]

Rash. Farewell Master *Scatter-good*: Come Lover, you're
too busie heere, I must tutor yee: Cast not your eye at the
table on each other; my Father will spie you without   1585
Spectacles, hee is a shrewd observer: doe you heare mee?
Ger. Very well sir.

1569-70 I ... Foole.] *as prose, Collier*; I ... part: / For ... Foole.
1572 Green's] *ed.*; Green's   1573 Greene's] *ed.*; Greene's   1578 on.]
Dodsley; on?   1580-1 O ... so.] *as prose, Collier*; O ... women: /
Custome ... so.   1582 SD [*Exeunt ... Scattergood.*]] *Reed*   1583 Master]
Hazlitt; M.   1585 other;] *Reed*; other   1586 hee ... mee?] *ed.*; *as one
line, Q1* (Hee)

Rash. Come then go wee togeather, let the Wenches alone.
/ Doe you see yonder fellow? [G3]
Ger. Yes: prethee what is hee? 1590
Rash. Ile give you him within, he must not now be
thought on: but you shall know him. *Exeunt Rash & Gerald.*
Gart. I have observ'd my sister, and her eye
Is much inquisitive after yond fellow;
Shee has examin'd him from head to foot: 1595
Ile stay and see the issue.
Joy. To wrastle gainst the streame of our Affection,
Is to strike Ayre, or buffet with the Winde
That playes upon us: I have striv'd to cast
This fellow from my thoughts, but still he growes 1600
More comely in my sight; yet a slave
Unto one worse condition'd then a Slave:
They are all gone, heer's none but hee, and I,
Now I will speake to him: and yet I will not.
Oh! I wrong my selfe, I will suppresse 1605
That insurrection *Love* hath traind in mee,
And leave him as he is: once my bold spirits
Had vowed to utter all my thoughts to him
On whom I setled my affection:
And why retyres it now? 1610
Sta. Fight *Love* on both sides; for on mee thou strik'st
Strokes that hath beat my heart into a flame:
She hath sent amorous glaunces from her eye,
Which I have backe returnd as faythfully.
I would make to her, but these servile Roabes, 1615
Curbes that suggestion, till some fitter time
Shall bring mee more perswadingly unto her.
Joy. I wonder why he stayes; I feare hee notes mee,
For I have publiquely betrayde my selfe,
By too much gazing on him: I will leave him. 1620
Gart. But you shall not; Ile make you speake to him
Before you goe. Doe you heare sir?

1592 SD *Exeunt*] *Reed*; *Exit* // *Rash*] *Q2*; *Rash.* 1598 Winde] *Q3*; Winde,
1611 SP *Sta.*] *Q2*; no period, *Q1* 1613 eye,] *Dodsley*; eye:

SC. XII] GREENE'S TU QUOQUE 59

Joy. What meane you sister?
Gart. To fit you in your kind, sister: doe you
Remember / how you once tyranizd over mee? [G3ᵛ] 1625
Joy. Nay prethee leave this jesting, I am out of the
  vaine.
Gart. I, but I am in: goe speake to your Lover.
Joy. Ile first be buried quicke.
Gart. How, ashamd?
S'fott, Itro, if I had set my affection
On a Collier, Ide nere fall backe, 1630
Unlesse it were in the right kind:
If I did, let mee be tyed to a Stake,
And burnt to death with Charcoale.
Joy. Nay then wee shall hate.
Gart. Yes marry shall you. Sister, will you speake 1635
to him?
Joy. No.
Gart. Doe you heare sir? heer's a Gentlewoman would
speake with you.
Joy. Why Sister, I pray Sister. 1640
Gart. One that loves you with all her heart, yet is
ashamd to confesse it.
Sta. Did you call, Ladyes?
Joy. No sir, heer's no one cald.
Gart. Yes sir twas I, I cald to speake with you. 1645
Joy. My Sister's somewhat frantique; there's no regard
  to
Be had unto her clamors: Will you yet leave?
In fayth you'le anger mee.
Gart. Passion: Come backe foole lover, turne againe
and kisse your belly full, heer's one will stand yee. 1650

1624-5 To ... doe you / Remember ... mee?] *ed.*; To ... remember /
How ... mee? 1626 Nay ... vaine.] *as one line, Collier*; Nay ...
iesting, / I ... vaine. 1628-33 How ... Charcoale.] *as verse, ed.*;
as prose, Q1 (How ... S'fott ... on ... vnlesse ... if ... and)
1629 S'fott,] *Dodsley*; S'fott 1636 him?] *Q3*; him: 1641-2 One ...
it.] *as prose, Collier*; One ... heart, / Yet ... it. 1647 Be]
ed.; be

Sta. What does this meane troe?

Joy. Yes, is your humor spent?

Gart. Come, let me goe, Birds that want the use of Reason and of Speech, can couple together in one day; and yet you that have both, cannot conclude in twentie: now Sister I am even with you, my venome is spit; as much happinesse may you enjoy with your lover as I with mine: and droope not wench, nor never be ashamd of him; the man will serve the turne, though he be wrapt in a blew Coate, Ile warrant him: come. 1660

Joy. You're merrely disposed, Sister.

Exeunt Wenches. /

Sta. I needs must prosper, Fortune & Love worke for [G4] mee:
Be moderate my Joyes; for as you grow
To your full height, so Bubbles waxeth low.   *Exit.*

[SCENE XIII]

Enter Spendall, Sweatman, and Tickleman.

Tick. Will my sweete *Spendall* be gone then?   1665

Spend. I must upon promise; but Ile be heere at supper: Therefore Mistris *Sweatman*, provide us some good cheare.

Sweat. The best the Market will yeeld.

Spend. Heer's twentie shillings; I protest I have left my selfe but a Crowne for my spending mony: for indeed I intend to be frugall, and turne good husband.   1671

Tick. I, marry will you, you'le to play againe, & loose your Monie and fall to fighting; my very heart trembles to thinke on it: how if you had been kild in the quarrell? of my fayth I had been but a dead woman.   1675

1653-60 Come ... come.] *as prose, Reed*; Come ... of / Reason ... day; / And ... twentie: / now ... spit, / As ... mine: / And ... him, / The ... wrapt / In ... come. 1656 spit;] *Dodsley*; spit, 1658 him;] *Dodsley*; him, 1660 him:] *Dodsley*; him, 1661 SD Exeunt] *Q3*; Exit 1663-4 Be ... grow / To ... low.] *Q3*; Be ... height, / So ... low. 1670 Crowne] *Dodsley*; Crowne, 1672 I,] *Dodsley* (Ay,); I 1674 quarrell?] *Dodsley*; quarrell,

SC. XIII]   GREENE'S TU QUOQUE

Spen. Come, come, no more of this; thou dost but dissemble.
Tick. Dissemble? do not you say so; for if you doe, Gods my judge Ile give my selfe a gash.
Spend. Away, away, prethee no more: farewell.   1680
Tick. Nay busse first: Well, there's No adversitie in the world shall part us.

Enter Sergiants.

Spend. Thou art a loving Rascall; farewell.
Sweat. You will not fayle supper?
Spend. You have my word; farewell.   1685
1.Ser. Sir, wee arrest you.
Spend. Arrest mee, at whose suite?
2.Ser. Marry there's suites enough against you, Ile warrant you.
1.Ser.   Come, away with him.   1689
Spend. Stay, heare mee a word.
2.Ser.   What doe you say? /
        [*They stand aside, talking.*]

Enter Purssnet.   [G4^v]

Tick. How now *Purssnet*, why com'st in such haste?
Purss. Shut up your doores, and barre young *Spendall*
        out,
And let him be cashieard your companie:
He is turnd Banquerout, his wares are ceazd on,
And his shop shut up.   1695
Tick. How, his wares ceazd on? thou dost but jest, I
        hope.
Purss. What this tongue doth report, these eyes have
        seene:
It is no *Aesops* fable that I tell,
But it is true, as I am faythfull Pander.   1699

1681-2 Nay ... there's / No ... us.] *ed.*; Nay ... Well, / There's
... vs. 1690 SD [*They stand aside, talking.*]] *ed.* 1693 companie:]
ed.; companie, 1697 seene:] *ed.*; seene,

Sweat. Nay I did ever thinke the prodigall would prove
A Banquerout; but hang him, let him rott
In prison, he comes no more within these doores
I warrant him.
Tick.   Come hither? I would
He would but offer it, weele fier him out
With a pox to him.
Spend. [*To the Sergiants.*] Will you doe it?   1705
To carrie me to prison, but undoes me.
1.Sar. What say you fellow *Gripe*, shall we take his 40.
shillings?
2.Sar. Yes fayth, we shall have him againe within this
weeke.   1710
1.Sar. Well Sir, your 40 shillings, and weele have some
compassion on you.
Spend. Will you but walke with me unto that house,
And there you shall receave it.
Sar. What, where the women are?   1715
Spend. Yes sir.   [*They come forward.*]
Sweat. Looke yonder, if the ungratious rascall
Be not comming hither, betwixt two *Sargiantes*:
He thinkes belike, that weele relieve him;
Let us goe in, and clap the doores against him.   1720
Purss. It is the best course Mistres *Tickleman*.
Tick. But I say no, you shall not stirre a foote,
For I will talke with him.
Spend.   *Nan*, I am come
Even in the Minute that thou didst professe /
Kindnesse unto mee, to make tryall of it.   [H1] 1725

1703-05 Come ... would / He ... weele ... out / With ... him.] *ed.*;
Come ... it, / Weele ... him. 1703 hither?] *ed.*; hither, 1705 SD
[*To the Sergiants.*]] *ed.* // it?] *Q3*; it; 1706 me.] *Q3*; me? 1708
            (lings.
shillings?] *Dodsley*; shil-   1711 shillings,] *ed.*; shillings?
1716 SP *Spend.*] *Q2*; no period, *Q1* // SD [*They come forward.*]] *ed.*
1717-20 Looke ... him.] *verse relined, ed.*; Looke ... hither, /
Betwixt ... belike, / That ... in, / And ... him. 1721 *Tickleman.*]
Q3; *Tickleman?* 1722 SP *Tick.*] *Q2*; no period, *Q1* 1723 him.] *Q2*; him,
1725 it.] *Dodsley*; it,

Adversitie thou Sees layes hands upon mee,
But Fortie shillings will deliver mee.
Tick. Why you Impudent Rogue, do you come to me for
    Mony?
Or do I know you? what acquaintance pray,
Hath ever past betwixt your selfe and mee?   1730
Sar. Zounds do you mocke us, to bring us to these
women that do not know you?
Sweat. Yes in good Sooth, (Officers I take't you're)
Hee's a meere stranger heere: onely in charitie,
Sometimes we have relieved him with a meale.   1735
Spend. This is not earnest in you? Come, I know
My guiftes and bountie cannot be soone buried:
Goe prethee fetch Fourtie shillings.
Tick. Talke not to mee (you slave) of Fourtie shillings;
For by this light that shines, aske it againe,   1740
Ile send my Knife of an earrand in your Guttes:
A shamelesse Roge to come to mee for Money.
Sweat. Is he your Prisoner, Gentlemen?
Sar. Yes marry is hee.
Sweat. Pray carry him then to Prison, let him smart
    for't,   1745
Perhaps twill tame the wildnesse of his youth,
And teach him how to lead a better life:
Hee had good counsell heere, I can assure you,
And if a would a tooke it.
Purss. I told him still my selfe, what would insew.   1750
Spend. Furies breake loose in mee: Sargeants, let me
    goe,
Ile give you all I have to purchase freedome
But for a lighting while, to teare yond Whore,
Baud, Pander, and in them, the Divell:

1727 mee.] *Dodsley*; mee, 1738 shillings.] *Q3*; shillings? 1739 SP
Tick.] *Q2*; *no period, Q1* 1742 Money.] *Q3*; Money? 1751-56 Furies ...
place.] *as verse, ed.*; *as prose, Q1* (Furies ... Ile ... but ...
Baud ... for ... nor) 1752 have] *Dodsley*; have, 1754 Baud] *Q1(c)*;
Ba(?u)d *Q1(u)*

64 GREENE'S TU QUOQUE [SC. XIII

For there's his Hell, his habitation; 1755
Nor has hee any other locall place.
Sar. No sir, weele take no Bribes.

       Takes Spendals Cloake.

Spend. Honest Sargeants, give me leave to unlade
A heart ore-chargd with griefe; as I have a soule,
Ile not breake from you. / 1760
Thou Strumpet, that wert borne to ruine men, [H1^v]
My fame, and fortune: be subject to my Cursse,
And heare mee speake it: Mayst thou in thy youth,
Feele the sharpe Whippe; and in thy Beldame age,
The Cart: when thou art growne to bee 1765
An old Upholster unto *Venerie,*
(A Bawd I meane, to live by Fether-beds,)
Mayst thou be driven to sell all thou hast
Unto thy *Aqua vite* Bottle; that's the last
A Bawd will part withall; and live so poore, 1770
That being turnd forth thy house, mayst die at doore.
Ser. Come sir, ha you done?
Spend. A little further give mee leave, I pray,
I have a charitable Prayer to end with.
May the *French* Canniball eate into thy flesh, 1775
And picke thy bones so cleane, that the report
Of thy Calamitie, may draw resort
Of all the common Sinners in the towne,
To see thy mangled Carcasse: and that then,
They may upon't, turne honest; Bawd, say Amen. 1780

     Exeunt [Spendall and Sergiants].

Sweat. Out upon him wicked villaine, how he blaspheames.
Purss. Hee will be damn'd for turning Heretique.
Tick. Hang him Banquerout rascall, let him talke in
    Prison,

1757 SD *Takes Spendals Cloake.*] after l. 1757, *Reed*; after l. 1756,
Q1 1769 Bottle] *ed.*; *Bottle* 1780 SD *Exeunt [Spendall and
Sergiants].*] *ed.*; *Exit.* 1781 blaspheames.] *Dodsley*; blspheames;

The whilst weele spend his Goods: for I did never
Heare, that men tooke example by each other. 1785
Sweat. Well, if men did rightly consider't, they should
    find,
That Whores and Bawdes are profitable members
In a Common-wealth: for indeed, tho wee somewhat
Impaire their Bodyes, yet wee doe good to their Soules;
For I am sure, wee still bring them to Repentance. 1790
Purse. By *Dis*, and so wee doe.
Sweat.   Come, come, will you *Dis* before?
Thou art one of them, that I warrant thee
Wilt be hangd, before thou wilt repent.   *Exeunt*. /

[SCENE XIV]

Enter Rash, Stayns and Geraldine.   [H2]

Rash. Well, this Love is a troublesome thing, *Jupiter*
blesse mee out of his fingers: ther's no estate can 1795
rest for him: Hee runnes through all Countries, will travell
through the *Ile of Man* in a minut; but never is quiet till
hee come into *Middle-sex*, and there keepes his Christmas:
Tis his habitation, his mantion; from whence, heele never
out, till hee be fierd.   1800
Ger. Well, do not tyranize too much, least one day he
make you know his Deitie, by sending a shaft out of a
sparkling eye, shall strike so deepe into your heart, that
it shall make you fetch your breath short againe.
Rash. And make mee cry, O eyes no eyes, but two   1805
celestiall Starres! A pox ont, Ide as leive heare a fellow
sing through the nose. How now Wench?

Enter Gartred.

Gart. Keepe your station; you stand as well for the

1791-3 Come ... repent.] *as verse, ed.; as prose*, *Q1* (Come ... thou
... wilt) 1791 before?] *Q3*; before: 1793 SD *Exeunt.*] *Dodsley*; *Exit*.
Sc. XIV OSD *Rash, Stayns*] *Q2*; *Rash Stayns* 1799-1800 Tis ... fierd.]
as prose, Reed; Tis ... whence, / Heele ... fierd. 1807 through]
Q2; throngh

incounter as may be: Shee is comming on; but as melancholy
as a Base-vyoll in Consort. 1810
Rash. Which makes thee as Sprightly as the Trebble. Now
dost thou play thy prize: heer's the honorable Sciense one
against another: Doe you heare Lover, the thing is done you
wot off; you shall have your Wench alone without any 1814
disturbance: now if you can doe any good, why so, the
Silver Game be yours, weele stand by and give ayme, and
hallow if you hit the Clout.
Sta. Tis all the assistance I request of you:
Bring mee but opportunatly to her presence,
And I desire no more: and if I cannot win her, 1820
Let mee loose her.
Gart. Well sir, let me tell you, perhaps you undertake
A harder taske then yet you doe imagine.
Sta. A taske, what to win a Woman, & have opportunitie?
I would that were a taske ifayth, for any man that 1825
weares his wittes about him: give me but halfe an houres /
conference with the coldest creature of them all, and [H2^V]
if I bring her not into a fooles Paradice, Ile pul out my
tongue, & hang it at her doore for a draw-latch. Udsfoot,
I'de nere stand thrumming of Caps for the matter; Ile
quickly make tryall of her if shee love: to have her Beautie
prays'd, Ile prayse it: if her Witte, Ile commende it: if
her good parts, Ile exalt them. No course shall scape me;
for to whatsoever I saw her inclind too, to that would I
fit her. 1835
Rash. But you must not doe thus to her, for shee's a
subtile flouting rogue, that will laugh you out of
countenance, if you solicit her ceriously: No, talke me to
her wantonly, slightly & carelesly, and perhaps so you may
prevaile as much with her, as wind does with a Sayle,

1809 melancholy] *Reed*; melancholy, 1811-12 Which ... dost] *as prose,*
ed.; Which ... Trebble. / Now dost 1818 you:] *ed.*; you, 1824-33
A ... them.] *as prose, Reed*; A ... opportunitie? / I ... his / wittes
... houres / Conference ... all, / And ... Paradice, / Ile ... draw-
latch. / Vdsfoot ... matter, / Ile ... loue: / To ... Witte, / Ile
... them. 1830 matter;] *Reed*; matter,

carry her whither thou wilt, Bully.   1841

Enter Joyce.

Sta. Well sir, Ile follow your instruction.
Rash. Do so. And see she appeares; fall you two off
from us, let us two walke togeather.
Joy. Why did my enquiring eye take in this fellow,   1845
And let him downe so easie to my heart;
Where like a Conquerour he ceases on it,
And beates all other men out of my Bossome?
Rash. Sister, you're well met: Heer's a Gentleman
desires to be acquainted with you.   1850
Joy. See the Servingman is turnd a Gentleman.
That villanous Wench my Sister, has no mercy:
Shee and my Brother has conspired together
To play upon me; But Ile prevent their sport:
For rather then my tongue shall have scope to speake 1855
Matter to give them mirth, my heart shall breake.
Rash. You have your desire sir, Ile leave you; Grapple
with her as you can.
Sta. Lady, God save you. [*Aside.*] She turns her backe
upon the motion, ther's no good to be done by braying
for her, I see that; I must plunge into a passion: now for
a peece of *Hero* and *Leander*: t'were excellent; and prayse be
to my memorie, / it has reacht halfe a dozen lines for   [H3]
the purpose: Well, shee shall have them.

    One is no Number; Maydes are nothing then   1865
    Without the sweete societie of Men.
    Wilt thou live single still? one shalt thou bee,

1843-4 Do ... togeather.] *as prose, Collier*; Do ... vs, / Let ...
togeather. 1849-50 Sister ... you.] *as prose, Collier*; Sister ...
met, / Heer's ... you. 1849 met:] *ed.*; met, 1851 Gentleman.]
Dodsley; Gentleman, 1852 mercy:] *ed.*; mercy, 1853-56 Shee ...
breake.] *as verse, ed.*; *as prose, Q1* (Shee ... to ... for ... matter)
1857-8 You ... can.] *as prose, ed.*; You ... you; / Grapple ... can.
1859 SP *Sta.*] *Q2*; *Sat.* 1859-64 Lady ... them.] *as prose, ed.*;
Lady ... motiõ, / Ther's ... that; / I ... and / *Leander* ...
memorie, / It ... purpose: / Well ... them. 1859 you.] *ed.*; *period
uncertain, Q1* // SD [*Aside.*]] *ed.*

68   GREENE'S TU QUOQUE   [SC. XIV

          Though never singling Hymen couple thee.
          Wild Savages that drinke of running Springs,
          Thinkes Water farre excells all other things.   1870
          They that dayly taste neat Wine, despise it.
          Virginitie albeit some highly prize it,
          Compard with Marriage, had you tryde them both,
          Differs as much as Wine and Water doth.
[Aside.] No? Why then have at you in another kind. 1875
By the fayth of a Souldier (Lady) I doe reverence the ground
that you walke upon: I will fight with him that dares say
you are not faire: Stabbe him that will not pledge your
health; and with a Dagger pierce a Vaine, to drinke a full
health to you; but it shall be on this condition, that
you shall speak first.   1881
[Aside.] Uds-foot, if I could but get her to talke once,
halfe my labour were over: but Ile try her in an other
vaine.
          What an excellent creature is a Woman without a tongue?
          But what a more excellent creature is a Woman
          That has a tongue, and can hold her peace?
          But how much more excellent and fortunate a creature
          Is that man, that has that Woman to his wife? 1889
[Aside.] This cannot choose but madde her; And if any
thing make a Woman talke, tis this. It will not doe tho yet.
I pray God they have not guld mee: But Ile try once againe.
          When will that tongue take libertie to talke?
          Speake but one word, and I am satisfied:

1868 couple] Q1(c); coup^a_ae Q1(u) 1870 things.] Q2; thing. 1873
Marriage,] Dodsley; Marriage; 1874-5 doth. / No?] Hazlitt; doth. No?
1875, 1882 SD [Aside.]] ed. 1875-6, 1881-2 kind. / By [,] first. /
[...] Uds-foot,] Q1 (This lineation between prose passages is un-
altered from Q1, as it seems intended to set off successive passages
in a stylistic tour de force.) 1876-81 By ... first.] not indented,
ed.; indented as in verse passages such as ll. 1865-74, Q1 1885-9
What ... wife?] as verse, ed.; as prose, Q1 (What ... But ... that
... But ... is) 1889-90 Is ... Woman ... wife? / [...] This
... her; And if any] ed.; Woman ... wife? This ... her; / And] Q1
1890, 1896 SD [Aside.]] ed. 1892 I ... againe.] as one line, ed.;
... I ... mee: / But ... againe.

SC. XIV]   GREENE'S TU QUOQUE   69

  Or doe but say but *Mum*, and I am answerd? 1895
[*Aside*.] No sound? no accent? Is there no noyse in Woman?
Nay then without direction I ha don.
I must goe call for helpe.   [*Leaves her*.]
Rash. How, not speake? /
Sta. Not a sillable, night nor sleepe, is not [H3^V] 1900
more silent: Shee's as dumbe as *Westminster* Hall, in the
long vacation.
Rash. Well, and what would you have mee doe?
Sta. Why, make her speake.
Rash. And what then? 1905
Sta. Why, let mee alone with her.
Rash. I, so you sayd before: Give you but opportunitie,
and let you alone, you'd desire no more: but come, Ile try
my cunning for you: See what I can doe. How doe you Sister,
I am sory to heare you are not well. This Gentleman 1910
tels mee you have lost your tongue; I pray let's see: if you
can but make signes whereabout you lost it, weele goe & looke
for't: in good fayth Sister, you looke very pale; in my
conscience tis for griefe: will you have any comfortable
Drinkes sent for? [*Aside*.] This is not the way; come
walke, seeme earnest in discourse, cast not an eye towards
her, and you shall see weaknesse worke it selfe. 1917
Joy. My heart is swolne so big, that it must vent,
Or it will burst: Are you a Brother?
Rash. Looke to your selfe Sir, 1920
The Brazen head has spoke, and I must leave you.
Joy. Has shame that power in him, to make him fly:

1898 SD [*Leaves her*.]] *Hazlitt* 1900-2 Not ... vacation.] *as prose*,
ed.; Not ... silent: / Shee's ... vacation. 1900 sillable] *Q1*(c);
sillabe *Q1*(u) 1907-17 I ... it selfe.] *as prose*, *Collier*; I ...
opportunitie, / And ... come, / Ile ... doe. / How ... well, / This
              (pale, /
... see? / If ... it, / Weele ... very ... In ... haue / Any ...
way; / Come ... eye / Towards ... it selfe. 1907 before:] *ed*.;
before, 1910 well.] *Dodsley*; well, // Gentleman] *Dodsley*; Gent.
1911 tongue;] *Dodsley*; tongue, // pray] *Q1*(c); dray *Q1*(u) // let's]
Dodsley; lels // see:] *ed*.; see? 1913 for't] *Dodsley*; fort' //
pale;] *Reed*; pale, 1915 for?] *Dodsley*; for, // SD [*Aside*.]]
Hazlitt // This] *ed*.; this

And dare you be so impudent to stand
Just in the face of my incensed anger?
What are you? why doe you stay? who sent for you?   1925
You were in Garments yesterday, befitting
A fellow of your fashion; has a Crowne
Purchast that shyning Sattin of the Brokers?
Or ist a cast Suite of your goodly Maisters?
Sta. A Cast suite, Lady?   1930
Joy. You thinke it does become you: fayth it does not,
A Blew Coat with a Badge, does better with you.
Goe untrusse your Maisters Poynts, and doe not dare
To stop your Nose when as his Worship stinkes:
T'as been your breeding.   1935
Sta. [*Aside.*] Uds' life, this is excellent; now she talkes. /
Joy. Nay, were you a Gentleman, and which is more,   [H4]
Well Landed, I should hardly love you:
For, for your Face, I never saw a worse,   1940
It lookes as if't were drawne with yellow Oacker
Upon blacke Buckram: and that Haire
Thats on your Chin, lookes not like Beard,
But as ift had been smeard with Shoomakers Wax.
Sta. [*Aside.*] Udsfoot, sheele make mee out of love   1945
with my selfe.
Joy. How dares your Basenes once aspyre unto
So high a fortune, as to reach at mee?
Because you have heard, that some have run away   1949
With Butlers, Horskeepers, and their fathers Clearks,
You forsooth, cockerd with your owne suggestion,
Take heart upon't, and thinke mee, (that am meate,
And set up for your Maister) fit for you.
Sta. [*Aside.*] I would I could get her now to hold her
    tongue.

1929 Maisters?] *Reed*; Maisters.   1935 T'as] *Q3*; Ta's   1936 SD [*Aside.*]] *Hazlitt*   1938 Gentleman,] *Dodsley*; Gentleman: // more,] *Q2*; more;   1945, 1954, 1959 SD [*Aside.*]] *Hazlitt*   1948 mee?] *ed.*; mee: 1950 Clearks,] *ed.*; Clearks;

Joy. Or cause, some times as I have past along, 1955
And have returnd a Curtcie for your Hatt,
You (as the common trickes is) straight suppose,
Tis Love, (sir reverence, which makes the word more beastly.)
Sta. [*Aside.*] Why, tis worse then scilence.
Joy. But wee are fooles,
And in our reputations we find the smart on't: 1960
Kindnesse is tearmd Lightnesse in our sex:
And when we give a Favour, or a Kisse,
Wee give our Good names too.
Sta. Will you be dumbe againe?
Joy. Men you are cald, but you're a viperous brood, 1965
Whom we in charitie take into our bosomes,
And cherish with our heart, for which you sting us.
Sta. Uds' foot, Ile fetch him that waked your tonge,
To lay it downe againe. [*Fetches Will Rash.*]
Rash. Why how now man?
Sta. O relieve mee, or I shall loose my hearing. 1970
You have raysde a Furie up into her tongue:
A Parliament of women could not make /
Such a Confused noyse as that she utters. [H4^V]
Rash. Well, what would you have mee do?
Sta. Why make her hold her tongue. 1975
Rash. And what then?
Sta. Why then let me alone againe.
Rash. This is very good Ifayth: first give thee but 1978
oppertunitie, and let thee alone: then make her but Speake,
and let thee alone: now make her hold her tongue, and

1956 Hatt,] *Q3*; Hatt; 1958 sir reverence,] *Dodsley*; sirreuerence,
Q1(c); sirreuerenc, *Q1*(u) 1959-60 But ... fooles, / And ... we ...
on't:] *ed.*; But ... reputations / We ... on't: 1961 Kindnesse] *Q2*;
Kindnesse, // Lightnesse] *Q2*; Lightnesse, 1964 againe?] *Q2*; againe.
1967 heart,] *ed.*; heart: // which] *Q3*; which, 1969 SD [*Fetches Will
Rash.*]] *Hazlitt* 1970 relieve] *Q2*; reliue // hearing.] *ed.*; hearing,
1971 tongue:] *Collier*; tongue 1974 SP *Rash.*] *Q2*; *no period*, *Q1*
1975 SP *Sta.*] *Q3*; *Sat.* 1978 is] *Q1*(c); si *Q1*(u) // Ifayth:] *Collier*;
I fayth, 1980-3 let ... did.] *as prose*, *Reed*; let / Thee ... then /
Let ... let / Thee ... mee, / The ... away, / Walke ... did. 1980
tongue] *Q2*; tougue

then let her alone: By my troth I thinke I were best to let
thee alone indeed: but come, follow mee, the Wild-cat shall
not carry it so away: walke, walke, as we did.
Joy. What, have you fetcht your Champion? what can he
    do?
Not have you, nor himselfe from out the storme   1985
Of my incensed rage; I will thunder into your eares,
The wrongs that you have done an innocent Mayde:
Oh you're a cupple of sweet--What shall I call you?
Men you are not; for if you were,
You would not offer this unto a Mayde.   1990
Wherein have I deserved it at your handes?
Have I not been, alwayes a kind Sister to you
And in signes & tokens shewed it? Did
I not send Money to you at *Cambridge* when   1994
You were but a Freshman, wrought you Purses and Bandes;
And since you came to th' Inn's a Court, a faire
Payre of Hangers? Have you not taken Rings
From mee, which I have been faine to say I have lost,
When you had paund them, and yet was never
Beholding to you for a payre of Gloves?   2000
Rash. A Womans tongue I see, is like a Bell,
That once being set a going, goes it selfe.
Joy. And yet you to joyne with my sister against mee,
Send one heere to play upon mee, whilst
You laugh and leere, and make a pastime on mee: 2005
Is this Brotherly done? No it is Barberous,
And a *Turke* would blush to offer it to a Christian:
But I will thinke on't, and have it written

1981 troth] *Q2*; torth 1982 Wild-cat] *Q1(c)*; wild Catt *Q1(u)* 1983
away:] *ed.*; away, 1984 SP *Joy.*] *Q2*; *no period, Q1* 1988 sweet--]
Dodsley; sweet: 1991-2 handes? / Have] *Dodsley*; handes? Haue 1992-
2000 Have ... Gloves?] *as verse, ed.*; *as prose, Q1* (Haue ... & ...
I ... you ... and ... payre ... from ... when ... be- / holding)
1996 to th'] *Dodsley*; toth' 1999 them,] *ed.*; them: 2001 SP *Rash.*]
Q1(c); *no period, Q1(u)* 2003-7 And ... Christian:] *verse relined,
ed.*; And ... mee, / Send ... you ... leere, / And ... is ... done? /
No ... & ... Chri- / stian: 2008-9 But ... memories.] *as verse, ed.*;
as prose, Q1 (but ... in)

SC. XIV]   GREENE'S TU QUOQUE   73

In my heart, when it hath slipt your memories.
Rash. When will your tongue be wearie? /   2010
Joy. Never.
Rash. How, never? Come talke, and Ile talke with you:
Ile try the nimble footmanship of your tongue;
And if you can out-talke mee, yours be the victorie.

*Heere they two talke and rayle what they list;
then Rash speakes to Stayns.*

Rash. Uds' foot, dost thou stand by, and doe   2015
nothing? Come talke, and drowne her clamors.

*Heere they all three talke, and Joyce gives
over, weeping, and Exit.*

Gerald. Alas, shee's spent yfayth: now the stormes
over.
Rash. Uds' foot, Ile follow her as long as I have any
breath.   2020
Gart. Nay no more now Brother, you have no compassion,
you see shee cryes.
Sta. If I do not wonder she could talke so long, I am a
villaine; she eats no Nuts I warrant her: sfoot, I am almost
out of breath with that little I talkt: well Gentlemen,
Brothers I might say; for shee and I must clap hands upon't:
a match for all this. Pray goe in; and Sister, salve the
matter, collogue with her againe, and all shall be well:
I have a little businesse that must be thought upon, and
tis partlie for your mirth; therefore let mee not (tho
absent) be forgotten: Fare well.
Rash. We will be mindfull of you sir, fare you well.
                                    [*Exit Staines.*]

2012 you:] *Collier*; you, 2013 nimble] *Q2*; ninble 2015 SP *Rash.*] *ed*.;
All speake. 2016 SD *over*,] *ed*.; ouer 2021-2 Nay ... cryes.] *as
prose, ed.*; Nay ... compassion, / You ... cryes. 2023-31 If ...
                        (laine, /
Fare well.] *as prose, Reed*; If ... vil-   She ... breath / With
... say; / For ... this. / Pray ... her / Againe ... businesse / That
... mirth; / Therefore ... forgotten: / Fare well. 2024 villaine;]
        (laine,
ed.; vil-   2025 Gentlemen,] *ed*.; Gent. 2032 SD [*Exit Staines.*]] *ed*.

Ger. How now man, what tyerd, tyerd? 2033
Rash. Zounds, and you had talkt as much as I did, you
would be tyrd I warrant: What, is shee gone in? Ile to
her againe whilst my tongue is warme: and if I thought I
should be usde to this exercise I woulst eate every morning
an ounce of Lickorish. *Exeunt.*

[SCENE XV]

*Enter Lodge the maister of the Prison,
and Hold-fast his man.*

Lodge. Have you sumd up those Reckonings?
Hold. Yes Sir. 2040
Lodg. And what is owing mee?
Hold. Thirtie-seven pound odd monie. / [11ᵛ]
Lodg. How much owes the *Frenchman*?
Hold. A fourtnights Commons.
Lodg. Has *Spendall* anie monie? 2045
Hold. Not any sir: and he has sold all his Cloaths.

Enter Spendall.

Lodg. That fellow would wast Millions, if he had them;
Whilst he has Monie, no man spends a pennie:
Aske him monie, and if he say he has none,
Be plaine with him, and turne him out o' th Ward. 2050

Exit Lodg.

Hold. I will sir. Maister *Spendall*,
My Maister has sent to you for monie.
Spend. Monie, why does he send to mee? does he thinke
I have the Philosophers Stones, or I can clip
Or coyne? How does he thinke I can come by monie? 2055
Hold. Fayth sir, his occasions are so great, that hee
Must have monie, or else he can buy no Victuals.
Spend. Then we must starve, belike: Udsfoot thou seest

2038 SD *Exeunt.*] *Reed; Exit.* Sc. XV OSD *Hold-fast*] *Q3; Lock-fast*
2052 sent to] *Q2;* sentto

I have nothing left, that will yeeld mee two shillings.
Hold. If you have no monie, 2060
You're best remove into some cheaper Ward.
Spend. What Ward should I remove in?
Hold.   Why to the Two-pennie Ward,
Is likliest to hold out with your meanes:
Or if you will, you may goe into the Holl,
And there you may feed for nothing. 2065
Spend. I, out of the Almes-basket, where Charitie
     appeares
In likenesse of a peece of stinking Fish,
Such as they beat Bawdes with when they are Carted.
Hold. Why sir, doe not scorne it, as good men as your
     selfe,
Have been glad to eate Scraps out of the Almsbasket. 2070
Spend. And yet slave, thou in pride wilt stop thy nose,
Scrue and make faces, talke contemptibly of it,
And of the feeders; surely groome.

             Enter Fox.

Hold. Well sir, your mallapertnes will get you nothing.
     Fox.
Fox. Heere. / 2075
Hold. A prisoner to the Holl, take charge of him, [I2]
And use him as scurvily as thou canst: you shall
Be taught your duetie sir, I warrant you.
Spend. Hence slavish tyrants, instruments of torture,
There is more kindnesse yet in Whores, then you, 2080
For when a man hath spent all, hee may goe
And seeke his way, theyle kicke him out of dores,
Not keepe him in as you doe, and inforce him
To be the subject of their crueltie.
You have no mercie; but be this your comfort, 2085

2059-60 I ... clip / Or ... monie?] *ed.*; I ... coyne? / How ... monie?
2062-65 Why ... nothing.] *as verse, ed.*; *as prose,* Q1 (Why ... is
 ... or ... and) 2067 Fish,] *Dodsley*; Fish: 2073 And] *ed.*; and
2074 SP *Hold.*] Q2; *no period,* Q1 2076-8 A ... you.] *as verse, ed.*;
as prose, Q1 (A ... and ... be) 2082 dores,] *Reed*; dores;

               The punishment and torturs which you doe
               Inflict on men, the Divels shall on you.
           Hold. Well sir, you may talke, but you shall see
               The end, and who shall have the worst of it. *Exit Hold.*
           Spend. Why villaine, I shall have the worst, I know
                            it,   2090
               And am prepard to suffer like a *Stoicke,*
               Or else (to speake more properly) like a Stocke;
               For I have no sence left: dost thou thinke I have?
           Fox. Zounds, I thinke hee's madde?   2094
           Spend. Why, thou art i'th right; for I am madde indeed,
               And have been madde this two yeare. Dost thou thinke
               I could have spent so much as I have done
               In wares and credite, had I not been madde?
               Why thou must know, I had a faire estate,
               Which through my ryot, I have torne in peeces,   2100
               And scattered amongst Bawdes, Buffoons, and Whores,
               That fawnd on mee, and by their flatteries,
               Rockt all my understanding faculties
               Into a pleasant slumber, where I dreampt
               Of nought but joy and pleasure: never felt   2105
               How I was luld in sensualitie,
               Untill at last, Affliction waked mee:
               And lighting up the Taper of my soule,
               Led mee unto my selfe, where I might see   2109
               A minde and body rent with Miserie. *A Prisoner within.*
           Pris. Harry Fox, Harry Fox.
           Fox. Who calles? /
                            Enter Prisoners.   [I2ᵛ]
           Pris. Heer's the Bread and Meate-man come.
           Fox. Well, the Bread and Meate-man may stay a little.
           Pris. Yes indeed *Harry,* the Bread and Meat-man may 2115
               stay: But you know our stomacks cannot stay.

2087 Inflict] *Q2;* Iuflict 2088-9 Well ... it.] *verse relined, ed.;*
Well ... the end, / And ... it. 2089 end,] *Q1(c);* end; *Q1(u)* // SD
Hold.] *Q3;* Lock. 2104 slumber,] *ed.;* slumber; 2109 my selfe,]
Dodsley; my selfe; 2114 Meate-man] *Q2;* Meate-man, 2115-6 Yes ...
stay.] *as prose, Collier;* Yes ... stay: / But ... stay. 2115 Meat-
man] *Q2;* Meat-man,

Enter Gatherscrap with the Basket.

Fox. Indeed your Stomacke is alwayes first up.
Pris. And therefore by right, should be first served:
I have a stomacke like *Aqua fortis*, it will eate any thing:
O father *Gatherscrap*, here are excellent bits in the   2120
Basket.
Fox. Will you hold your Chops further? by and by youle
drivell into the Basket.
Pris. Perhaps it may doe some good, for there may be a
peece of powderd Beefe that wants watering.   2125
Fox. Heere sir, heer's your share.
Pris. Heer's a bit indeed: whats this to a *Gargantua*
stomack?
Fox. Thou art ever grumbling.
Pris. Zounds, it would make a Dogge grumble, to   2130
want his Victuals: I pray give *Spendall* none, hee came into
th' Holl but yester-night.
Fox. What, doe you refuse it?
Spend. I cannot eate, I thanke you.
Pris. No, no, give it mee; hee's not yet seasond   2135
for our companie.
Fox. Devide it then amongst you.   *Exeunt Fox &*
                                        Prisoners.
Spend. To such a one as these are must I come,
Hunger will draw mee into their fellowship,
To fight and scramble for unsaverie Scraps,   2140
That come from unknowne hands, perhaps unwasht:
And would that were the worst; for I have noted,
That nought goes to the Prisoners, but such food
As either by the weather has been tainted,
Or Children, nay sometimes full paunched Dogges,   2145
Have overlickt, as if men had determind

2118 SP Pris.] Q2; Bris. // first] Q2; fire 2120-1 O ... Basket.]
as prose, ed.; as separate verse line, Q1 2122 further?] Dodsley;
further; 2123 Basket.] Dodsley; Basket? 2124 good,] ed.; good;
2131-2 into th'] ed.; into'th 2137 SD Exeunt] Reed; Exit 2138 are]
Collier; are,

That the worst Sustenance, which is Gods Creatures,
How ever they're abusde, are good enough /
For such vild Creatures as abuse themselves. [I3]
O what a Slave was I unto my Pleasures? 2150
How drownd in Sinne, and overwhelmd in Lust?
That I could write my repentance to the world,
And force th' impression of it in the hearts
Of you, and my acquaintance, I might teach them
By my example, to looke home to Thrift, 2155
And not to range abroad to seeke out Ruine:
Experience shewes, his Purse shall soone grow light,
Whom Dice wastes in the day, Drabs in the night:
Let all avoyde false Strumpets, Dice, and Drinke;
For hee that leaps in Mudde, shall quickly sinke. 2160

Enter Fox and Longfield.

Fox. Yonder's the man.
Long. I thanke you. How is it with you, sir. What,
On the ground? Looke up, there's comfort towards you.
Spend. Belike some charitable Friend has sent a
 Shilling.
What is your Businesse?
Long.   Libertie. 2165
Spend. There's vertue in that word; Ile rise up to you.
Pray let mee heare that chearefull word againe.
Long. The able, and wel-minded Widdow *Raysby*,
Whose hand is still upon the poore mans Box,
Hath in her Charitie remembred you: 2170
And beeing by your Maister seconded,
Hath taken order with your Creditors
For day and payment; and freely from her Purse,
By mee her Deputie, shee hath dischargd 2174
All Duties in the House: Besides, to your necessities,
This is bequeathd, to furnish you with Cloaths.

2160 SD *Longfield*] *Q2*; *Long field* 2162-3 I ... you.] *verse relined,
ed.*; I ... you. / How ... on ... ground? / Looke ... you. 2162 What,]
Dodsley; What 2164 Shilling.] *Dodsley*; Shilling, 2173 day] *Q3*; day,

SC. XVI]   GREENE'S TU QUOQUE   79

Spend. Speake you this seriously?
Long. Tis not my practise to mocke Miserie.
Spend. Be ever praysed that Devinitie,
That has to my oppressed state raysd Friends: /   2180
Still be his blessings powred upon their heads: [13^v]
Your hand, I pray,
That have so faythfully performd their willes:
If ere my industrie, joynd with their loves,
Shall rayse mee to a competent estate,   2185
Your name shall ever be to mee a friend.
Long. In your good wishes, you requite mee amply.
Spend. All Fees, you say, are payd? there's for your
    love.
Fox. I thanke you sir, and glad you are releast.

                                                     Exeunt.

                    [SCENE XVI]

              Enter Bubble gallanted.

Bub. How Apparell makes a man respected; the very   2190
children in the streete do adore mee: for if a Boy is
throwing at his Jacke-alent chaunce to hit mee on the
shinnes, why I say nothing but *Tu quoque*, smile, and forgive
the Child with a becke of my hand, or some such like token:
so by that meanes, I do seldome goe without broken   2195
shinnes.

              Enter Stains like an Italian.

Sta. The blessings of your Mistres fall upon you,
And may the heat and spirit of Her lip,
Endue her with matter above her understanding,
That she may only live to admire you,   2200
Or as the *Italian* sayes; *Que que dell fogo Ginni Coxcombie.*

2181 Still] *Dodsley*; still   2189 SD Exeunt.] *Reed*; Exit.   2193 shinnes,]
Dodsley; shinnes: // why] *Dodsley*; Why 2193 but] *Dodsley*; but,
2198 Her lip,] *Q2* (Her-lip,); Hee-lip, 2200-1 That ... *Coxcombie.*]
verse relined, ed.; That ... or ... sayes; / *Que ... Coxcombie.*

Bub. [*Aside.*] I doe wonder what language he
speakes. Doe you heare my friend, are not you a Conjurer?
Sta. I am sir, a perfect Traveller, that have trampled
over the face of this uneverss, and can speake *Greeke*
and *Latine* as promptly as my owne naturall Language: I have
composd a Booke, wherein I have set downe all the Wonders of
the world that I have seene, and the whole scope of my
Jornies, togeather with the miseries and lowsie fortunes I
have endured therein.   2210
Bub. O Lord Sir, are you the man? give me your
hand: How doe yee: in good fayth I thinke I have heard of
you.   2213
Sta. No sir, you never heard of mee: I set this day
footing / upon the Wharffe, I came in with the last [I4]
peale of Ordinance, and dind this day in the Exchange amongst
the Marchants. But this is frivelous and from the matter:
you doe seeme to be one of our *Genteell* spirrits that doe
affect *Genorositie*: Pleaseth you to be instituted in the
nature, Garb, and habit of the most exactest Nation in
the world, the *Italian*: whose Language is sweetest, Cloaths
neatest, and haviour most accomplisht: I am one that have
spent much monie, and time, which to me is more dear then
monie, in the observation of these things: and now I am
come, I will sit me downe and rest, and make no doubt,
but by qualitie, to purchase and build, by professing this
Art, or humane Science (as I may tearme it,) to such 2227
Honorable and Worshipfull personages as meane to be peculiar.

2202 SD [*Aside.*]] *ed.* 2202-3 I ... Conjurer?] *as prose, ed.*; I ...
speakes. / Doe ... Coniurer? 2204-10 I ... therein.] *as prose*,
Collier; I ... ouer / The ... and / *Latine* ... Language: / I ...
downe / All ... seene, / And ... the / Miseries ... therein. 2205
uneverss,] *Q2* (vniuers,); vneuerss. 2211-3 O ... you.] *as prose*,
ed.; O ... hand: / How ... you. 2216 man?] *Q3*; man; 2214-28 No ...
peculiar.] *as prose, Collier*; No ... footing / Vpon ... Ordinance, /
And ... Marchants. / But ... seeme / To ... *Genorositie*: / Pleaseth
... habit, / Of ... *Italian*: / Whose ... hauiour / Most ... monie, /
And ... the / Obseruation ... come, / I ... doubt, / But ... Art, /
Or ... Honorable / And ... peculiar. 2214 mee:] *ed.*; mee, 2220
Garb,] *Q3*; Garb. // habit] *Dodsley*; habit, 2221 whose] *ed.*; Whose
2223 time,] *Dodsley*; time;

Bub. [*Aside.*] This fellow has his tongue at his fingers
endes: But harke you sir, is your *Italian* the finest
Gentleman?   2231
Sta. In the world *Signeor*, your *Spaniard* is a meere
Bumbard to him: hee will bounce indeed; but hee will burst:
But your *Italian* is smooth and loftie, and his language is
Cozen germane to the *Latine*.   2235
Bub. Why then hee has his *Tu quoque* in his salute?
Sta. Yes sir, for it is an *Italian* word as well as a
Latine, and infoldes a double sence: for one way spoken, it
includes a fine Gentleman like your selfe; and another way,
it imports an Asse, like whom you will.   2240
Bub. [*Aside.*] I would my man *Jarvis* were heere, for hee
understands these thinges better then I. You will not serve?
Sta. Serve? no sir, I have talkt with the great *Sophy*.
Bub. I pray sir, whats the lowest price of being
Italianated?   2245
Sta. Sir, if it please you, I will stand to your bounty:
And marke me, I will set your face like a Grand signeors, and
you shall march a whole day, untill you come opounctly to
your Mistris, and not disrancke one hayre of your phisnomie.
Bub. I would you would doe it Sir: if you will   2250
stand to my Bounty, I will pay you, as I am an *Italian tu
quoque*. /
Sta. Then sir, I will first disburthen you of your [14^V]
Cloake, you will be the nimbler to practise: Now sir,
observe mee: Goe you directly to the Lady to whom you
devote your selfe.   2256
Bub. Yes sir.

2229 SD [*Aside.*]] *ed.* 2229-31 This ... Gentleman?] *as prose, ed.*;
This ... endes: / But ... Gentleman? 2234 smooth and] *Q2*; smoothand
// language is] *Q2*; language is, 2237-40 Yes ... will.] *as prose,
Collier*; Yes ... *Latine*, / And ... spoken, / It ... selfe; / And
... will. 2241 SD [*Aside.*]] *Hazlitt* 2243 Serve?] *ed.*; Serue,
2244 pray] *Q2*; pary 2246-9 Sir ... phisnomie.] *as prose, Collier*;
Sir ... bounty: / And ... signeors, / And ... opounctly / to ...
Mistirs, / And ... phisnomie. 2249 Mistris] *Q2*; Mistirs 2250 Sir:]
ed.; Sir, 2251 Italian] *Q2*; Itatian 2253-6 Then ... selfe.]
as prose, Collier; Then ... Cloake, / You ... mee, / Goe ... selfe.
2255 mee:] *Collier*; mee,

Sta. You shall set a good stay'd face upon the matter then. Your Band is not to your Shirt, is it?
Bub. No sir, tis loose.   2260
Sta. It is the fitter for my purpose. I will first remoove your Hatte: it has been the fashion (as I have heard) in *England*, to weare your Hatte thus in your eyes; But it is grosse, naught, inconvenient, and proclaymes with a loude voyce, that hee that brought it up first, stood in feare of Sargiants. Your *Italian* is contrarie, hee doth advance his Hatte, and sets it thus.   2267
Bub. Excellent well: I would you would set on my head so.
Sta. Soft, I will first remove your Band, and set   2270 it out of the reach of your eye; it must lie altogeather backward: So, your Band is well.
Bub. Is it as you would have it?
Sta. It is as I would wish; onely sir, this I must   2274 condition you off; in your affront or salute, never to moove your Hatte: But heere, heere is your curtesie.
Bub. Nay I warrant you, let mee alone; if I perceive a thing once, Ile carrie it away: Now pray sir, reach my Cloake.
Sta. Never whilst you live, sir.   2280
Bub. No, what doe your *Italians* weare no Cloakes?
Sta. Your *Signeors* never: you see I am unfurnisht my selfe.

Enter Sir Lyo., Will Rash, Geraldine, Widdow, Gartred, and Joyce.

Bub. Sa'y so? prethee keepe it then. See, yonder's the companie that I looke for; therefore if you will set my face of any fashion, pray doe it quickly.   2286
Sta. You carry your face as well as eare an *Italian* in

2261 It ... purpose.] *as prose, Collier; as separate verse line, Q1*
2262 Hatte:] *ed.*; Hatte,   2265 voyce,] *Dodsley*; voyce;   2281 *Italians*] *Q2*; *Iltalians*   2283 SD *Lyo.,*] *Dodsley*; *Lyo.*   2286 quickly.] *Q3*; quickly?

the world; onely inrich it with a Smyle, and tis incompara-
ble: and thus much more: at your first apparance, you shall
perhaps / strike your acquaintance into an extasie,   [K1]
or perhaps a laughter: but tis ignorance in them, which will
soone be overcome, if you persever.   2292
Bub. I will persever, I warrant thee; onely doe thou
stand aloofe and be not seene, because I would have them
thinke I fetcht it out of my owne practise.   2295
Sta. Do not you feare, Ile not be seene, I warrant you.
                                                     Exit.
Lyo. Now *Widdow*, you are welcome to my house,
And to your owne house too; so you may call it:
For what is mine, is yours: you may command
Heere as at home, and be as soone obayde.   2300
Wid. May I deserve this kindnesse of you, sir?
Bub. Save you Gentlemen: I salute you after the *Italian*
fashion.
Rash. How, the *Italian* fashion? Zounds, he has drest
him rarely.   2305
Lyo. My sonne *Bubble*, I take it?
Rash. The nether part of him I thinke is hee,
But what the upper part is, I know not.
Bub. [*Aside.*] By my troth hee's a rare fellow, he sayd
true: They are all in an extasie.   2310
Gart. I thinke hee's madde?
Joy. Nay that can not bee; for they say, they that are
madde, loose their wits: and I am sure he had none to loose.

                    Enter Scattergood.

Lyo. How now sonne *Bubble*, how come you thus   2314
attyrde? What, do you meane to make your selfe a laughing

2288 world;] Reed; world, 2289 more:] ed.; more, // apparance] ed.
(after Q1); apparace 2293 SP Bub.] Q2; no period, Q1 2299-2300
For ... command / Heere ... obayde.] ed.; For ... heere, / As ...
obayde. 2300 Heere] Dodsley; heere, 2302 Gentlemen] ed. (after
Dodsley); Gent. // Italian] Q2; Italiau 2304 fashion] Dodsley;
fashion 2305 rarely.] Dodsley; rarely 2309 SD [Aside.]] Hazlitt
2314-16 How ... ha?] as prose, ed.; possibly intended as verse, Q1
(How ... attyrde? / What ... ha?)

stocke, ha?
Bub. [*Aside.*] Um; Ignorance, ignorance.
Ger. For the love of laughter, looke yonder, another
Hearing in the same pickle.
Rash. The tother Hobby-horse I perceive is not   2320
forgotten.
Bub. Ha, ha, ha, ha.
Scat. Ha, ha, ha, ha.
Bub. Who has made him such a Coxcombe troe? An *Italian*
tu quoque?   2325
Scat. I salute you according to the *Italian* fashion.
Bub. Puh, the *Italian* fashion? the tatterd-de-malian
fashion hee meanes.
Scat. Save you sweete bloods, save you.
Lyo. Why but what Jigge is this?   2330
Scat. Nay if I know father, would I were hangd,
I am e'ne as Innocent as the Child new borne.
Lyo. I but sonne *Bubble*, where did you two buy your
Felts?
Scat. Felts? By this light, mine is a good Beaver: 2335
It cost mee three pound this morning upon trust.
Lyo. Nay, I thinke you had it upon trust: for no man
that has any shame in him, would take mony for it: behold
Sir.
Scat. Ha, ha, ha.   2340
Lyo. Nay never doe you laugh, for you're i'th same
blocke.
Bub. Is this the *Italian* fashion?
Scat. No, it is the Fooles fashion:
And we two are the first that follow it.   2345
Bub. Et tu quoque, are we both cozend? Then lets shew
our selves brothers in adversitie, and imbrace.
Lyo. What was hee that cheated you?

2317 SD [*Aside.*]] Hazlitt   2318-19 For ... pickle.] *as prose, ed.*;
For ... yonder, / Another ... pickle.   2324-5 Who ... quoque?]
as prose, ed.; Who ... troe? / An ... quoque. // quoque?] *Q3*; quogue.
2341 SP *Lyo.*] *Q3*; *no period, Q1*   2346-7 Et ... imbrace.] *as prose,
Collier*; Et ... cozend: / Then ... imbrace.   2346 cozend?] *Q3*;
cozend:

SC. XVI]   GREENE'S TU QUOQUE   85

Bub. Marry sir, he was a Knave that cheated mee.
Scat. And I thinke he was no honest man that   2350
cheated mee.
Lyo. Doe you know him againe, if you see him?

                     Enter Stayns.

Bub. Yes I know him againe, if I see him: But I doe not
know how I should come to see him. O *Jarvis, Jarvis*, doe
you see us two, *Jarvis*?   2355
Sta. Yes sir, very well.
Bub. No, you doe not see us very well; for we have been
horribly abused: Never were *Englishmen* so guld in *Italian*,
as we have been.
Sta. Why sir, you have not lost your Cloake and   2360
Hatte?
Bub. Jarvis you lie, I have lost my Cloake and
Hatte: And therefore you must use your credite for another.
Scat. I thinke my old Cloake and Hatte must be glad to
serve mee till next quarter day.   2365
Lyo. Come, take no care for Cloakes, Ile furnish you: /
To night you lodge with mee, to morrow morne   [K2]
Before the Sunne be up, prepare for Church,
The Widdow and I have so concluded on't:
The Wenches understand not yet so much,   2370
Nor shall not, untill bedtime: then will they
Not sleepe a wincke all night, for very joy.
Scat. And Ile promise the next night, they shall not
sleepe for joy neither.
Lyo. O Maister *Geraldine*, I saw you not before: 2375
Your Father now is come to towne, I heare.
Ger. Yes Sir.

2350 man] *Q2*; man,   2351 mee.] *Dodsley*; mee,   2352 SD *Stayns.*] *Q2*;
possible comma, Q1   2353-5 Yes ... Jarvis?] *as prose, Collier*; Yes
... him: / But ... him. / O ... Iaruis?   2357-9 No ... been.] *as
prose, Collier*; No ... well; / For ... abused: / Neuer ... been.
2361 Hatte?] *Q3*; Hatte.   2362-3 Jarvis ... another.] *as prose, ed.*;
Iaruis ... Hatte: / And ... another.   2364 Hatte] *Q3*; Hatte,   2366
care] *Q2*; car(?e)   2371 they] *Q3*; they,   2373-4 And ... neither.] *as
prose, Collier*; And ... night, / They ... neither.   2376 heare.] *Q3*;
heare?

Lyo. Were not my businesse earnest, I would see him:
But pray intreat him breake an howers sleepe
To morrow morne, t'accompanie mee to Church;   2380
And come your selfe I pray along with him.

Enter Spendall.

Ger. Sir, I thanke you.
Lyo. But looke, heere comes one, that has but lately
Shooke off his Shackles. How now sirra, wherefore come you?
Spend. I come to crave a pardon sir, of you,   2385
And with heartie and zelous thankes
Unto this worthy Lady, that hath given mee
More then I ere could hope for: Libertie.
Wid. Be thankfull unto Heaven, and your Maister:
Nor let your heart grow bigger then your Purse,   2390
But live within a limit, least you burst out
To Ryot, and to Miserie againe:
For then t'would loose the benefite I meant it.
Lyo. O you doe graciously, tis good advice:
Let it take roote sirra, let it take roote.   2395
But come *Widdow* come, and see your Chamber;
Nay your companie too, for I must speake with you.
Spend. Tis bound unto you Sir.   *Exeunt [Sir Lionel,*
                                       Widow, Spendall].
Bub. And I have to talke with you too, Mistris
Joyce: / Pray a word.   [K2ᵛ] 2400
Joy. What would you, Sir?
Bub. Pray let me see your hand: the line of your
Maydenhead is out. Now for your Finger; upon which Finger
will you weare your wedding Ring?
Joy. Upon no Finger.   2405
Bub. Then I perceive you meane to weare it on your

2383-4 But ... lately / Shooke ... you?] *ed.*; But ... one, / That
... Shackles. / How ... you? 2398 SD *Exeunt*] Reed; *Exit* // [*Sir* ...
Spendall]] *ed.*; SD *after l.* 2398, *ed.*; *after l.* 2397, *Q1* 2399-2400
And ... word.] *as prose, ed.*; And ... *Ioyce:* / Pray ... word. 2403
Finger;] *Q1(c)*; *possible comma, Q1(u)* 2406-7 Then ... come.] *as
prose, ed.*; *possibly intended as verse, Q1* (Then ... thumb. / Well
... come.)

SC. XVI] GREENE'S TU QUOQUE 87

thumb. Well, the time is come sweet *Joyce*, the time is come.
Joy. What to doe, sir?
Bub. For mee to tickle thy *Tu quoque*; to doe the act
Of our forefathers: therefore prepare, provide, 2410
To morrow morne to meete mee as my Bride. *Exit.*
Joy. Ile meete thee like a Ghost first.
Gart. How now,
What matter have you fisht out of that foole?
Joy. Matter as poysning as Corruption,
That will without some Antidote strike home 2415
Like blew Infection to the very heart.
Rash. As how, for Gods sake?
Joy. To morrow is the appoynted Wedding day.
Gart. The day of doome it is?
Ger. T'would be a dismall day indeed to some of us. 2420
Joy. Sir, I doe know you love mee; and the time
Will not be dallyed with: bee what you seeme,
Or not the same: I am your Wife, your Mistris,
Or your Servant, indeed what you will make mee:
Let us no longer wrangle with our Wittes, 2425
Or dally with our Fortunes; lead mee hence,
And carry mee into a Wildernesse:
Ile fast with you, rather then feast with him.
Sta. What can be welcommer unto these armes?
Not my estate recoverd is more sweete, 2430
Nor strikes more joy in mee, then does your love.
Rash. Will you both kisse then upon the bargaine?
Heer's two couple on you; God give you joy,
I wish well to you, and I see tis all the good 2434
That I can doe you: And so to your shiftes I leave you./
Joy. Nay Brother, you will not leave us thus, I [K3]
    hope.

2409-10 For ... act / Of ... provide,] *ed.*; For ... of our /
forefathers ... prouide, 2411 Bride] *Q2*; Brde 2412-13 How now, /
What ... foole?] *ed.*; *as one line*, *Q1* (what) 2424 Servant,] *ed.*;
Seruant; 2430 recoverd] *Dodsley*; recouerd, 2432 bargaine?] *Dodsley*;
bargaine, 2434-5 I ... good / That ... you.] *ed.*; I ... that ...
you: / And ... you.

Rash. Why what would you have me do? you meane to run
Away togeather: would you ha me run with you,
And so loose my Inheritance? no, trudge, trudge
With your backes to mee, and your bellies to them:
away.   2440
Ger. Nay I prethee be not thus unseasonable:
Without thee wee are nothing.
Rash.   By my troth,
And I thinke so too: you love one another
In the way of Matrimonie, doe you not?
Ger. What else man?   2445
Rash. What else man? why tis a question to be askt;
For I can assure you, there is an other kind of love:
But come follow mee, I must be
Your good Angell still: Tis in this braine
How to prevent my Father, and his brace   2450
Of Beagles: you shall none of you be bid to night:
Follow but my direction, if I bring
You not, *To have and to hold, for better for worse*,
Let me be held an Eunuch in wit, and one
That was never Father to a good Feast.   2455
Gart. Wee'le be instructed by you.
Rash.   Well, if you bee,
It will be your owne another day. Come follow mee.

*Spendall meetes them, and they looke strangely
upon him, and Exeunt.*

Spend. How ruthlesse men are to adversitie:
My acquaintance scarce will know mee, when wee meet

2437-2440 Why ... away.] *as verse, ed.; as prose,* Q1 (Why ... away
... and ... with) 2437 do?] *Dodsley*; do, 2438 togeather:] *Hazlitt*;
togeather, 2439 Inheritance?] *Dodsley*; Inheritance: 2442-4 By ...
not?] *as verse, ed.; as prose,* Q1 (By ... and ... in) 2444 In] *ed.*;
in Q1(c); sn Q1(u) 2448-55 But ... Feast.] *verse relined, ed.*; But
... your ... still: / Tis ... how ... brace / Of ... to night: /
Follow ... you not, / To ... let ... an / Eunuch ... that ... Feast.
2456-7 Well ... mee.] *verse relined, ed.*; Well ... it ... day. /
Come ... mee. 2457 SD strangely] Q2; strngely // Exeunt] *ed.*; Exit
2458 adversitie:] *ed.*; aduersitie,

They cannot stay to talke, they must begone; 2460
And shake mee by the hand as if I burnt them:
A man must trust unto himselfe, I see;
For if hee once but halt in his estate,
Friendship will proove but broken Crutches to him:
Well, I will leane to none of them, but stand 2465
Free of my selfe: and if I had a spirit
Daring to act what I am prompted too,
I must thrust out into the world againe, /
Full blossomd with a sweete and golden Spring: [K3^v]
It was an argument of love in her 2470
To fetch mee out of Prison, and this night,
She claspt my hand in hers, as who should say,
Thou art my Purchase, and I hold thee thus:
The worst is but repulse, if I attempt it:
I am resolvd, my Geneus whispers to mee 2475
Goe on and win her, thou art young and active:
Which she is apt to catch at, for there's nought
That's more unsteadfast, then a womans thought. [Exit.]

[SCENE XVII]

Enter Sir Lyo., Will Rash, Scatter-good, Bubble,
Widdow, Gartred, Joyce, Phillis, and Servant.

Lyo. Heere's ill lodging *Widdow*: but you must know,
If wee had better, wee could affoord it you. 2480
Wid. The lodging Sir, might serve better Guestes.
Lyo. Not better, *Widdow*, nor yet welcommer:
But wee will leave you to it, and the rest.
Phyllis, pray let your Mistris want not any thing.
Once more Good night, Ile leave a kisse with you. 2485
As earnest of a better Guift to morrow.
Sirrah, a Light.
Wid. Good rest to all.

2478 SD [*Exit.*]] Reed Sc. XVII OSD *Lyo.,*] *Dodsley*; *Lyo,* 2479 SP
Lyo.] *Q1(c); no period, Q1(u)* 2484 thing.] *Dodsley*; thing, 2486
morrow.] *Q2*; morrow,

Bub. Et tu quoque, forsooth.
Scat. God give you good-night, forsooth, 2490
And send you an early resurrection.
Wid. God-night to both.
Lyo. Come, come away, each Bird unto his nest,
To morrow night's a time of little rest. *Exeunt.*

Manent Widdow and Phillis.

Wid. Heere untie: soft, let it alone, 2495
I have no disposition to sleepe yet:
Give mee a Booke, and leave mee for a while,
Some halfe houre hence, looke into mee.
Phil. I shall forsooth. *Exit Phillis.* /

Enter Spendall. [K4]

Wid. How now, what makes this bold intrusion? 2500
Spend. Pardon mee Lady, I have busines to you.
Wid. Busines? from whom? is it of such importance
That it craves present hearing?
Spend. It does.
Wid. Then speake it, and be briefe.
Spend. Nay gentle *Widdow*, be more plyant to mee. 2505
My suite is soft and courtious, full of love.
Wid. Of love?
Spend. Of love.
Wid. Why sure the man is madde? bethinke thy selfe:
Thou hast forgot thy errand. 2510
Spend. I have indeed, faire Lady; for my errand
Should first have been delivered on your lippes.
Wid. Why thou impudent fellow, unthrift of shame,
As well as of thy purse; What has moovd thee
To prosecute thy ruine? hath my bountie, 2515
For which thy Maister was an orator,

2489 forsooth.] *Q2*; forsooth . 2494 SD *Exeunt.*] *Dodsley*; *Exit.* //
Manent] *Dodsley*; *Manet* 2495 let it] *Q1(c)*; letit *Q1(u)* 2496
disposition] *Q2*; diposition 2502 Busines?] *ed.*; Busines, // whom?]
Dodsley; whom, 2506 courtious,] *ed.*; courtious: 2509 selfe:]
Dodsley; selfe, 2510 errand.] *Dodsley*; errand?

Importund thee to pay mee with abuse?
Sirra retire, or I will to your shame,
With clamors rayse the house, and make your Maister
For this attempt, returne you to the Dungion, 2520
From whence you came.
Spend. Nay then I must be desperate:
Widdow, hold your Clapdish, fasten your Tongue
Unto your Roofe, and do not dare to call,
But give mee audience, with feare and silence:
Come kisse mee: No? 2525
This Dagger has a poynt, doe you see it?
And be unto my suite obedient,
Or you shall feele it too: For I will rather
Totter, hang in cleane Linnen, then live to scrub
It out in lowsie Lynings. Goe too, kisse: 2530
You will? why so: Againe: the third time? /
Good, tis a sufficient Charme: Now heare mee: [K4^V]
You are rich in Mony, Lands, and Lordships,
Mannors, and fayre Possessions, and I have not so much
As one poore Coppy-hold to thrust my head in. 2535
Why should you not then have compassion
Upon a reasonable handsome fellow,
That has both youth and livelihood upon him;
And can at midnight quicken and refresh
Pleasures decayed in you? You want Children, 2540
And I am strong, lusty, and have a backe
Like *Hercules*, able to get them
Without the helpe of Muscadine and Eggs:
And will you then, that have inough,
Take to your Bed a bundle of diseases, 2545
Wrapt up in threescore yeares, to lie a hawking,
Spitting, and coffing backwards and forwards
That you shall not sleepe; but thrusting forth

2517 Importund] *Q3* (Importun'd); Importure 2528-31 Or ... time?]
verse relined, ed.; Or ... too: / For ... totter ... Linnen, /
Then ... it ... Lynings. / Goe ... time? 2532 mee:] *ed.*; mee,
2537 Upon] *Q2*; vpon

Your face out of the Bed, be glad to draw
The Curtaines, such a steame shall reeke 2550
Out of this dunghill. Now what say you?
Shall we without further wrangling clap it up,
And goe to Bed togeather?
Wid. Will you heare mee?
Spend. Yes with all my heart,
So the first word may bee, Untrusse your Poynts. 2555
Knocke within.
Zounds one knocks: do not stirre I charge you,
Nor speake, but what I bid you:
For by these Lippes, which now in love I kisse,
If you but struggle, or but rayse your voyce,
My arme shall rise with it, and strike you dead. 2560
Go too, come on with mee, and aske, who's there?
Wid. It is my Mayde.
Spend. No matter, doe as I bid you: say, Who's there?
Wid. Who's there?
Within Phillis. Tis I, forsooth. 2565
Spend. If it be you, forsooth, then pray stay, /
Till I shall call upon you. [Ll]
Wid. If it be you, forsooth, then pray you stay,
Till I shall call upon you.
Spend. Very well, why now I see 2570
Thou'lt proove an obedient wife: come, let's undresse.
Wid. Will you put up your naked weapon sir?
Spend. You shall pardon mee (Widdow) I must have you
grant first.
Wid. You will not put it up? 2575
Spend. Not till I have some token of your love.
Wid. If this may be a testimonie take it. *Kisse him.*
By all my hopes I love thee, thou art worthy
Of the best widdow living: thou tak'st the course;
And those that will win widdowes must doe thus. 2580

2555 SD *Knocke within.*] ed.; after mee? in l. 2553, Q1 2561 aske,]
ed.; aske 2562 is] Q2; i(?s) 2566 stay,] Q2; stay. 2571 wife:]
ed.; wife, 2575 up?] *Reed*; vp. 2579 living:] *Hazlitt*; liuing,

SC. XVII]   GREENE'S TU QUOQUE   93

Spen. Nay, I knew what I did, when I came with my
naked weapon in my hand; but come, unlace.
Wid. Nay my deare love, know that I will not yeeld
My body unto lust, untill the Priest
Shall joyne us in *Hymens* sacred nuptiall rites.   2585
Spend. Then set your hand to this, nay 'tis a contract
Strong and sufficient, and will holde in Lawe.
Heere, heere's pen and incke, you see I come provided.
Wid. Give me the penne.
Spend.   Why here's some comfort:
Yet write your name faire I pray,   2590
And at large; why now 'tis very well:
Now widdow you may admit your Maid,
For i'th next roome I'le goe fetch a nappe.
Wid. Thou shalt not leave me so, come pre thee sit,
Wee'l talke a while, for thou hast made my heart   2595
Dance in my bosome I receive such joy.
Spend. Thou art a good wench yfaith, come kisse upon't.
Wid. But will you be a loving husband to me,
Avoyde all naughty company, and be true
To me, and to my bedde?   2600
Spend. As true to thee, as Steele to Adamant. /
           Binde him to the poast.   [L1^v]
Wid. I'le binde you to your word, see that you be,
Or I'le conceale my bagges: I have kinsfolkes,
To whom I'le mak't over, you shall not have a penny.
Spend. Push, pre thee doe not doubt me: 2605
How now, what meanes this?
Wid. It means my vengeance; nay sir, you are fast,
Nor doe not dare to struggle, I have libertie,
Both of my tongue and feet, I'le call my maid:
Phillis come in, and helpe to triumph,   2610

                    Enter Phillis.

2587 Lawe.] *Dodsley*; Lawe, 2589 comfort:] *ed.*; comfort, 2591 well:]
ed.; well, 2593 nappe] *Q3*; napppe 2601 SD *Binde*] *Q1* (catchword /
Bind / L1) // poast.] *Q1(c)*; poas . *Q1(u)* 2603 bagges:] *Dodsley*;
bagges, 2604 have] *Q2*; bave 2605 me:] *Q2*; me,

Over this bolde Intruder: wonder not wench,
But goe unto him, and ransacke all his pockets,
And take from thence a Contract which he forc'd
From my unwilling fingers.
Spend. Is this according to your oath?   2615
Phillis. Come sir, I must search you.
Spend.   I pre thee do.
And when thou tak'st that from me, take my life too.
Wid. Hast thou it gerle?
Phill.   I have a paper heere.
Wid. It is the same, give it me: looke you sir,
Thus your new fancied hopes I teare asunder: 2620
Poore wretched man, t'hast had a golden dreame,
Which guilded o're thy calamitie:
But being awake thou findst it ill laid on,
For with one finger I have wip'd it off: 2624
[*To Phillis.*] Goe fetch me hither the Casket that containes
My choicest Jewells, and spread them heere before him;
Looke you sir:
Heere's gold, pearle, rubies, saphires, diamonds;
These would be goodly things for you to pawne,
Or revell with amongst your Curtizans,   2630
Whilst I and mine did starve: why dost not curse,
And utter all the mischiefes of thy heart,
Which I know swells within thee? powre it out,
And let me heare thy fury. /
Spend.   Never, never: [L2]
When ere my tongue shall speake but well of thee,   2635
It prooves no faithfull servant to my heart.
Wid. False traitor to thy maister, and to me,
Thou liest, there's no such thing within thee.
Spend. May I be burn'd to uglinesse, to that
Which you and all men hate, but I speake truth.   2640

2611 Intruder:] *ed.*; Intruder, 2614 fingers.] *Q2*; fingers: 2615 oath?] *Dodsley*; oath. 2616 SP *Phillis.*] *Q2*; *no period, Q1* 2619 me:] *ed.*; me, 2625 SD [*To Phillis.*]] *ed.* 2628 diamonds;] *Q2*; diamonds ; 2633 thee?] *Q3*; thee,

Wid. May I be turn'd a monster, and the shame
Of all my Sex,——and if I not beleeve thee:
Take me unto thee, these, and all that's mine;
Were it thrice trebled, thou wert worthy all:
And doe not blame this triall, cause it shews   2645
I give my selfe unto thee, am not forc'd,
And with't a love, that ne'r shall be divorc'd.
                                        [*Unties him.*]
Spend. I am glad 'tis come to this yet, by this light
Thou putt'st me into a horrible feare:
But this is my excuse: know that my thoughts   2650
Were not so desperate as my actions seem'd,
For fore my dagger should ha drawne one droppe
Of thy chaste blood, it should have sluc'd out mine:
And the cold point strucke deepe into my heart:
Nor better be my fate, if I shall move   2655
To any other pleasure but thy love.
Wid. It shall be in my Creed: but lett's away,
For night with her blacke Steeds drawes up the day. *Exeunt.*

[SCENE XVIII]

*Enter Rash, Staines, Geraldine, Gartred, Joyce, and
a Boy with a Lanthorne.*

Rash. Softly Boy, softly, you thinke you are upon firme
ground, but it is dangerous; you'l never make a good   2660
thiefe, you rogue, till you learne to creepe upon all foure:
if I do not sweate with going this pace: every thing I see,
mee thinkes, should be my father in his white beard.
Sta. It is the property of that passion, for feare
Still shapes all things we see to that we feare. /   2665
Rash. Well said Logicke: sister, I pray lay hold   [L2^V]
of him, for the man I see is able to give the Watch an

2642 thee:] *ed.*; thee, 2643 mine;] *ed.*; mine, 2647 a love,] *ed.*;
aloue, *Q1(c)*; alone (*possible period*) *Q1(u)* // SD [*Unties him.*]] *ed.*
2666-8 Well ... for ... they] *as prose, Collier*; Well ... him, /
For ... they 2666 Logicke:] *Dodsley*; Logicke,

answere, if they   *Enter Spendall, Widdow, and Phillis.*
should come upon him with Interrogatories: zownds wee are
discovered! boy, come up close, and use the property of
your Lanthorne: what dumbe shew should this be?   2671
Geral. They take their way directly, intend nothing
gainst us.
Sta. Can you not discerne who they are?
Joyce. One is *Spendall.*   2675
Gart. The other is the Widdow as I take it.
Sta. T'is true, and that's her maid before her.
Rash. What a night of conspiracie is heere, more
villanie? there's another goodly mutton going, my father is
fleeced of all; griefe will give him a box yfaith, but
'tis no great matter, I shall inherit the sooner: nay soft
sir, you shall not passe so currant with the matter, I'le
shake you a little: who goes there?
Spend. Out with the Candle! who's that askes the
       question?
Rash. One that has some reason for't.   2685
Spend. It should be, by the voyce, yong *Rash.*
Why we are honest folkes.
Rash. Pray where do you dwell? not in towne I hope.
Spend. Why we dwell, zownds where doe we dwell?
I know not where.   2690
Rash. And you'l be married you know not when: zownds
it were a Christian deed to stoppe thee in thy journy: hast
thou no more spirit in thee, but to let thy tongue betray
thee? Suppose I had beene a Constable, you had beene in a
fine taking, had you not?   2695
Spend. But my still worthy friend,
Is there no worse face of ill bent towards me,
Then that thou merrily putt'st on?
Rash. Yes, heere's foure or five faces more, but ne'r an

2670 discovered!] *Dodsley*; discouered, 2680 all;] *Reed*; all, 2681
sooner:] *ed.*; sooner, 2683 a little] *Q2*; alittle 2684 Candle!]
Hazlitt; Candle, 2691 when:] *ed.*; when, 2694 thee?] *Dodsley*; thee.
2698 on?] *Q3*; on.

SC. XIX]   GREENE'S TU QUOQUE   97

ill one, though never an excellent good one: Boy, up 2700
with your lanthorne of light, and shew him his associats, all
running away with the flesh as thou art: goe yoake together,
you may be oxen one day, and draw all together in a plough:
go march / together, the Parson staies for you, pay him [L3]
royally: come, give me the Lanthorne, for you have   2705
light sufficient, for night has put off his blacke Cappe, and
salutes the morne: now farewell my little children of *Cupid*,
that walke by two and two as if you went a feasting: let mee
heare no more words, but be gone.
Spend. & Sta. Farewell.   2710
Gart. & Joyce. Farewell brother.   [*Exeunt.*] *Manet Rash.*
Rash. I, you may crie farewell, but if my father should
know of my villanie, how should I fare then? but all's one,
I ha done my sisters good, my friends good, and my selfe
good, and a generall good is alwaies to be respected 2715
before a particular: ther's eight score pounds a yeare
saved, by the conveyance of this widdow. I heare footesteps:
now darkenesse take me into thy armes, and deliver me from
discovery.   *Exit.*

[SCENE XIX]

Enter Sir Lyonell.

Lyonell. Lord, lord, what a carelesse world is this,
neyther Bride nor Bridegroome ready, time to goe to Church,
and not a man unroosted: this age has not seene a yoong
Gallant rise with a candle, we live drowned in feather-beds,
and dreame of no other felicitie: this was not the life when
I was a yong man: what makes us so weake as wee are 2725

2700 good one:] *ed.*; good one, 2702 art:] *ed.*; art, 2703 plough:]
ed.; plough, 2705 royally:] *ed.*; royally, 2707 morne:] *ed.*; morne,
2711 SP *Joyce.*] *Dodsley*; *no period, Q1* // SD [*Exeunt.*]] *Reed* 2716
particular:] *ed.*; particular, 2717 widdow.] *Q3*; widdow, //
footesteps:] *Collier*; footesteps, Sc. XIX OSD *Sir*] *Q2*; *sir* 2720 SP
Lyonell.] *Q2*; *no period, Q1* 2722 unroosted:] *Reed*; vnroosted,
2725 man:] *ed.*; man,

now? a feather-bed: what so unapt for exercise? a feather-
bed: what breedes such paines and aches in our bones? why a
feather-bed or a wench, or at least a wench in a feather-bed:
is it not a shame, that an olde man as I am should be up
first, and in a wedding day? I thinke in my conscience
there's more mettall in laddes of three score, then in boyes
of one and twenty. 2732

Enter Baskethilt.

Why *Baskethilt.*
Bask. Heere sir.
Lyon. Shall I not be trussed to day? 2735
Bask. Yes sir, but I went for water.
Lyon. Is *Will Rash* up yet?
Basket. I thinke not sir, for I heard no body stirring
in the house. 2739
Lyon. Knocke sirra at his chamber. *Knocke within.* /
The house might be plucked downe and builded againe [L3^v]
Before hee'd wake with the noyse. *Rash aloft.*
Rash. Who's that keepes such a knocking, are you madde?
Lyon. Rather thou art drunke, thou lazy slowch,
That mak'st thy bed thy grave, and in it buriest 2745
All thy youth and vigor; up for shame.
Rash. Why 'tis not two a clocke yet.
Lyo. Out sluggish knave 'tis neerer unto five:
The whole house has out-slept themselves,
As if they had drunk Wilde poppy: Sirra, goe 2750
You and raise the maides, and let them call
Upon their mistresses.
Bask. Well sir, I shall. *Exit.*

Enter Scattergood and Bubble.

Scatt. Did I eate any Lettice to supper last night, that
I am so sleepie? I thinke it be day light, brother *Bubble.*

2730 day?] *Q3*; day, 2732 SD, 2733 *Baskethilt.*] *Dodsley*; *Basket hilt.*
2740 chamber.] *Q2*; chamber, 2748 five:] *Reed*; fiue, 2749-52 The ...
mistresses.] *as verse, ed.*; *as prose, Q1* (The ... as ... you ...
vpon) 2754 sleepie?] *Dodsley*; sleepie,

Bub. What sai'st thou brother? heigh ho! 2755
Lyon. Fie, fie, not ready yet? what sluggishnesse
Hath seiz'd upon you? why thine eyes are close still.
Bub. As fast as a Kentish oyster: surely I was begotten
in a Plumb-tree, I ha such a deale of gumme about mine eies.

Enter Baskethilt.

Lyon. Lord how you stand! I am asham'd to see 2760
The Sunne should be a witnesse of your slouth:
Now sir, your haste?
Bask. Marry sir, there are guests comming to accompany
you to church.
Ly. Why this is excellent, men whom it not concerns 2765
Are more respective then we that are maine Actors.
Bub. Father *Rash*, be not so outrageous, we will goe in
and buckle our selves, all in good time: how now! what's
this about my shinnes?

Enter old Geraldine, and Long-field.

Scatt. Me thought our shankes were not fellowes, we 2770
have metamorphosed our stockings for want of splendor.
Bub. Pray what's that *Splendor*?
Scatt. Why 'tis the Latin word for a Christmasse candle.

Exeunt.

Lyon. O Gentlemen, you love, you honour mee: welcome, /
Welcome good Master *Geraldine*, you have taken paines [L4]
To accompany an undeserving friend. 2776

Enter Phillis.

Old Ger. You put us to a needelesse labour sir,
To runne and winde about for circumstance,
When the plaine word, I thanke you, would have serv'd.
Lyon. How now wench, are the females ready yet? 2780

2758-9 As ... eies.] *as prose*, Reed; As ... a / Plumb-tree, / I ...
eies. 2758 oyster:] *ed.*; oyster, 2759 SD *Enter Baskethilt.*] Reed;
Enter Seruant. 2761 slouth:] *ed.*; slouth, 2762 haste?] *Q3*; haste.
2768 time:] *ed.*; time, 2773 candle.] *Q2*; candle // SD *Exeunt.*]
Reed; *Exit.*; SD *after l.* 2771, *Q1* 2774 mee:] *ed.*; mee, 2775 Welcome]
ed.; welcome

The time comes on upon us, and we runne backward:
We are so untoward in our busines, we thinke
Not what we have to doe, nor what we doe.
Phill. I know not sir whether they know what to doe, but
I am sure they have beene at Church well-nie an houre:
they were afraid you had got the start of them, which
made them make such haste.   2787
Lyon. Is't possible? what thinke you Gentlemen?
Are not these wenches forward? is there not vertue in a man
Can make yong Virgins leave their beddes so soone?   2790
But is the widdow gone along with them?
Phill. Yes sir, why she was the ring-leader.
Lyo. I thought as much, for she knowes what belong's
    to't.
Come Gentlemen, me thinkes 'tis sport to see
Yong wenches run to church before their husbands: 2795

              En. Rash.

Faith we shall make them blush for this ere night:
A sirra, are you come? why that's well said;
I marl'd indeede that all things were so quiet,
Which made me thinke th'ad not unwrapt their sheets:

          Enter Servant with a cloake.

And then were they at Church I holde my life: 2800
Maides thinke it long untill ech be made a wife.

       *Enter Spend., Sta., Geraldine, Widdow,
             Gartred, and Joyce.*

Hast thou my cloake knave? well said, put it on,
Wee'l after them; let me goe hasten both,
Both the Bridegroomes forward, wee'l walke a little
Softly on afore: but see, see, if they be not come   2805

2782-3 We ... we thinke / Not ... doe.] *ed.*; We ... busines, / We ...
not ... doe. 2785 houre:] *ed.*; houre, 2788 Is't] *Dodsley*; I'st //
possible?] *Dodsley*; possible, 2790 Can] *Q2*; can // soone?] *Q3*;
soone. 2793 to't.] *Q3*; to't, 2801 SD *Spend., Sta.,*] *Reed*; *Spend.
Sta.* 2804 a little] *Q3*; alittle

To fetch us now, we come, we come,
Bid them returne and save themselves this labour.
Rash. [*Aside.*] Now have I a quartane ague upon me. /
Lyonell. Why how now! why come you from Church [L4^V]
To kneele thus publikely? what's the matter?   2810
Ger. We kneele sir for your blessing.
Lyon.   How, my blessing!
Master *Geraldine*, is not that your sonne?
Old Ger. Yes sir, and that I take it is your daughter.
Lyon. I suspect knavery, what are you?
Why doe you kneele hand in hand with her?   2815
Sta. For a fatherly blessing too sir.
Lyon. Hoy day! 'tis palpable, I am gull'd, and my sonne
Scatter-good and *Bubble* fool'd: you are married?
Spend. Yes sir, we are married.   2819
Lyon. More villanie! every thing goes the wrong way.
Spend. We shall goe the right way anone, I hope.
Lyon. Yes marry shall you, you shall eene
To the Counter againe, and that's the right way for you.
Wid. O you are wrong,
The prison that shall hold him are these armes.   2825
Lyon. I doe feare that I shall turne stinckard,
I do smell such a matter: you are married then?

Enter Scatter-good and Bubble.

Spend. Ecce signum, heere's the wedding Ring t'affirme
          it.
Lyon. I beleeve the knave has druncke Ipocras,
He is so pleasant.
Scat.   God morrow Gentlemen.   2830
Bub. Tu quoque to all: what, shall we goe to
Church? Come, I long to be about this geare.

2808 SD [*Aside.*]] *ed.* 2809-10 Why ... Church / To ... matter?] *as verse, ed.; as prose, Q1* (to) 2810 publikely?] *ed.;* publikely, 2811-12 How ... sonne?] *as verse, ed.; as prose, Q1* 2818 fool'd:] *Dodsley*; fool'd, 2822-3 Yes ... eene / To ... you.] *as verse, ed.; as prose, Q1* (to) 2826-7 I doe ... then?] *as verse, ed.; as prose, Q1* 2831-2 *Tu* ... geare.] *as prose, ed.; Tu* ... Church? / Come ... geare.

Lyon. Doe you heare me, will you two goe sleepe againe?
Take out the tother nap, for you are both
Made Cockescombes, and so am I.
Scatt.   How, Cockes-combes!   2835
Lyon.   Yea Cockes-combes.
Scatt. Father, that word Cockes-comb goes against my stomacke.
Bub. And against mine, a man might ha digested a Wood-
cocke better. /   2840
Lyon. You two come now to goe to church to be
          married,   [M1]
And they two come from Church, and are married.
Bub. How, married! I would see that man durst marry her.
Ger. Why sir, what would you doe?   2845
Bub. Why sir I would forbid the banes.
Scatt. And so would I.
Lyon.   Doe you know that youth in Sattin?
Hee's the penner that belongs to that Inck-horne.
Bub. How, let me see, are not you my man *Gervase*?
Sta. Yes sir.   2850

               Enter a Sergeant.

Bub. And have you married her?
Sta. Yes sir.
Bub. And doe you thinke you have usde me well?
Sta. Yes sir.
Bub. O intollerable rascall! I will presently be   2855
made a Justice of Peace, and have thee whipp'd: goe fetch
a Constable.
Sta. Come, y'are a flourishing Asse; Sergeant take
       him to thee,

2833-5 Doe ... againe? / Take ... both / Made ... I.] *as verse, ed.;*
as prose, Q1 (Doe ... take ... made)   2847-8 Doe ... Sattin? / Hee's
... Inck-horne.] *as verse, ed.; as prose, Q1* (hee's)   2847 Sattin?]
Dodsley; Sattin, 2850, 2852, 2854, 2858, 2862 SP *Sta.] Dodsley; Scat.*
2856 whipp'd:] *ed.;* whipp'd,   2858-9 Come ... thee, / He ...
pageantry.] *as verse, ed.; as prose, Q1* (Come ... he ... pageantry.)

He has had a long time of his pageantry.
Lyon. Sirra let him goe, I'le be his baile, 2860
For all debts which come against him.
Sta. Reverend sir, to whom I owe the duty of a sonne,
Which I shall ever pay in my obedience:
Know that which made him gracious in your eyes,
And guilded over his imperfections, 2865
Is wasted and consumed even like ice,
Which by the vehemence of heate dissolves,
And glides to many rivers, so his wealth,
That felt a prodigall hand, hote in expence,
Melted within his gripe, and from his coffers, 2870
Ranne like a violent streame to other mens:
What was my owne, I catch'd at.
Lyon. Have you your morgage in?
Sta. Yes sir.
Lyon. Stand up, the matter is well amended:
Master *Geraldine*, you give sufferance to this match? 2874
Old Ger. Yes marry doe I sir, for since they love, /
I'le not have the crime lie on my head, [M1^{V}]
To divide man and wife.
Lyon. Why you say well, my blessing fall upon you.
Wid. And upon us that love Sir *Lyonell*. 2879
Lyon. By my troth since thou hast tane the yong knave,
God give thee joy of him, and may he prove
A wiser man then his Master.
Sta. Sergeant, why dost not carry him to prison?
Serg. Sir *Lyonell Rash* will baile him.
Lyon. I baile him knave! wherefore should I baile
  him? 2885
No, carry him away, I'le relieve no prodigalls.
Bub. Good Sir *Lyonell*, I beseech you sir, Gentlemen, I
pray make a purse for me.

2860-1 Sirra ... baile, / For ... him.] *as verse, ed.; as prose, Q1*
(for) 2871 mens:] *ed.*; mens, 2873 SP Sta.] *Dodsley*; Scat. //
amended:] *ed.*; amended, 2874 match?] *Dodsley*; match. 2878 upon you.]
Q2; vpon you, 2879 Sir] *Q2*; sir 2887 Sir] *Reed*; sir

Serg. Come sir, come, are you begging?
Bub. Why that does you no harme, *Gervase*, master I   2890
should say; some compassion.
Sta. Sergeant, come backe with him:
Looke sir, heere is your livery:
If you can put off all your former pride,
And put on this with that humilitie   2895
That you first wore it, I will pay your debts,
Free you of all incombrances,
And take you againe into my service.
Bub. Tenter-hooke let mee goe, I will take his worships
offer without wages, rather then come into your clutches
againe; a man in a blew coate may have some colour for his
knavery, in the Counter he can have none.   2902
Lyon. But now Master *Scatter-good*, what say you to this?
Scat. Marry I say 'tis scarce honest dealing for any man
to Conny-catch another mans wife, I protest wee'l not
put it up.   2906
Sta. No? which we?
Scatt. Why *Gartred* and I.
Sta. Gartred? why shee'l put it up.
Scatt.   Will she?
Ger. I that she will, and so must you.
Scatt.   Must I? /   2910
Ger. Yes that you must.   [M2]
Scatt.   Well, if I must, I must;
But I protest I would not, but that I must:
So *vale, vale: Et tu quoque.*   *Exit.*
Lyon. Why that's well said,
Then I perceive we shall wind up all wrong: 2915
Come Gentlemen, and all our other guests:

2890 harme,] *ed.*; harme   2892 Sergeant] *ed.*; Sergeants   2892-3
Sergeant ... him: / Looke ... livery:] *ed.*; *as one verse line, Q1*
(Sergeants ... looke ... is / your liuery,)   2892 him:] *ed.*; him,
2893 livery:] *ed.*; liuery,   2903 Master] *Hazlitt*; M.   2907 No?] *ed.*;
No,   2909 Gartred?] *ed.*; Gartred,   2910 you.] *Q2*; *possible comma, Q1*
2911-13 Well ... quoque.] *verse relined, ed.*; Well ... must; but ...
not: / But ... quoque.   2912 not,] *Dodsley*; not:

Let our well-temper'd bloods taste *Bacchus* feasts,
But let us know first how these sports delight,
And to these, Gentlemen, each bid good night.
Rash. Gentles, I hope, that well my labor ends, 2920
All that I did was but to please my friends.
Ger. A kind enamouret I did strive to prove,
But now I leave that, and pursue your love.
Gart. My part I have performed with the rest,
And though I have not, yet I would doe best. 2925
Sta. That I have cheated through the Play, 'tis true,
But yet I hope, I have not cheated you.
Joyce. If with my clamors I have done you wrong,
Ever hereafter I will hold my tongue.
Spend. If through my riot I have offensive beene, 2930
Henceforth I'le play the civil Citizen.
Wid. Faith all that I say, is, how ere it happe,
Widdowes like Maids sometimes may catch a clappe.
Bub. To mirth and laughter henceforth I'le provoke ye,
If you but please to like of *Greenes Tu quoque.* 2935

FINIS.

2919 these, Gentlemen,] *ed.*; these Gentlemen 2931 I'le] *Q1(c)*; I le
Q1(u) 2933 Maids] *Q1(c)*; M ids *Q1(u)*

PRESS-VARIANTS

[Copies of *Q1* collated: BM (British Museum, press-mark C. 34. c. 19), Bodl (Bodleian Library, shelfmark 4°. T. 36. ART [4]), CSmH (Huntington Library), DFo (Folger Shakespeare Library), MH (Harvard University Library: sigs. H2-H3^v in this copy contain 78 unique variants, almost certainly due to interleaving from a copy of *Q2*; hence, leaves H2 and H3 are defective in this copy and accordingly, their variants are disregarded), NNP (Pierpont Morgan Library). The corrected precedes the uncorrected form in each lemma.]

Sheet B (outer forme)
Sig. B4^v
    II.249 tongue:] tongue,
Corrected: CSmH
Uncorrected: BM, Bodl, DFo, MH, NNP

Sheet C (inner forme)
Sig. C4
    V.526 inuite] inuite
Corrected: BM, Bodl, DFo, MH, NNP
Uncorrected: CSmH

Sheet D (outer forme)
Sig. D2^v
    VII.694 him.] him
Corrected: BM, Bodl, MH
Uncorrected: CSmH, DFo, NNP
Sig. D4^v
    IX.868 *Ser.*] *Ser*
Corrected: BM, Bodl, CSmH, DFo, MH
Uncorrected: NNP

Sheet E (outer forme)
Sig. E2^v
    IX.998, 1004 *Bubble*] *Bubleb*
Corrected: Bodl, DFo, NNP
Uncorrected: BM, CSmH, MH

Sheet E (inner forme)
Sig. E1^v
    IX.930 I] I'
Corrected: BM, Bodl, CSmH, NNP
Uncorrected: DFo, MH

Sheet G (outer forme)

Sig. G1
    XII.1474 wealth] weath
Corrected: Bod1, DFo, NNP
Uncorrected: BM, CSmH, MH

Sheet H (outer forme)
  First State Corrected: BM, Bod1, DFo, NNP
  Uncorrected: CSmH

Sig. H3
    XIV.1868 couple] coup^a_ae

  Second State Corrected: CSmH, DFo, MH

Sig. H1
    XIII.1754 Baud] Ba(?u)d
Sig. H4^v
    XIV.2001 *Rash*.] *Rash*
  Third State Corrected: Bod1, CSmH, DFo, MH, NNP
Sig. H4^v
    XIV.1978 is] si
        1982 Wild-cat] wild Catt
        *1983 carry] Carry (*addendum to Textual Notes)
        *2003 mee,] mee. (*addendum to Textual Notes)

Sheet H (inner forme)

Sig. H3^v
    XIV.1900 sillable] sillabe
        1911 pray] dray
Corrected: Bod1, CSmH, DFo, NNP
Uncorrected: BM
Sig. H4
    XIV.1958 sirreuerence] sirreuerenc
Corrected: Bod1, CSmH, DFo, MH, NNP
Uncorrected: BM

Sheet I (inner forme)

Sig. I2
    XV.2089 end,] end;
Corrected: BM, Bod1, DFo, MH, NNP
Uncorrected: CSmH

Sheet K (outer forme)

Sig. K2^v
    XVI.2403 Finger;] *possible comma*
Corrected: Bod1. CSmH, MH, NNP
Uncorrected: BM, DFo
Sig. K3
    XVI.2444 in] sn
Corrected: Bm, CSmH, DFo, MH, NNP
Uncorrected: Bod1

Sheet K (inner forme)

Sig. K3^v
    XVII.2479 *Lyo*.] *Lyo*
Corrected: BM, CSmH, DFo, MH, NNP
Uncorrected: Bod1

XVII.2495 let it] letit
Corrected: BM, Bod1, CSmH, DFo, NNP
Uncorrected: MH

       Sheet L (outer forme)
Sig. L3
 *XVIII.2714 ha] ha' (*addendum to Textual Notes)
Corrected: Bod1, CSmH, DFo, MH, NNP
Uncorrected: BM

       Sheet L (inner forme)
Sig. L1^v
 XVII.2601 *poast.*] *poas* .
Corrected: BM, Bod1, CSmH, MH, NNP
Uncorrected: DFo
Sig. L2
 XVII.2647 aloue,] alone (*possible period*)
Corrected: BM
Uncorrected: Bod1, CSmH, DFo, MH, NNP

       Sheet M (inner forme)
Sig. M2
 XIX.2931 I'le] I le
  2933 Maids] M ids
Corrected: BM, Bod1, DFo, MH, NNP
Uncorrected: CSmH

HISTORICAL COLLATION

[Editions collated: 1st. 4° (*Q1*, 1614); 2nd. 4° (*Q2*, 1622); 3rd. 4° (*Q3*, n.d.); Dodsley (*D*, in *A Select Collection of Old Plays*, 1st. ed., 1744, III, 1-85); Reed (*R*, in *A Select Collection of Old Plays*, 2nd. ed., 1780, VII, 3-120); *A* [?] (in *The Ancient British Drama*, 1810, II, 538-573; this ed. almost always follows *R* except for orthographic variants, and is noted only when it contains substantive or semi-substantive variants differing from *R*); Collier (*C*, in *A Select Collection of Old Plays*, 3rd. ed., 1825, VII, 1-99); Hazlitt (*H*, in *A Select Collection of Old English Plays*, 4th. ed., 1875, XI, 173-289). Only substantive and semi-substantive variants are recorded; obvious errors are not recorded. Lemmata are taken from the present text. Omission of siglum indicates agreement with lemma.]

[TP]

6. Jo.] *Iohn Q2*; JOSEPH *D*
7. for *John Trundle*. 1614.] by *M. Flesher*. (n.d.) *C* [TP of 3rd. 4°, *Q3*]

[DRAMATIS PERSONAE]

[*Heading and list first given by D.*]
1. SIR LIONEL RASH] Sir Lionel *R*
3. OLD GERALDINE] *C, H*; om. *D, R*
21. AMBUSH, a broker] *ed.*; om. *D-H*
23. GARTRED] GERTRUDE *H* (*not hereafter noted*)
29-31. A ... SERVANTS] *ed.*; DRAWERS &c. *D-H*

To the Reader.

1-13,
17-18. Om. *D* up to there in 1. 13 and after *Citty* in 1. 17.
5. frontispice] *Q2-3*; frontispire *Q1*; frontispiece *R-H*; om. *D*
9. howsoever, since it] *Q1-2*; howsoever it *Q3*; howsoever, it *R-H*; om. *D*
15. applaudent] *Q1*; aplaudent *Q2*; applauded *Q3-H*
16. greater grace at the Court] better Grace at Court *D*

Upon the death of Thomas Greene.

Title] om. *D*
2. (Greene)] *Q1-3*; Green *D, C, H*; green *R*

[SCENE I]

[*Play not previously divided into scenes.*]

111

HT.	*Greenes Tu Quoque.*] *Q1-3*; GREEN'S TU QUOQUE: OR, THE CITY GALLANT. *D-C*; THE CITY GALLANT. *H*
OSD.	Master] *H*; M *Q1*; M. *Q2-3*; Mr. *D-C* (*not hereafter noted*)
1.	SP *Spend.*] *D-H*; Francis. *Q1-3*
3.	SP *Spend.*] *D-H*; Fran. *Q1-3*
5.	toward] *Q1-3*; towards *D-H*
11.	man that you] man you *H*
14.	sir.] sir? *C*, *H*
16.	quaifes] *Q1-2*; quoifes *Q3-C*; coifs *H* handkerchers] *Q1-3*; handkerchiefs *D-H* (*not hereafter noted*)
25.	or whether] or whither *Q3* SD *He*] *Q1-3*; Spendall *D-H*
28.	randevows] *Q1-3*; rendezvous *D-H*
35.	pray send] pray you send *Q2* this] *Q1-3*; the *D-H*
38.	truth, sir.] *Q1-2*; truth. *Q3-H*
39.	SD [*Aside.*]] *H*; om. *Q1-C*, ed.
42.	SD *Exit wench.*] *D-H*; after l. 41, *Q1-3*
44.	wonderous] *Q1*, *Q3*; wondrous *Q2*, *D-H*
64.	it had] is had *Q3*
68.	glasse] *Q1-3*; gloss *D-H*
78.	so?] *Q3-H*; so; *Q1*; so, *Q2* SD chapman. *Exeunt ... Long.*] *R-H*; after flatter? in l. 79, *Q1-D*
85.	meritst] merits *Q3-R*
90.	you will] you you will *Q2*
94.	againe?] *D-H*; againe. *Q1-3*
99.	SD [*Exit Gartred.*]] *D-H*; om. *Q1-3*
102.	seemst] *Q1-2*; seemest *Q3-H*
112.	SD [*Points to his heart.*]] *H*; om. *Q1-C*
117.	What say?] *Q1-2*; What say you? *Q3-H*
130.	of Knighthood] of my Knighthood *C*, *H*
148.	the Aldermen] th' aldermen *H*
151.	*Tamberlaine* to] *Q1-3*; Tamerlane to *D-C*; Tamerlane [did] to *H*

[SCENE II]

156.	eat] ate *H* (*not hereafter noted*)
157.	nor never] *Q1-3*; nor ever *D-H*
162.	sent him] *Q1*, *Q3*; sent me *Q2*; send him *D-H*
168.	How now! *Bubble*] *Q1-D*; How now, *Bubble Q2*; How now, *Bubble*! *R-H*
175.	usuring] vsurping *Q2*
184.	heare] heard *Q2*
191.	mine] *Q1-3*; my *D-H*
194.	SD *Enter a Messenger.*] *Q1-2*; *Enter Messenger. Q3-H*
214.	SD [*Aside.*]] ed.; om. *Q1-H*
225.	SD [*Aside.*]] ed.; om. *Q1-H*
237.	has] hath *D-H*
243.	of money] of my money *D-H*
248.	SD [*Aside to Blank.*]] ed.; [*Aside.*] *H*; om. *Q1-C* lov'st] lovest *A*
253.	Butcher.] *Q3-H*; Butcher? *Q1-2*
263.	SD [*Aside.*]] *H*; om. *Q1-C*
266.	service?] *D-H*; ser- / uice, *Q1-3*
268.	it be] it may be *H*
274.	Knights] Knight *Q2*
275.	christen] *Q1-3*; Christian *D-H* (*not hereafter noted*)

HISTORICAL COLLATION 113

[SCENE III]

OSD. study,] *R-H*; study *Q1-D*
285. flames] flame *R-H*
288. mother] *Q1-2*; mothers *Q3-H*
294. Why] *D-H*; We *Q1-3*
295. employment?] *D-H*; employment, *Q1, Q3*; employment. *Q2*
305. dost love] Dost thou love *D-H*
306. fairer thrice] thrise fairer *Q2*
307. Whom] Who *D-H*
317. borne and bred] bred and born *D-H*
332. sits] sit *D-H*
336. SD [Aside to Longfield.]] ed.; om. *Q1-H*
338. SD [To Geraldine.]] ed.; om. *Q1-H*
343. SD Exeunt.] *R-H*; Exit. *Q1-D*

[SCENE IV]

345. us up a] us a *D-H*
350. SD [Exit.]] *R-H*; om. *Q1-D*
361. SD Ipocras. [Exit.]] *H*; om. *Q1-C, ed.*
367. curmogin] curmudgeon *H*
368. SD [Exit Drawer.]] ed.; om. *Q1-H*
372. Maior] Major *Q3*
374. prentices] Apprentices *D, R*
 whensoever] whenever *D-H*
376. Maligoe] Malaga *H* (so throughout)
377. know I] know that I *D-H*
380. fine] fiue *Q2*
382. fill us a] fill a *Q2*
388. Mistris] *Q2*; M *Q1, Q3*; mrs. *D*; Mrs. *R-C*; Mistress *H* (not hereafter noted)
393. ith] *Q1, Q3*; in ith *Q2*; i' the *D-H*
397. dar'st] darest *A*
398. the feather-beddes] *Q1-2*; thy feather-beddes *Q3-H*
405. Belzebub] Beelzebub *R-H* (not hereafter noted)
445. stand.] stand? *Q3, H*

[SCENE V]

471. t'was] *Q1-3*; 'twas *D, A-H*; 'was *R*
486. sleep'st] *Q1-3*; sleepest *D-H*
489. comfortablest] comfortable *A*
493. I'le] I *Q2, R*
497. left] felt *C*
502. SD [She makes a grimace.]] *H*; om. *Q1-C, ed.*
511. um] *Q1-3*; 'em *D-H* (not hereafter noted)
512. harlotries] *Q1-3*; harlots *D-H*
516. SD dissemble. [Aside.]] *H*; om. *Q1-C, ed.*
518. like] loue *Q2*
522. of a] of his *Q2*
531. er't] *Q1-3*; ere it *D-H*
540. councell] *Q1-3*; council *D*; counsel *R-H*
541. Sister, know] Sister, [you] know *H*
544. rites] *Q1-2*; rights *Q3-A, H*; rigdts *C*

551. i'th] *Q1-3*; in the *D-H*

[SCENE VI]

559. cheerefully things] cheerefully doe things *Q2*
563. in's] i'th *Q2*
566. flowrie] *Q1-D*; flowery *R-H*
577. Y'are] *Q1-3*; You are *D-H*
580. y'are] *Q1-3*; you are *D-H*
589. heere's] *Q1-3*; here is *D-H*
599. youle] you *C, H*
601. scurvily you were best;] *Q1-D*; scurvily; you were best *R, A*; scurvily: you were best *C, H*
603. SD [*Exit Gartred.*]] *ed.*; om. *Q1-H*
607. ha] *Q1, Q3*; haue *Q2, D-H*
608. SD *Enter Gart.* [*below*].] *H*; *Enter Gart.*, after l. 611, *Q1-H*
609. passion of] *Q1-3*; passion on *D-H*
645. SD him: *Enter Joyce* [*below*].] *H*; *Enter Joyce.*, after l. 645, *D-H*; after l. 642, *Q1-3*
646. furdest] *Q1-3*; farthest *D-H* (not hereafter noted)
647. wrastle] *Q1-3*; wrestle *D-H* (not hereafter noted)
653. together of your selves] together yourselves *C, H*
667. SD *Exeunt ambo.*] *Q1-D*; *Exeunt. R-H*

[SCENE VII]

683. vantage] *Q1-3*; advantage *D-H*
690. SD *Lionell, and Long-field*] *Q1-3*; *Lionel, Longfield D-H*
692. these two] this two *H*
693. hee's] *Q1-3*; he is *D-H*
697. him againe] *Q1-D*; him back again *R-H*
702. what, are these onions?] *Q1-D*; what are these, onions? *R-H*
705. onions Gentlemen,] *Q1-2*; onions, Gentlemen, *Q3*; onions. Gentlemen, *D-H*
710. into] *Q1-2*; to *Q3-H*
716. you.] *D-H*; you *Q1-3*
    SD *Gentlemen ... out.*] *ed.*; after l. 711, *Q1-R*; after l. 714, *C, H*
721. them] *Q1-3*; 'em *D-H*
735. SD *Enter Staines.*] *Q1-3*; after l. 734, *D-H*
747. whatsoe'r] *Q1-3*; whatsoever *D-H*
750. snacke] *Q1, Q3*; snap *Q2, D-H*
760. ith] *Q1, Q3*; in the *Q2*; i' the *D-H*
761. this] *Q1-3*; thus *D-H*
772. makes] *Q1-2*; make *Q3-H*
792. mine] *Q1-2*; my *Q3-H*

[SCENE VIII]

818. tell sir] *Q1-3*; tell it, sir *D-H*
829. further] *Q1-3*; farther *D-H* (not hereafter noted)
831. SD [*Aside.*]] *H*; om. *Q1-C*
835. lend] send *Q2*
840. deed?] *D-H*; deed. *Q1-3*

842. witnesse?] *D-H*; witnesse. *Q1-3*
847. SD [*Gives ... servant.*]] *ed.*; [*To* SERVANT.]] *H*; om. *Q1-C*
    For] *Q1-C*; There's for *H*
848. SP *Ser.*] BLANK. *H*
    I'le ... you.] I thank you, sir. I'll ... you. (*line added*) *H*
849. you] we *Q2*
851. SD both. [*Exeunt ... Servant.*]] *ed.*; [*Exit.*]] after *l. 850, H*; om. *Q1-C*
862. SD *Exit Spend.*] *Q1-2*; om. *Q3*, *D*; *Exit. R-H*

[SCENE IX]

867. a clocke] o'clock *C*, *H* (*not hereafter noted*)
871. i'th] *Q1-3*; in th' *D-R*, *C-H*; in the *A*
878. you true sir] you sir *Q2*
879. mine] *Q1-3*; my *D-H*
881. I'm] *Q1-D*; I am *R-H*
886. sawest] *Q1-3*; saw'st *D-H*
897. ye] *Q1-3*; you *D-H*
899. Th'ast] *Q1-3*; Thou hast *D-H*
900. throughly] *Q1-3*; thoroughly *D-H*
911. fetch, sir,] *ed.*; fetch sir [?] *Q1-2*; fetch some *Q3-H*
913. smoake?] *D-H*; smoake. *Q1-3*
917. I had thought] *Q1-3*; I thought *D-H*
924. pence?] *Q3*, *H*; pence, *Q1-2*; pence! *D-C*
938. Udslid] *Q1-3*; Ud's life *D-H* (*not hereafter noted*)
942. mournavall] *Q1-3*; mournival *D-C*; murnival *H*
945. Udslid, I am] *Q1-3*; Ud's life! I'm *D-R*, *H*; Ud's life, I am *A*
967. SP *Spend.*] *Q1-D*; *Long. R-H*
    yfaith] *Q1-3*; 'faith *D-C*; faith *H*
972. scot] scut *Q2*
976. for't] *Q1-D*; for it *R-H*
981. whiles] *Q1-3*; whilst *D-H*
987,
988. as while a man] *Q1-3*; as a man *D-R*, *C-H*; as a might *A*
992. Broaker, *Ninni-hammer?*] *Q3*, *D*; Broaker *Ninni-hammer? Q1-2*; Broaker? *Ninni-hammer. R-H*
996. SD [*Exit Ninnihammer.*]] *ed.*; om. *Q1-H*
997. Looke you] *Q1-3*; Lookye *D*; Look ye *R-H*
998. Gamster:] *ed.*; Gamster, *Q1-3*; gamester? *D-H*
999. Tu quoque sir.] Tu quoque. *H*
1000,
1001. God ... quoque.] om. *H*
1026. the whole world] *Q1-3*; the world *D-H*
1077. last ever] last [for] ever *H*
1093. SD [*Aside.*]] *H*; om. *Q1-C*
    Umh] *Q1-3*; Hum *D-H*
1099. neare] neuer *Q2*
1100. meat's] meat is *Q2*
1109. SD *Exeunt] R-H*; *Exit Q1-D*
1121. ha] *Q1-3*; ha' *D*; have *R-H*
1124. y'are] y're *R-C*
1131. bloud] *Q1-3*; blood *D-H*

1148.   SD *Ex. omnes*] after l. 1148, *D-H*; after l. 1147, *Q1-3*

[SCENE X]

1162.   Th'art] *Q2-H*; Tha'rt *Q1*
1166.   q?] *D-H*; q, *Q1-3*
1171.   his] us *H*
1176.   give to each] *Q1-3*; give each *D-H*
1185.   Satires] *Q1-3*; satyrs *D-H*
1188.   that] and *H*
1197,
1201,
1203.   SD [*Aside.*]] *H*; om. *Q1-C, ed.*
1208.   in to] into *H*
1216.   y'are] *Q1-D*; you are *R-H*
1237.   SD [*To Longfield.*]] *D-C*; [*Aside to* LONGFIELD.] *H*; om. *Q1-3, ed.*
1248.   y'ould] you'd *H*
1262.   marke] *Q1-3*; work *D-H*
1271.   SD [*Aside.*]] *H*; om. *Q1-C, ed.*
1277.   Not see his] Not his *Q2*
1287.   SD [*Aside.*]] *H*; om. *Q1-C, ed.*
1297.   SD bosome. [*Aside.*]] *H*; om. *Q1-C, ed.*
1300.   shall shake] *Q1-3*; shall e'er shake *D-H*
1301.   SD [*Aside.*]] *H*; om. *Q1-C, ed.*
1305.   should] would *Q2*
1312.   to] *Q1-3*; unto *D-H*
1330.   SD [*Aside.*]] *H*; om. *Q1-C, ed.*
1334.   SD [*Kisses him.*]] *ed.*; om. *Q1-H*
1336.   SD [*Aside.*]] *H*; om. *Q1-C, ed.*
        who'ld] who'd *H*

[SCENE XI]

OSD.   [*Tothill Fields.*]] *H*; om. *Q1-C, ed.*
1360.   SP *Sta.*] om. *Q2*
1373.   It were] 'Twere *H*

[SCENE XII]

1379.   i'th] *Q1-3*; i' the *D-H*
1381.   guesse] *Q1-2*; guests *Q3-H*
1388.   SD *Exit Servant.*] *R-H*; after l. 1395, *Q1-D*
1395.   SD *Scattergood, Staines,* [*and Servant*].] *R-H*; *Scattergood, and Staines. Q1-D*
1401,
1402.   SD [*Exit Servant.*]] *R-H*; om. *Q1-D*
1418.   shew me a] *Q1-A*; shew a *C*; show a *H*
1431.   arrantest] *Q1-3*; errantest *D-H* (*not hereafter noted, including variants, e.g., l. 1465*)
1438.   SD heere: [*Kisses the elder.*]] *H*; om. *Q1-C, ed.*
1441.   SD [*Aside.*]] *ed.*; om. *Q1-H*
1470.   SD he: [*Aside.*]] *H*; om. *Q1-C, ed.*
1472.   SD [*Aside.*]] *ed.*; om. *Q1-H*
        chose] *D-H*; choose *Q1-3*

HISTORICAL COLLATION 117

1480. SD [Aside.]] H; om. Q1-C
1481. mee?] Q1-3; mee. D-H
1487. SD best. [Aside.]] H; om. Q1-C, ed.
    Jarvis] Q1-D; Gervase R-H (not hereafter noted)
1492. SD Lady: [Aside.]] H; om. Q1-C, ed.
1498. SD [Aside.]] H; om. Q1-C, ed.
    Augh] Q1-3; Ah D-H
1503. Boone] bon H
1504. SD has: [Aside.]] H; om. Q1-C, ed.
1505. and] Q1-3; an D-H
    Gentleman.] Q3-H; Gentleman? Q1-2
1514. SD [Exit Servant.]] ed.; om. Q1-H
1518. strooke] Q1-2; strucke Q3-H
    on the] Q1-3; o' th' D-R, C-H; o' the A
1527. whilst] while H
1534. I am] Q1-3; I'm D-H
1536. you] Q1-3; ye D-H
    SD more. [Whispers.]] H; om. Q1-C, ed.
1545. Guist] Q1; Guest Q2-H
1548. Ye're] Q1, Q3; Ye are Q2; You're D-H
1549. be long] belong Q3
1555. SD Exeunt] D-H; Exit Q1-3
1562. S'fott] Q1-2; S'foot Q3-H (not hereafter noted)
1578. on.] D-H; on? Q1-3
1582. SD [Exeunt ... Scattergood.]] R-H; om. Q1-D
1592. SD Exeunt] R-H; Exit Q1-D
    SD Rash] Q1-D; Will Rash R-H (not hereafter noted)
1596. SD issue. [Withdraws a little.]] H; om. Q1-C, ed.
1601. yet a slave] yet [is] a slave H
1605. I wrong] I [do] wrong H
1607. spirits] Q1-2; spirit Q3-H
1611. SD [Aside.]] H; om. Q1-C, ed.
1612. hath] Q1-2; have Q3-H
1613. eye] eyes Q2
1616. Curbes] Q1-3; Curb D-H
1618. SD [Aside.]] H; om. Q1-C, ed.
1625. over] o'er H
1627. goe speake] Q1-2; goe and speake Q3-H
1634. hate] Q1; ha'te Q2; haue't Q3-H
1648. In fayth] Q1-2; I faith Q3; I' faith D-H
1649. foole lover, turne] Q1-3; fool, lover, turn D; fool; lover, turn R-H
1652. Yes] Q1-3; Yet D-H
1654. and of Speech] and Speech Q2
1661. You're] Q1-3; You are D-H
    SD Exeunt] Q3-H; Exit Q1-2

[SCENE XIII]

1674. quarrell?] D-H; quarrell, Q1-3
1678. not you say] not say Q2
1679. Gods] God is H
1682. world] Q1, D-H; word Q2-3
    SD Enter Sergiants] after l. 1685, H
1685. SD [Exit. The Street.]] H; om. Q1-C, ed.

1688. suites] *Q1-2, R-C*; suite *Q3, D*
1690. SD say? [*They stand aside, talking.*]] *ed.*; *om. Q1-H*
       SD say? [*Sweatman's house. Another part of the street.*]] *H*; *om. Q1-C, ed.*
1694. He is] He's *H*
       Banquerout] bankrupt *H* (*not hereafter noted*)
1695. And his] And's *H*
1696. wares] *Q1-2*; ware *Q3-H*
1697. have] *Q1, D-H*; hath *Q2-3*
1703. hither?] *ed.*; hither, *Q1-2*; hither! *Q3-H*
1705. SD [*To the Sergiants.*]] *ed.*; *om. Q1-H*
1709. SD [*Aside.*]] *H*; *om. Q1-C, ed.*
1713. you] thou *Q2*
1714. shall] shalt *Q2*
1716. SD [*They come forward.*]] *ed.*; *om. Q1-H*
       SD [*They walk together to the house.*]] *H*; *om. Q1-C, ed.*
1721. Tickleman.] *Q3-H*; Tickleman? *Q1-2*
1726. Sees] *Q1-3*; seest *D-H*
1731. Zounds] Zwounds *Q2* (*not hereafter noted*)
1733. you're] *Q1-3*; you are *D-H*
1737. be soone] *Q1-2*; be so soone *Q3*; so soon be *D-H*
1738. shillings.] *Q3-H*; shillings? *Q1-2*
1742. Money.] *Q3-H*; Money? *Q1-2*
1749. a would a] *Q1, Q3*; he would haue *Q2, R-H*; he would ha' *D*
1755. his habitation] his local habitation *H*
1756. other locall place] other place *H*
1757. SD Bribes. Takes Spendals Cloake.] *R-H*; after l. 1756, *Q1-D*
1760. SD you. [*They loose him.*]] *H*; *om. Q1-C, ed.*
1761. men] me *D, H*
1764. Beldame] *Q1-D*; beldam *R-H*
1769. Aqua vite] *Q1*; Aqua vitae *Q2-H*
1780. SD Exeunt [*Spendall and Sergiants*].] *ed.*; Exit. *Q1-H*
1793. Wilt be] *Q1-3* (wilt); will be *D-C*; will, be *H*
       SD *Exeunt*] *D-H*; Exit *Q1-3*

[SCENE XIV]

1798. come] *Q1-D*; comes *R-H*
1801. least] *Q1-2*; lest *Q3-H*
1806. leive] *Q1-2*; lieve *Q3, R-C*; live *D*; lief *H*
1810. Consort] *Q1-D*; concert *R-H*
1814. off] of *A, H*
1817. hallow] *Q1-3*; holloo *D-R*; halloo *A-H*
1819. opportunatly] *Q1-3*; opportunely *D-H*
1825. would] wold *Q3*
1828. into a fooles] into fooles *Q2*
1834. inclind too, to that] *Q1-R*; inclined, to that *A-H*
1837. subtile] *Q1-D*; subtle *R-H*
       rogue] tongue *Q2*
1847. ceases] *Q1-3*; seizes *D-H*
1851. SD [*Aside.*]] *H*; *om. Q1-C, ed.*
1853. has] *Q1-3*; have *D-H*
1857. You have] You shall haue *Q2*
1858. SD [*Aside. Exit.*]] *H*; *om. Q1-C, ed.*
1859. SD you. [*Aside.*]] *ed.*; *om. Q1-H*

HISTORICAL COLLATION 119

1860. braying] *Q1-3*; praying *D-H*
1870. Thinkes] *Q1-2*; Thinke *Q3-H*
       other things] *Q2-C*; other thing *Q1*; earthly things *H*
1871. They] *Q1-2*; But they *Q3-H*
1875,
1882,
1890. SD [*Aside*.]] *ed*.; *om*. *Q1-H*
1895. answerd?] *Q1-2*; answerd. *Q3-H*
1896. SD [*Aside*.]] *ed*.; *om*. *Q1-H*
       Woman] *Q1-2*; Women *Q3-H*
1898. SD [*Leaves her*.]] *H*; *om*. *Q1-C*
1901. Westminster] Westminister *Q2*
1915. SD for? [*Aside*.]] *H*; *om*. *Q1-C*
1918. [*Aside*.]] *H*; *om*. *Q1-C*, *ed*.
1935. T'as] *Q3*; Ta's *Q1*; Tas *Q2*; 'Tas *D*, *R*; 'Thas *A*; 'T' as *C*;
       'T has *H*
1936. SD [*Aside*.]] *H*; *om*. *Q1-C*
1941. if't were] *Q1*, *Q3*, *R-A*; if twere *Q2*; if it were *D*;
       if 'twere *H*
1945. SD [*Aside*.]] *H*; *om*. *Q1-C*
1952. meate] meet *H*
1954. SD [*Aside*.]] *H*; *om*. *Q1-C*
1956. Curtcie] *Q1-3*; court'sie *D-C*; courtesy *H*
1957. trickes] *Q1-2*; tricke *Q3-H*
1959. SD [*Aside*.]] *H*; *om*. *Q1-C*
       tis] *Q1-3*; this is *D-H*
1965. you're] you are *Q2*
1969. SD againe. [*Fetches Will Rash*.]] *H*; *om*. *Q1-C*
1970. relieve] *Q2-H*; reliue *Q1*
1996. Inn's a Court] *Q1-3*; inns o' court *D*, *A-H*; inns of court *R*
2000. Beholding] *Q1-3* (beholding); beholden *D-H*
2014. SD then Rash] *Q1-3*; and then Rash *D-H*
2015. SP *Rash*.] *ed*.; *All speake*. *Q1-H*
2016. SD [*Enter GERTRUDE and GERALDINE*] *H*; *om*. *Q1-C*, *ed*.
       SD *over*,] *ed*.; *ouer Q1-H*
2025. Gentlemen,] *ed*.; Gent. *Q1-3*; gentle *D-H*
2032. SD [*Exit Staines*.]] *ed*.; *om*. *Q1-H*
2038. SD Exeunt] *R-H*; Exit *Q1-D*

[SCENE XV]

OSD. Hold-fast] *Q3-H*; Lock-fast *Q1-2*
2047. them] *Q1-3*; 'em *D-H*
2054. Stones] *Q1-2*; Stone *Q3-H*
2061. You're] *Q1-3*; You'd *D-H*
2063. Is] *Q1-2* (is); its *Q3*, *A*; it's *D-R*, *C-H*
2089. SD *Exit Hold*.] *Q3-D*; *Exit Holdfast R-H*; *Exit Lock*. *Q1-2*
2095. i'th] *Q1-3*; in the *D-H*
2096. this two yeare] *Q1-2*; this two yeares *Q3-C*; these two
       years *H*
2111. Harry] Henry *Q2* (*not hereafter noted*)
2112. SD *Prisoners*] *Q1-C*; PRISONER *H*
2113. SP *Pris*.] *Q1-D*, *A*, *H*; *Prisoners*. *R*, *C*
2118. first] *Q2-H*; fire *Q1*
2122. Chops] chaps *H*

2123. Basket.] *D-H*; Basket? *Q1-3*
2125. watering] watring *Q2*
2131,
2132. into th'] *Q1, Q3*; into the *Q2, D-H*
2137. SD *Prisoners*] PRISONER *H*
2138. come,] come? *D*
2148. are] is *H*
2149. vild] *Q1-2, H*; vile *Q3-C*
2154. you, and] you of *H*
2160. in Mudde] *Q1-2*; ith Mudde *Q3, D-H*
2170. remembred] *Q1-3*; remember'd *D-R, C-H*; remembered *A*
2189. and glad] *Q1-2*; and am glad *Q3-H*
      SD *Exeunt*] *R-H*; Exit *Q1-3*; Ex. *D*

[SCENE XVI]

2198. Her lip] *Q2, D-H*; Hee-lip *Q1, Q3*
2202. SD [*Aside.*]] *ed.*; *om. Q1-H*
2216. Ordinance] *Q1-3*; ordnance *D-H*
2218. Genteell] *Q1-2*; Gentile *Q3-H*
2221. *Italian?*] *D-H*; *Italian: Q1-3*
2222. haviour] *Q1*; behauiour *Q2-H*
2225,
2226. doubt, but by qualitie, to] *Q1-3* (But); doubt, / But to *D-A*; doubt, but to *C*; doubt but to *H*
2227. humane] *Q1-3*; human *D-H*
2229. SD [*Aside.*]] *ed.*; *om. Q1-H*
2230. harke you] *Q1-3*; harkye *D*; hark ye *R-H*
2241. SD [*Aside.*]] *H*; *om. Q1-C*
2248. opounctly] *Q1*; opunctly *Q2, D-H*; oponctly *Q3*
2249. phisnomie] *Q1-3*; physiognomy *D-H*
2253. disburthen] disburden *Q2*
2268. set on] *Q1-3*; set it on *D-H*
2271. eye] *Q1-3*; eyes *D-H*
2275. condition] *Q1-3*; caution *D-H*
      off] *Q1-3*; of *D-H*
2284. Sa'y] *Q1, Q3*; Say *Q2*; Sa' ye *D*; Say ye *R-H*
2286. quickly.] *Q3-H*; quickly? *Q1-2*
2289. apparance] *ed.*; apparace *Q1*; appearance *Q2-H*
2294. would have] *Q1-3*; would not have *D-H*
2295. thinke I] *Q1-3*; think but I *D-H*
2302. Gentlemen] *D-H*; Gent. *Q1-3*
2309. SD [*Aside.*]] *H*; *om. Q1-C*
2309,
2310. SP *Bub*. By ... extasie.] *Q1-C*; [*Ger.*] By ... fellow. *Bub*. He ... ecstasy. *H*
2311,
2312. SD [*Aside.*]] *H*; *om. Q1-C, ed.*
2317. SD [*Aside.*]] *H*; *om. Q1-C*
2320. The tother] *Q1-3*; T'other *D-H*
2325. quoque?] *Q3-H*; quoque. *Q1-2*
2336. pound] *Q1*; pounds *Q2-H*
2352. SD *Enter Stayns.*] Enter STAINES [*in his own costume.*] *H*
2361. Hatte?] *Q3-H*; Hatte. *Q1-2*
2373. SD [*Aside.*]] *H*; *om. Q1-C, ed.*

2376.	heare.] *Q3-H*; heare? *Q1-2*
2391.	least] *Q1-3*; lest *D-H*
2393.	meant] *Q1-2*; meane *Q3-H*
2398.	SD *Exeunt*] *R-H*; *Exit Q1-D*; [*Sir* ... *Spendall*] ed.; om. *Q1-H*; SD *after* l. 2397, *Q1-H*
2403.	your Finger] *Q1-2*; your Fingers *Q3-H*
2410.	forefathers] forefather *Q3, D*
2411.	morne] morning *Q2*
2414.	poysning] *Q1, Q3*; poysoning *Q2, D-H*
2438.	ha] *Q1-3*; ha' *D*; have *R-H*
2455.	Feast] *Q1-2*; Ieast *Q3*; jest *D-H*
2457.	SD *and Exeunt*] ed.; *and Exit Q1-3*; *and go off D-H*
2468.	must] *Q1-3*; might *D-H*
2478.	SD [*Exit.*]] *R-H*; om. *Q1-D*

[SCENE XVII]

2480.	wee could] we'd *H*
2484.	want not] *Q1-2*; not want *Q3-H*
2492.	God-night] *Q1-3*; Good night *D-H*
2494.	SD *Exeunt. Manent*] *D-H*; *Exit. Manet Q1-3*
2498.	into] *Q1, Q3, D*; in to *Q2, R-H*
2510.	errand.] *D-H*; errand? *Q1-3*
2517.	Importund] *Q3-R, C-H* (Importun'd); Importuned *A*; Importune *Q1-2*
2538.	livelihood] *Q1-3*; liveliness *D-H*
2555.	SD Poynts. *Knocke*] *Knocks Q2*; SD *after* mee? in l. 2553, *Q1-2*; *after* you, in l. 2556, *Q3-H*
2566.	pray stay] *Q1-3, A*; pray you stay *D-R, C-H*
2568.	SD [*Repeats.*]] *H*; om. *Q1-C*, ed.
2575.	up?] *R-H*; vp. *Q1-D*
2577.	SD *Kisse*] *Q1-3*; *Kisses D-H*
2601.	SD *Binde*] *Q1, Q3*; *Bind Q2* (catchword / *Binds* / *K3*); *Binds D-H*
2603.	kinsfolkes] kinsfolk *H*
2605.	Push] *Q1-3*; Pish *D-H*
2610.	SD *Enter Phillis.*] *Q1-3*; *after* l. 2609, *D-H*
2615.	oath?] *D-H*; oath. *Q1-3*
2621.	t'hast] *Q1-2*; 'thast *Q3*; thou'st *D-H*
2622.	o're] *Q1-3*; over *D-H*
2625.	SD [*To Phillis.*]] ed.; om. *Q1-H*
2628.	pearle] *Q1-3*; pearls *D-H*
2633.	thee?] *Q3-H*; thee, *Q1-2*
2647.	with't a love] ed.; with't aloue *Q1(c)*; with't alone *Q1(u), Q2-3*; with it love *D-H* SD [*Unties him.*]] ed.; om. *Q1-H*
2649.	putt'st] puttest *Q2*
2651.	actions] action *C, H*

[SCENE XVIII]

2668.	SD *Enter ... Phillis.*] *Q1-D*; *after* Interrogatories: in l. 2669, *R-H*
2672.	directly, intend] directly, [and] intend *H*
2673.	gainst] *Q1-2*; against *Q3-H*

2684.	SD [Aside.]] H; om. Q1-C, ed.	
2693,		
2694.	betray thee?] D-H; betray thee. Q1-3	
2698.	on?] Q3-H; on. Q1-2	
2705.	Lanthorne] lanthorns C, H	
2711.	SD [Exeunt.]] R-H; after l. 2709, D; om. Q1-3	

[SCENE XIX]

2730.	day?] Q3-H; day, Q1-2	
2754.	sleepie?] D-H; sleepie, Q1-3	
2755.	sai'st] sayest H	
2759.	SD Enter Baskethilt.] R-H; Enter Seruant. Q1-D; after l. 2762, R-C; after l. 2761, H	
2761.	slouth] Q1; sloath Q2; sloth Q3-H	
2762.	haste?] Q3-H; haste. Q1-2	
2773.	SD Exeunt.] R-H; Exit. Q1-D; after l. 2771, Q1-2	
2799.	th'ad] th' had H	
2801.	untill] Q1-3; 'til D-H	
	SD Enter ... Joyce.] Q1-D; after l. 2807, R-H	
2808.	SD [Aside.]] ed.; om. Q1-H	
2817.	Hoy day] Q1-3; Hey day D-H	
	sonne] Q1-D; sons R-H	
2818.	married?] married. C, H	
2823.	Counter] Q1-D; Compter R-H (not hereafter noted)	
2829.	Ipocras] Ipozras Q2	
2830.	God] Q1-3; Good D-H	
2836.	Yea] Q1-2; Yes Q3-H	
2841.	come now] now are Q2	
2848.	penner] Q1-3; pen D-H	
2850,		
2852,		
2854,		
2858,		
2862.	SP Sta.] D-H; Scat. Q1-3	
2867.	vehemence] vehemency Q2	
2873.	SP Sta.] D-H; Scat. Q1-3	
2874.	you give] Q1-3; give you D-H	
	match?] D-H; match. Q1-3	
2892.	Sergeant] ed.; Sergeants Q1-H	
2909.	Gartred?] ed.; Gartred, Q1-3; Gartred; D; Gartred! R-H	
2919.	these, Gentlemen,] ed.; these Gentlemen Q1-H	
2935.	FINIS.] Q1-3; om. D-H	
	SD [Exeunt.]] A; om. Q1-R, C, H, ed.	

CRITICAL NOTES

Note on Documentation in Critical Notes:

Complete references to all works cited in the following Critical Notes, as well as in the Introduction, are provided in the Bibliography. The numbers cited in references to E.A. Abbott's *A Shakespearian Grammar*, 3rd. rev. ed. (1870; rpt. 1966), denote paragraph numbers rather than page numbers, just as they do in the work itself. All references to Shakespeare follow the text and act, scene and line numberings of *The Riverside Shakespeare*, ed. G.B. Evans et. al. (1974). Notes citing Sugden are references to E.H. Sugden, *A Topographical Dictionary to the Works of Shakespeare and His Fellow Dramatists* (1925). Notes citing Tilley are references to M.P. Tilley, *A Dictionary of the Proverbs in England in the Sixteenth and Seventeenth Centuries* (1950); citations to Tilley give the letters and numbers under which proverbial items are found, rather than page numbers.

[TP]

1. Greene's Tu quoque] See Introduction.

[DRAMATIS PERSONAE]

5. SPENDALL] Spend-all was a 16th-17th c. word for *spendthrift*.
13. PURSENET] Name of a thieving gallant in Thomas Middleton's *Your Five Gallants*, pub. 1608. Also a kind of net for catching rabbits, i.e. a "cony-catcher"--used allusively to mean "trickster," or "cheat."
21. AMBUSH, a broker] This character has three lines in Sc. IX (ll. 1070, 1072, 1076, SP *Amb.*), though his entrance and exit are not given. Ninnihammer does not refer to him when he enters with the money he was sent to get from Ambush earlier in the scene. The lack of explicit or implied stage directions here suggests authorial provenance.

[To the Reader.]

1. *gratulate*] to greet, salute.
2. *entirely*] wholly.
   Fellow] colleague, co-worker.
3. *being ... way*] having the opportunity.
5. *either*] each, (or) both of them.
   frontispice] Var. of *frontispiece*, here used to mean a *foreword*.
6. *For*] as for.
   Poem] (1) composition having some qualities in common with poetry, or including verse (as the play does); (2) hence, *work*.

123

8. *divulged*] published.
13. *censure*] judge.
14. *nature*] (1) character; (2) function, capacity (hence, *type*. Greene was his company's clown).
15. *applaudent*] applauded.
16. *of greater grace*] in greater favor, more approved.
    Court] This play was first performed at Court (see Introduction).
17. *character*] estimate of a person's qualities and reputation (*OED*, 13).
19. Thomas Heywood] Heywood was the principal playwright for Queen Anne's Men (see Introduction).

Upon the death of Thomas Greene.

1. *Floraes*] Flora was the Roman goddess of flowers.
2. (Greene)] See R.B. McKerrow (*An Introduction to Bibliography* ... , p. 318). The parentheses are used for emphasis.
3. W.R.] Reed (p. 539), infers that the author of the couplet was "probably William Rowley," who was a contributing playwright for Queen Anne's Men (see Introduction).

[SCENE I]

OSD. Mercers] A mercer was a textile dealer, "esp. ... silks, velvets, and other costly materials" (OED).
discovered] revealed, disclosed (perhaps by opening a curtain on a portion of the stage). G.F. Reynolds compares this SD with the opening SD in William Rowley's *A Shoemaker a Gentleman* (c. 1607-9): "Enter discouer'd in a Shop a Shoo-maker, his Wife spinning, Barnaby, two Iournimen." He conjectures that: "the discovery of these scenes ... might be taken to mean that the shop was on the rear stage or an arrangement of it" (*The Staging of Elizabethan Plays at the Red Bull Theater, 1605-1625*, p. 79).
Gartred] Var. of *Gertrude*, reflecting a contemporary pronunciation. (*Q1* of *Hamlet* intermittently has *Gertred*, and *Gertrad* appears in *Q2-4*.)

1, 3. SP *Spend.*] *Francis.* and *Fran.* respectively in *Q1-3*. Neither of these speech-prefixes is employed again, though Spendall is occasionally called "Frank" by other characters. The original speech-prefixes may indicate authorial provenance.

1. What lacke you] "The usual cry of the London huckster" (Tilley, L 20), *lacke* meaning *need* (as in l. 49).
   faire stuffes] good-looking woolens.
8. stirring humour] restless mood.
14. Marry] Orginally, the name of the Virgin Mary used as an oath; here, for emphasis, with the force of *to be sure*, (or) *indeed*.
16. quaifes] Also *coifs*, *quoifes*, etc.: close-fitting caps covering the entire head.
    handkerchers] handkerchiefs.
17. bonelace] "Lace, usually of linen thread, made by knitting upon a pattern marked by pins, with bobbins originally made of bone" (*OED*).
25. angell] A gold coin worth about 10 shillings, so named for its device of the archangel Michael standing upon, and

piercing, the dragon.
26. rascall] *OED* (3.b), cites this line as its earliest example of the word used without serious negative implications, here apparently in a playful way.
28. randevows] Var. of *rendezvous*.
noise] band, (or) consort.
45. and] if. Used for *an* (=*if*) throughout.
47. assist] accompany.
48. cheapen] (1) bargain for (?); (2) price (?).
53. affects] pleases.
56. demaund] ask (without peremptory connotation).
61. rellish too much] savor too much of.
67,
68. close wrought] tightly or densely woven, compact in texture and consistency.
68. glasse] Var. of *gloss*; i.e. *glaze*, *lustre*.
69. I,] ay.
73. Exchange] Probably not the Royal Exchange (est. 1570), but the New Exchange, opened by James I in 1609 ("Britain's Burse").
77. discharge] pay for.
78. chapman] buyer.
92. modest] (1) chaste; (2) inoffensive.
102. be ... seemst] Cf. Tilley, S 214 (*Be what thou would seem to be*).
107. Ile buy] I'd buy (see E.A. Abbott, *A Shakespearian Grammar*, 348).
custome] patronage.
113. Uds pitty] God's pity; a mild oath.
else] otherwise.
121. make ... wares] put the fabrics back in order.
123. shut up shop] i.e. shut up the shopwindows; hence, *close the shop to trade*. G.F. Reynolds speculates that this line indicates something was closed, perhaps a shutter (p. 79), though this would be less necessary than a counter and textile goods as props, judging from previous dialogue in this scene.
130. kinde] manner, fashion.
131,
132,
133. I ... purchac'd] There are numerous critical or satirical references in dramatic and non-dramatic literature of the time to the prolific sales of knighthoods during the reign of James I. (See B. Gibbons, *Jacobean City Comedy*, p. 58.)
132. all's one] no matter.
142. Strand] A street close to the Thames. "During the reign of James the Strand came to be the fashionable residential quarter of London, the West end of those days" (Sugden, p. 489).
143. *Fulham*] A village on the North bank of the Thames, known as a resort for gamesters. Hence, a "Fullam" was a kind of "loaded" die used for cheating (Sugden, p. 211). Staines uses such dice in Scene IX.
144. shift] change (one's lodging and/or position).
148. Alderman] London aldermen were both representatives of wards and magistrates. See J. Stow's *A Survay of London* (1598), pp. 61-2, 284 and *OED*, *ward*, sb.19.
152. meate] *food* generally, not necessarily just meat.

153. the which] which. (The definite article was often used with *which*, here considered an indefinite adjective. See Abbott, 270.)

[SCENE II]

156. eat] ate (pronounced *et*).
groat loaves] Coarse bread at fourpence per loaf. There were "penny loaves" at 1*d*.
out ... purse] i.e. that he paid for himself.
157. nor never] Elizabethan double negative, used of emphasis (see Abbott, 406).
159. cosoned] Var. of *cozened*; i.e. *cheated*.
160,
161. almes-basket] A basket containing scraps of food which were intended as public alms to be fed to penniless prisoners (as in Scene XV).
164. abroade] outdoors, at large.
165. Serjeants] arresting officers.
take ... me] come to recognize me (thereby, arrest me on sight on a creditor's suit). This passage in 11. 164-5 (dare ... me), is probably an echo from *Ram-Alley* by L. Barry (pub. 1611), the almost certain source for much of Scene XVII of this play: "I dare not walk the streets, / For I dwindle at a sergeant in buff ... " (ed. C.E. Jones, Materials for the Study of the Old English Drama, Vol. 23, 1952, 11. 1693-4).
166,
167. Ireland ... Westchester] Ireland and Virginia were refuges for fugitives from justice and those without prospects. So was *Westchester* (later Chester), because of its distance from London, and its convenience for passage to Ireland (Sugden, p. 559).
172. entertainement] employment.
188,
189,
190. Wapping ... handkerchers] Bubble is referring to the method used to execute pirates at Wapping, a London district on the West bank of the Thames, south of London Docks. "The first erection at W. was a gallows at execution dock ... where pirates and others were hung up at low water and left for the rising tide to drown" (Sugden, p. 556). Described in Stow's *Survay* (1598), p. 347.
192. dominiere] Var. of *domineer*; i.e. *revel*.
193. Tyburne] Tyburn was the site of the public gallows for Middlesex County until 1783. Ll. 193-4 recall the proverbial *to be hanged on a fair (one's own) gallows* (see Tilley, G 18, G 19).
209. next] nearest.
211. that] An implied stage direction: Bubble gives him a coin.
212. SD Enter ... knockes] G.F. Reynolds (p. 118), notes that as the SD indicates that the messenger knocks after entering, there must have been doors on stage.
220. what ... doe] what business have you.
222. I ... mercy] I beg your honor's pardon.
228. by this light] An asseverative phrase: *by this (good) light*,

i.e. *daylight*. Var. of *by God's light* or *'Slight*.
Scrivener] notary, clerk who draws up contracts. Blank, in addition, is a *money scrivener*, one who takes in money to put out at interest, and lends money on security; this is how Bubble's uncle acquired Staines's mortgage and country properties.
235. What] who (see Abbott, 254).
236. poore] humble (as in l. 266).
237,
238. He ... eares.] Petty robbers were sometimes punished by having one or both ears cut off.
240. putting out] lending out at interest or on security. Bubble equates "putting out" with "spending," which accounts for the misunderstanding in ll. 242-3, 245-6.
256. cheapen] bargain for, haggle for.
259. *aqua vitae*] Popularly, *brandy*, *whisky*, etc. Orginally, an alchemical term for ardent spirits or unrectified alcohol.
261. *Rosa solis*] Originally, a cordial made from or flavored with the juice of the sundew plant; here, brandy laced with spices and/or sugar.
268. brownest] i.e. cheapest, most humble. *Brown bread* was made of rye or of mixed rye and wheat, cheaper than white bread, made of wheaten flour only.
269. smallest] weakest, thinnest. This is either an allusion to *small beer*, beer of a weak or poor quality, or to diluted wine.
272. stand ... for] dispute, (or) haggle with you over.
275. behaviour] conduct; hence, *character*.
christen] Var. of *Christian*.
279. dutifull] forthcoming, willing to render what is due you.
281. behaviour] deportment, manners (such as the instruction Staines gives in Scene VII, ll. 760-77).

[SCENE III]

OSD. as] as if (see Abbott, 107).
as ... reading] G.F. Reynolds (p. 156), speculates that this SD may indicate a study setting on stage.
282,
283. As ... burne] Cf. Tilley, C 297 (*The burnt child dreads the fire*).
284. fondly] foolishly.
285. turne] (1) turn away (from them); (2) divert, (or) deflect (them).
286. well avoyde] adequately avoid (them): i.e. "I could hardly avoid them."
287. whenas] when.
290. distinguish] perceive clearly, recognize: i.e. make a distinction between the kinds and qualities of things.
291. conceit] conceive, apprehend; hence, *realize*, (or) *conclude*.
292. smoothest meanings] most affable (or) pleasant intentions, (or) purposes.
294. Why] Dodsley's emendation is accepted in lieu of *We* in *Q1-3*.
295. So] such.
sad] deplorable, unsatisfactory.
297. *Petrarkes*] Francesco Petrarca (1304-74).
cunning Quill] skillful pen.

301. away] desist, no more.
302. conjure] (1) appeal to; (2) charge, constrain.
304. want'st] (1) desirest; (2) needest, (or) lackest.
305. turtle] i.e. turtle-dove.
312. protest] An asseveration with the force of *declare*, (or) *affirm*.
319. for pride] so far as pride is concerned.
319,
320. the woman ... her] An allusion to a long *exemplum* in P. Stubbes's *The Anatomie of Abuses* (1595 ed.), pp. 43-4. It concerns a young woman of Antwerp who, frustrated that she could not get her ruffs starched and set to her liking, swore that the devil might take her if she ever wore ruffs again. Thereupon, the devil appeared to her as a young man, set her ruffs to her satisfaction, and then broke her neck, transforming her into a deformed corpse. Later, when her coffin was opened, "they found the body to be taken away, and a blacke Catte very leane & deformed sitting in the Coffin, setting of great ruffes, and frizling of haire, to the great feare and woonder of all the beholders" (p. 44). (During the period, both men and women wore the circular collars known as *ruffs*, which were starched, pleated, or frilled, and made of lace, muslin, or other fine fabrics.)
322. flowt] mock, jeer, be contemptuous of.
322,
323. court-waiting ... progresse] A woman in attendance at Court, accompanying the monarch "on progress," i.e. on a royal visit with a predetermined itinerary.
324. villainous] scurrilous, malicious.
324,
325,
326. for ... legges] *Ballads* in 1. 325 is equivalent to *scurrilous attacks*. The sense of the passage is: "she has such an inventory of invective that she will make scurrilous ballads on the calves of your legs alone."
328. turne] change (i.e. *soften* as preparation for tanning, so that "turne" has the connotation of *changing her color*--altering her behavior, if not her nature).
332. vertues sits] An example of a third person plural verb ending in -*s*, a common Elizabethan inflection (see Abbott, 333).
333. liberally] insolently, licentiously.
339,
340. will ... aire?] i.e. rather than be combative, will you take your cloak and sword and cool off outside?
340,
341. feare thy infection] am apprehensive about your disease (presumably, because of its hopelessness rather than its contagiousness).
343. thoughts] expectations; hence, *aspirations*.

[SCENE IV]

OSD. *Drawer*] tapster.
344. sirra] Form of address used for inferiors.
345. Ipocras] Var. of *Hippocras*: a cordial made of wine and flavored

349. with spices.
pottle] a two-quart tankard.
357. fore-part] An ornamental covering for the breast worn by women; a stomacker.
364. stuffe] woolen cloth.
367. curmogin] Var. of *curmudgeon*: skinflint, miser.
371,
372. doe ... bee] have no doubt that I'll be (see Abbott, 122).
373. Pageants] Temporary structures carried on moving cars as part of a public triumph or celebration.
375. Shrovetuesday] Shrove Tuesday, the day before Ash Wednesday, was a holiday for apprentices, and often called *pancake day* (allusively, a time of merriment).
376. Maligoe] i.e. *Malaga*, a white wine exported from Málaga.
377. zownds] Var. of '*Swounds*: *by God's (Christ's) wounds*; an oath.
386. *Stix*] Greek mythological river of Hades over which departed souls were ferried to the shore of the underworld. As in several other passages, Pursenet swears an oath by something related to the infernal.
388. charge] pledge (with probable bawdy pun on *charge* meaning *to assail sexually*. Cf. Shakespeare, *2H4*, II.iv.120-21, and see E. Partridge, *Shakespeare's Bawdy*, rev. and enl. ed., 1968, p. 78).
389. Doe ... Sergeant] i.e. I would pledge him even under threat of arrest (playing on *charge* to mean *accuse* or *arrest*).
391. wanton] (1) amorous, (or) amorously playful (see Partridge, p. 214); (2) giddy.
392. bawd] procuress.
a carowse] a toast (a full draught to Spendall's health).
399. clowted creame] clotted cream, obtained by "scalding" or heating milk.
rampallion] ruffian, villainous (appearance). Cf. Shakespeare, *2H4*, II.i.59, where, as here, it is applied to a woman, which is rare. The word is apparently derived from "ramp," a low, vicious wanton (see Partridge, p. 172 and Shakespeare, *Cym.*, I.vi.134).
407. good words] i.e. give him good (affable) words. From the elliptical expression in Latin *bona verba*, which has the force of "do not speak so fiercely."
409. complaining] lamenting, plaintive.
410. Supersedeas for] check on. In law, a *supersedeas* is a writ commanding the stay of legal proceedings or suspending the powers of an officer.
413. stand ... bookes] be put on account, i.e. a "charge account."
417. shall's] shall we (go).
420. gingling] Var. of *jingling*: full-pursed, "well-heeled."
421. of] on (see Abbott, 175).
423. Primero] A game of cards, fashionable from about 1530 to 1640.
426,
427,
428. but ... humors] Cf. Tilley, F 178, M 233. Possibly, this passage was influenced by *1H4*, II.iv.92-5. *Humors* in l. 428 = *moods, dispositions*; hence, *occasions*.
428. game] gamble, play.
429. swaggerer] a blustering, insolent quarreller.

430. drabbe] womanize, associate with harlots.
whoore-master] whoremonger, womanizer.
434. angry ... roaring boy] The *roaring boys* were gangs of riotous young men, feared for impulsive and intimidating violence.
435. Eolus defend us] an invocation to *Aeolus*, the Roman god of the winds.
442,
443. pickled oysters worke] Apparently, the pickled oysters he has eaten have resulted in a sudden "call of nature."
448. naked ... out] swords, (or) knives are unsheathed. (Probably a *double-entendre* on *tool*, the male generative organ, in which case, the phrase would also mean, "they are both incensed to violence," or "their dander's up." Cf. Shakespeare, *Rom.*, I.i.31-3 and see Partridge, p. 202.)

[SCENE V]

OSD. *sola*] alone.
451. When as] when.
455. By which] which.
use] practice.
456. for to] to (see Abbott, 152).
460. still] always, ever.
462. sleights] tricks, artifices.
464. Arts] wiles.
465. to ... will] to a desire that pleases us.
470. boy ... Bird-bolt] i.e. Cupid. A *bird-bolt* was a kind of blunt-headed arrow used for shooting birds, allowed children because of its relative harmlessness. Cf. Shakespeare, *Ado*, I.i.42; *LLL*, IV.iii.23; *TN*, I.v.93.
471. passion] a passionate speech or outburst (cf. l. 1287).
472. proper] handsome, well-favored.
473. blacke] dark.
475. convey you] carry you off secretly (i.e. help you to elope).
479. protested] affirmed, vowed.
480,
482. discover] reveal.
484. love-passions] love poems or other literary compositions or passages expressing strong (romantic) emotion.
485. speakest ... booke] repeatest (them) every morning from memory.
486,
487. houre ... Bell-man] an hour after the town crier or night-watchman calls the hour (most probably, 2 AM).
489. for] on account of.
490. for] because of.
492. loose] lose; i.e. *waste*.
497. unknowne] Figuratively, *uncounted*; i.e. *incalculable*.
499. unthrift] spendthrift, prodigal.
503. nimble-chappes] Special collocation for *a talkative person*. Earliest citation in *OED*.
505. Water] A play on words: *Walter* was pronounced *Water* (Hazlitt, p. 201), which Joyce would prefer to being called Mrs. Bubble.
508. Were ... pleasde] if you don't mind.
510. right tricke] characteristic deception, (or) capriciousness.
511. motion'd] proposed.

512. forsooth] truly (used ironically here).
when] while, whereas.
harlotries] silly wenches (as in l. 1393). Cf. Shakespeare, *1H4*, III.i.196, and *Rom.*, IV.ii.14. In fact, ll. 510-24 and 530-1 in this scene are reminiscent of *Rom.*, III.v.126-95, in which Capulet tries to force Paris on Juliet.
513. runne into] incur.
514. Eate ... oate-meale] A popular remedy for "chlorosis," also called the "green-sickness" or "virgins' disease" (*OED*, *chalk*, sb.7). A form of anaemia, "the Elizabethan dramatists emblemized it as a sign of a girl's lovesickness, or of vague desire, for a man" (Partridge, p. 117. See *Rom.*, III.v.156-7).
cry ... corners] Figurative phrase for *secretly grieve from unsatisfied longing*.
520. tyres] dresses, apparel (i.e. *attires*).
522. draw] persuade, entice.
523. Carroach] Var. of *caroche* or *carosse*: a stately or luxurious coach, representative of the later "carriage" for town use.
528. to ... coarse] Var. of *corse*, i.e. *corpse*: to pay my respects to the deceased.
543. answeres] (1) satisfies (my hopes); (2) responds to (my feelings).
546. slight] disdain.
547. The ... esteem'd] A variant of several similar proverbial expressions (cf. Tilley, A 12, F 47, M 20).
548. Things ... deem'd] Proverbial: Tilley (T 201), cites this line as an example.
554. goe to] An exhortation with the force of *come on!*
556. finde in] find it in.

[SCENE VI]

562. *Elizeum*] In Greek mythology, the abode of the blessed.
563. King of flames] Phoebus-Apollo, the sun-god in Greek mythology.
564. answer] satisfy.
565. comfortable] (1) cheering; (2) sustaining (both these senses reinforce the simile expressed in ll. 567-8).
567. illustrate] illustrious, resplendent.
568. wrappes] Var. of *raps*: transports, (or) carries up out of oneself. SD *aloft*] i.e. in the gallery over the back of the stage.
573. What] Interjectionally, "as an exclamation of surprise ... sometimes mixed with indignation ... usually followed by a question" (*OED*, B.2).
575. consumption] a wasting disease (perhaps "lovesickness"), not specifically tuberculosis in the 17th c.
581. doe the feat] "do the deed"; i.e. become my first lover (see Partridge, p. 95).
583. meere immodestie] sheer indecency.
603. uds foot] by God's (Christ's) foot: an oath.
605. geare cotton] business succeed.
607. ha boorded] have boarded; i.e. *have taken her, made love to her* (using the metaphor of boarding a vessel. See Shakespeare, *Ado*, II.i.142-3, Partridge, p. 68).
by this] by this time.
617. withall] with.
629. call's] calls (or possibly, but not probably, *calls us*).

633. conjure] adjure.
635. fasten] hold.
639. love] value.
640. Wilde-witted] rash, impulsive.
643. dearer] more highly esteemed, valued. Cf. Tilley, T 201 and ll. 642-3.
646. at furdest] i.e. at (the) furthest: farthest away. (The sense is: "you're as far away as possible from doing what you intended").
648. Passion] An allusive asseveration here, perhaps *passion of me*! (almost certainly not intended to characterize Geraldine.)
650. stand you] stand to you; i.e. *submit*, (or) *accede to you*.
653. be naught] A quibble on (1) come to nothing, and (2) have illicit sex together (see Shakespeare, *R3*, I.i.99-100, and Partridge, p. 95).
659. faces] courage, nerve (to say so and/or to do it).
663. conclude] consummate (your relationship).
667. SD *ambo*] both.

[SCENE VII]

669. they] i.e. the guests.
674. trencher] plate, platter.
677. man ... man] servant to my servant.
        for] despite.
679,
680. The ... flesh] Proverbial: see Tilley, B 520, who cites this line as an example.
682. The ... sweeter] Proverbial: Tilley (D 188), cites this line as an example.
685. broad-cloth] Inexpensive, usually woolen material.
686. Watling-streete] See Sugden, p. 558, and Stow's *Survay*, pp. 200, 280. Stow describes "Watheling streete" as follows: "True it is, that at this present as of olde time also, the inhabitants thereof were and are, wealthy Drapers, retailors of woollen cloathes both broad and narrowe, of all sortes, more then in any one streete of this Citie" (p. 280).
687. Draper] A dealer in woolen cloth, and by extension, in other textiles.
        for] as for.
690. freeze] (1) coarse woolen cloth with a nap, usually on only one side; (2) leather made imperfectly because of abrasions. Most often, *frieze-coated* meant someone wearing a coat of frizzed, brown or russet leather, so that this is probably the material and color described here.
707. sweeten your conceits] cheer your thoughts. Cf. Shakespeare, *Lr.*, IV.vi.130-1.
715. stomacke] appetite.
719. puddings ... dole] *Puddings* here are either a mixture made from the internal organs of animals or a kind of sausage. There is probably a play on *dole*, meaning both (1) food given to the local poor as charity; (2) sorrow (so that the phrase also means "puddings to alleviate sorrow").
729. fellow] fellow-servant.
732. be brave] i.e. wear gaudy and cheerful apparel.

733. rattle it] to make a rattling noise while walking rapidly; hence, *to display oneself ostentatiously*. First citation in OED of this sense of the verb (*rattle*, v.4).
734. Sculler] boatman (*sculls* were oars).
735. blacke carnation velvet] (1) dark red velvet (?); (2) smooth-textured black velvet (?).
736. *Tu quoque*] Latin for *you also*. The phrase was a proverbial retort to one's accuser, meaning *you are such another* (see Tilley, A 250, and *OED*, which cites the title of the play as its first citation of this expression).
743. seven ells] The English ell waa equivalent to 45 inches. Hence, Bubble is buying almost 9 yards of taffeta alone.
746. Cutlers] For making ornamental daggers and/or swords as part of a gentleman's equipage.
750. snacke] snap (allusively, one who works with dexterity and "flair").
752. fit you] furnish, provide you (with all suitable things); perhaps with a play on "fit you" in the sense of "be too much for you."
754. sawsie] unruly, impertinent.
 as] that.
759. let ... worst] Cf. Tilley, W 914 (*Let him do his worst*).
 his] its (see Abbott, 228).
762. Ordinary] (1) "an eating-house or tavern where public meals are provided at a fixed price; (2) in the 17th c. the more expensive *ordinaries* were frequented by men of fashion, and the dinner was usually followed by gambling; hence the term was often used as synonymous with 'gambling house'" (*OED*, sb.14.b). Obviously, Staines is using the word in the latter sense. In Scene IX, however, gambling precedes the dinner.
766. action] stance, attitude.
 carelesse] (1) unconcerned; (2) complacent, carefree.
767. as] as if (see Abbott, 107).
 engins] weapons.
769. tell] (1) count; (2) disclose (as in l. 1042).
772. a ... hand] a discreet, (or) circumspect nature together with generosity, (or) liberality.
 makes] Third person plural in -s, here with a compound subject (see Abbott, 333).
773. testerne] Var. of *tester*: colloquial for a *sixpence*.
788. gives Armes] Literally, *to show armorial bearings*; hence, *present myself*, (or) *greet others* is the intended sense here (with a possible play on *give arms = advance a hand in greeting*).
791. preferred] advanced, promoted.
793,
794. run ... for't] i.e. incur debts on credit. (Staines is now in an ideal position to run up bills on credit as Bubble's newly-created steward.)
802. vary shapes] change my appearance, assume disguises.
 shift] (1) stratagem, subterfuge; (2) change (?).
804. *Proteus*] In Greek and Roman mythology, a sea-god fabled to assume various shapes. See Tilley, S 285.

[SCENE VIII]

OSD. *Rackets*] tennis rackets.

806. Rubber] (1) a hard brush or cloth to wipe one's clothes clean (?); (2) a towel for drying oneself (?).
811. SD *another*] Apparently *a servant* (such vagueness suggests authorial provenance, rather than prompt-copy).
812. Phaeton] In Greek mythology, the driver of the sun-chariot. *Erebus*] The underworld in Greek and Roman mythology.
812,
813. it went ... Line] L. 864 makes clear that Pursenet is describing play in indoor tennis, so that the phrase means either that: (1) Spendall's shots hit just above the wall markers and/or bounced inside the floor marker just before the back wall; or (2) Pursenet is possibly describing the *line of chase*, i.e. the second impact on the floor (or in a gallery) of a ball which the opponent has not returned (see Stone, "English Sports and Recreations," p. 21). In either case, Spendall is being complimented for making good shots that were not easily returned.
816. has] who has (see Abbott, 244).
818,
821,
829. tell] count.
819. Bond ready] deed prepared. The *bond* here is really a *promissory note*.
822. What ... given] What date have you stipulated for the bond to come due?
824. light] (1) of little weight; (2) bright; (3) pure.
828. warrant] promise, assure (with play on *warrant* = *assurance* in l. 829).
830. Condition] stipulation, provision.
Obligation] (1) contract, agreement; (2) liability.
832. royall *Caesar*] Cf. Shakespeare, *JC*, III.ii.244.
833. Duckes and Drakes] i.e. reckless squandering (on trifles). Orginally, *duck-and-drake* referred to the pastime of skipping stones over water. *OED* cites this line as its first example of the expression used in the sense of *profligacy*, but Tilley records it as a proverbial expression used in this sense as early as 1581 (D 632).
837. merry Greekes] i.e. merry fellows (cf, Tilley, G 454, M 901).
838. *Stukely*] Thomas Stukely (or Stucley) was an adventurer, celebrated in *The Famous History of the Life and Death of Captain Thomas Stukeley* (pub. 1605), and in George Peele's *Battle of Alcazar* (pub. 1594), in which battle he was killed in 1578 (*DNB*, XIX, 123-6).
Sherley] Could refer to any of three brothers of this family, but most probably refers to Sir Anthony Shirley (or Sherley), who became ambassador to Persia, and published his account of his Persian adventures (*His Relation of His Travels into Persia*) in 1613 (*DNB*, XVIII, 121-4).
839. Royalty] munificence, generosity (*OED*, 3).
843. your hand] i.e. sign the bond as a witness. Cf. ll. 843-4 (your ... *Brutus*) and Shakespeare, *JC*, II.i.86 ff. and III.i.184 ff.
854. And] Adversative, equivalent to *but* (*OED*, II.7.b).
stay] wait.

[SCENE IX]

OSD. *Gallant*] finely dressed.
874. Fill] fill my pipe.
876. unrip't] revealed. (This line is the sole example cited by the *OED* of this reflexive and figurative use of the verb *unrip*, 2.b.)
879, 880. whispered ... Barbarie] i.e. suggested to my mind that I escape to the Barbary coast (to "turne pyrate," as in ll. 186-7).
882, 883. prosper ... invention] succeed in your plan and continue most successfully in your (more immediate) scheme.
890. take ... him] draw another into your scheme along with him.
893. crosse ... silver] Scattergood swears by the figure of a cross stamped on one side of his silver coins. In 17th-c. colloquial speech, *crosses* was often used to mean *coins*.
894. hilts ... sword] i.e. another form of swearing by the cross.
895. coach-horse ... captaine] i.e. a mark to be drawn in with my principal quarry. (Cf. Tilley, S 816, and less directly relevant, S 309.)
920. Gleeke] A card-game played by three persons.
922. gleeke] trick, prevail over.
924. a crowne] i.e. 5 shillings (60*d*., rather than the 12*d*. that Longfield suggested as "stakes" for the game).
925. spoile] impair (connoting *tax*); cf. Tilley, B 602 (*To beat [cudgel] one's brains*).
927. Honnor] i.e. The last of the eight cards forming the common stock, which alone is turned up for trumps on which the players wager or "pass," is a king, one of the five "honor" cards in gleek. "Every card in the pack has a numerical value attached to it, reckoned to the respective winners of them in the Tricks. The Honours are counted as follows: Tib, the Ace, fifteen points; Tom, the Knave, nine; Tiddy, the Four, four; and the King and Queen, three points each" (J.S. McTear, "Gleek: A Forgotten Old Game," *The Gentleman's Magazine*, Vol. 287 [October, 1899], p. 365. This article reproduces two 17th-c. descriptions of gleek, J. Cotgrave's from *Wits Interpreter* [1662], and C. Cotton's from *Compleat Gamester* [1674] on pp. 361-3, and follows with a synopsis of the game on pp. 364-7).
930. Why ... thirteene] Scattergood has commenced bidding on the suit or "ruff"--in this case, hearts--and is betting that he will hold more consecutive cards in this suit than either of the other players will hold in any other suit (see McTear, p. 366).
935. ha't for me] take it for my part (i.e. "I pass").
937. Take ... you] i.e. pick up the card you have bid for.
938. out-brav'd] out-bid (in modern gaming slang, "bluffed out").
939. vie] bet, wager on (the suit: the bettor must put in two "counters," i.e. two times the stakes, here, two crowns. See McTear, p. 366).
940. I'le ... it] I'll wager nothing on it (i.e. "I pass").
942. mournavall] Var. of *mournival*: a set of four aces, kings, queens, or knaves (jacks). In ll. 942-4, Staines and Longfield

	are calling for payment on cards they already hold. The holder of a *mournival* of aces is entitled to the payment of eight "counters" from each opponent (here, a total of 16 crowns). See McTear, p. 366.
	gleek] A set of three court cards of the same rank (e.g. three queens) in one hand in the game of gleek. The *OED* cites this line as its earliest example of the noun used in this sense.
942, 943.	gleek of queens] Entitled to half the sum for the corresponding *mournival*, in this case, a total of four crowns from the two opposing players. See McTear, p. 366.
944.	gleeke of knaves] three jacks (entitled to a total of two crowns from the opposing players. See McTear, p. 366).
945.	gleek't] outplayed, beaten.
953.	wilde hand] As in modern gin rummy, no sets of similar cards in threes or fours (*gleeks* or *mournivals*), and not enough cards in one suit to carry a "ruff" (and little to build on, in order to form them in time to win the game).
956.	as ... me] as I hope for God to save me.
960.	stockes] (1) funds (sums set apart for play); (2) the cards on the table forming the players' "common stock"; hence, allusively, *how go the cards?* (?)
964.	heere's ... pounds] i.e. there is here, (or) see here, all of five pounds lost.
967.	SP *Spend.*] Reed and subsequent editors through Hazlitt give this line to *Longfield*, though there seems to be no apparent need to change the *Q1* reading, as it is both logical in the dialogue and in character for Spendall to speak this line.
970.	madd'st wagges] ruinously imprudent fellows.
972, 973.	scot and lot] completely, entirely. Proverbial: see Tilley, S 159.
973.	all ... else] all sorts of expenses besides (with a possible play on *dueties* = *sexual debts*).
980.	pent-house] roof of a lean-to, annex (to give shelter from the rain).
990.	Novum] From Latin *novem* (= "nine"). A game of dice played by five or six persons, the two principal throws being nine and five (cf. Shakespeare, *LLL*, V.ii.544-5).
992.	Broaker] pawnbroker.
994, 995.	twenty marks] A mark was equal to 2/3 of one pound sterling (an amount, not a coin). Hence, Scattergood expects to receive almost 14 pounds on the diamond.
1012.	salute] greet each other, exchange salutations.
1016.	*Gemini*] The constellation also referred to as "Castor and Pollux," inseparable twins.
1017.	Shall I desire] may I ask.
1027.	SD *with Ambush the Broker*] This character is given three lines in this scene (ll. 1070, 1072, 1076), but is given neither an entrance nor exit in *Q1* or in any subsequent edition. It seems most logical that Ambush should enter with Ninnihammer, who was previously sent to him. Although this would have Ambush on stage for some time without speaking, it seems likely that he would follow the gaming in the hope of finding new prey, which

in fact he does with Spendall. (The absence of SDs here,
particularly of Ambush's entrance, is another indication of
authorial provenance.)
1030. I ... dice] i.e. It's my "roll" (my turn to throw the dice).
set] put down your wagers, "place your bets."
1032. mad-cap] reckless, impulsive person (i.e. Joyce).
1033. For me, fix] I stake, (or) put my money on (this number).
1038. Bakers dozen] i.e. thirteen. The *OED* cites this line as its
earliest example of this expression.
1051. condition] character; i.e. *identity*.
1056. The ... soone] An exclamation meaning, *it's as soon the devil
as he* (i.e. from his appearance, I'd as soon believe him to be
the devil as himself).
1058. playes upon] "practices upon"; i.e. *cheats*.
1061. fresh bale] new set. A *bale* was a set of dice used in any
special game, usually a set of three, as here in the game of
Novum.
1064. chafing] fretting, complaining. Ironically, Bubble inappropriately acts on Staines's advice on how to behave while Staines
is gulling him.
1068,
1069. is ... fellow?] This rhetorical question does not necessarily
express a suspicion of being cheated, but is most probably
mere chafing against bad luck. Still, a proverb to describe
a knave in the 17th c. was: "He's as honest a man as any in the
cards when all the kings are out" (Tilley, M 67).
1072. Upon ... pawne] i.e. on an item of equal value as collateral.
1074. three pile velvet] velvet of treble thickness; hence, *velvet
of the highest quality*.
1087. chanc'd with] (1) at risk against; (2) lucky in relation to
(? see *OED*, "chance," v.3).
1091. at] (1) against; (2) to prevail over.
SD *Drawes all*] = withdraws, i.e. *takes all bets to himself* (?).
Cf. 1. 1121 ("drawne" = "taken").
1094. grossely] palpably.
1095. gull'd] cheated.
1119. respect ... credite] regard for your reputation.
1123. Cockes-comb] i.e. head. Here, connotes *fool's head*, as a
cockscomb (or *coxcomb*) was the cap worn by a professional fool,
resembling a cock's comb in shape and color.
1124. But] except.
prating Jacke] boasting knave, (or) idle-chattering, ill-
mannered fellow.
1125. Nor ... clubbes] i.e. nor is it your reliance on calling for
assistance. Two Shakespearean examples of *clubs* used to mean
assistance are found in *1H6*, I.iii.84, and *H8*, V.iii.51.
("Prentices and clubs" was the rallying cry for the London
apprentices.) For the irregular sequence of tenses from 1.
1125 through 1. 1127, see Abbott, 370, and in this construction,
involving the conditional tense in 1. 1126, Abbott, 371.
1130. Soft] not so fast.
1140. Maze in Tuttle] Sugden describes *Tuttle* or *Tuttle Fields* as
follows: "A large piece of open land in Westminster on the
left bank of the Thames, S. of Tothill St. ... Tournaments
were held there, and wagers of battle decided; and till the

	end of the 17th cent. it was a common place for duels.... There was an artificial maze which was frequented by pleasure-seekers" (p. 535). A *maze* here is a network of winding and intercommunicating paths and passages (*OED*), in this case, probably with artificial gardens.
1142.	Single rapier] A thrusting sword (*single* here meaning they would fight without accompanying daggers, gauntlets or bucklers held in their left hands for defense. See L. Stone, "English Sports and Recreations," p. 12).

[SCENE X]

1149, 1150.	thou speak'st ... thinkst] Cf. Tilley, S 725 (*To speak [not to speak] as one thinks*).
1155.	with] from.
1157.	nice ... tricks] coy and reserved wiles (connoting *affectations* here).
1159.	plaine dealing] straightforwardness. Tilley cites this line as an example of the proverbial expression, "plain dealing is a jewel" (P 381).
1160.	And ... Jewell] A possible play on *jewel*, allusively, as "chastity incarnate in the maidenhead" (Partridge, p. 128 and see Shakespeare, *Per.*, IV.vi.154-5).
1162.	should] shall. See Abbott, 326.
1165, 1166.	to ... q] i.e. to come on time more propitiously to play his part (*q* is a spelling of *cue*, i.e. the right time to come "on stage").
1166.	withdraw] retire (to somewhere close by, but out of sight).
1167.	Close, close] i.e. let us be secret (unobserved) and quiet.
1170.	Auroraes] Aurora was the Roman goddess of dawn.
1171.	her delight] joy of her.
1173.	taske] chide, reprove.
1174.	flaring] fitfully shining.
1186.	call] enjoin.
1188.	that] so that.
1189.	take] enjoy, experience.
1190.	But you are] that you are not.
1194.	my ... woman] i.e. I was never inconstant or vacillating (see Tilley, W 653, W 673, W 674, W 698).
1197.	terrible] (1) as an intensive for *tyrannizing*: hence, *exceedingly*; (2) dreadful.
1198.	to turne Turke] i.e. to become an idolator (applied to Geraldine, not to Gartred). Proverbial: see Tilley, T 609.
1200.	fond] foolish, irrationally doting.
1203.	shee's ... nothing] Proverbial: see Tilley, N 258, who cites this line.
1204.	jade] horse.
1208.	in love] on love.
	come in to] accede to, fall in with.
1210.	scurvily] shabbily, contemptuously.
1218.	take the course] choose the right way (cf. 1. 2579).
1219.	goe ... bush] Proverbial: see Tilley, B 742.
1220.	keepe ... verse] make a fuss, much ado with (your) verses.

1224,
1225. Who ... respected] See Tilley, A 12, F 47.
1228. close] out of sight.
1230. with such terrour] so dreadfully.
1232. tedious] painful.
1251. have tane] has taken, reached. Subjunctive, complete present: see Abbott, 366.
his] its.
full height] climax.
1253. Mercurie] Among other attributes, Mercury was the protector of traders and thieves, as well as the god of eloquence and feats of skill; hence, he was associated with trickery and subterfuge. In addition, as a "Mercury" was colloquially a "go-between" in amorous affairs, the god Mercury might be associated here with the attributes of a matchmaker.
1261. contemn'd] scorned.
deluded] beguiled, toyed with.
1262. generall marke] common destiny, (or) purpose.
1274. not] not of.
1285. so] if, provided that.
1296. strength and pollicie] force and cunning.
1301. come ... awake] Cf. Matthew, ix:5-6.
1302. with ... baggage] i.e. entirely, cleanly. (Orginally, *bag and baggage* was military slang denoting *with all belongings*, i.e. *without surrender of anything*. Possibly, there is a bawdy pun intended, *bag and baggage = male genitalia*. See Partridge, p. 134.)
1306. on] of.
1308. Tho ... spirites] i.e. even if all his life-blood had been emptied out of his body. *Vital spirits* was frequently used in the plural form during the period to refer to the force that sustained life (*OED*).
1315. heere's ... Song] Proverbial: see Tilley, E 126.
1320. Colliar] Var. of *collier*: here, not a coal miner, but a *coal carrier* and/or a *maker and seller of wood charcoal*.
fall backe] retreat; hence, *lose heart, hesitate*. (As the following phrase makes clear, Joyce intends a *double-entendre*, *fall back* also meaning *submit sexually*. See Partridge, p. 103 and Shakespeare, *Rom.*, I.iii.42.)
1321. kinde] way.
1323. mad] reckless, wildly impulsive.
1325. lie ... manger] i.e. live in reckless abundance (connoting *abandon* here). Proverbial: see Tilley, R 4.
1326. forbid the banes] To "forbid the banns" is to make a formal objection to the proclamation or public notice given in church of an intended marriage.
1327,
1328. must be great] can be intimate, "thick with" (each other. *OED*, *great*, 19); hence, *can be bound together*.
1328. specially you sister] Suggests a play on *great = pregnant* (i.e. "great with child").
swearing] (1) exchanging oaths or vows; (2) protesting (?).
1333. qualitie] temper, consistency.
trickes] turns, quirks.

[SCENE XI]

1339. This be] let this be.
1340. of] from.
1342. French doublet] A *doublet* was a close-fitting body garment for men; a *French doublet* may refer either to a fashion of the time, or possibly, to a *brigandine*, or *doublet of defense*, i.e. metal plates covered with cloth or leather.
1345. Mauritanian Moore] Loosely, a warrior of Northwestern Africa. "In the Middle Ages, and as late as the 17th c., the Moors were commonly supposed to be mostly black ... and hence the word was often used for 'negro'" (*OED*. Hence, *Moor* here = *Blackamoor*, with Spendall giving the popular notion of the appearance of African warriors).
1348. Guild-hall] As well as the hall where trade-guilds met, a meeting-place for the town and corporation, often synonymous with "town-hall"; hence, used allusively for the general body of citizens in the town.
1354. thy armes] your sword.
1355. Have] Subjunctive form: see Abbott, 361 and *OED* (*have*, 4.a).
1364. Sblood] An oath: *by God's* (*Christ's*) *blood*.
1367. bent] determined.
1369. offer't] attempt it.
1371. motion] proposal.

[SCENE XII]

1380. the vaults unstop'd] the drain, (or) sewer, (or) privy's opened up (i.e. *is leaking*).
1381. guesse] An old variant for *guests* (used only for the plural).
1387. fustian] Coarse cloth made of cotton and flax.
1388. wait] be in attendance to serve.
1389. stirre and talke] bestir myself and give directions.
1391. Pimliko] Pimlico: "A place of entertainment in Hogsdon much resorted to by the Londoners of the 17th cent. for the sake of the fresh air and the cakes and ale for which it was famous" (Sugden, p. 412).
1392. Derby ale] The ale of Derby, a town 110 miles north of London (Sugden, p. 150), was proverbial for its excellence: see Tilley, A 101, who cites this line.
1393. puling] pining.
   harlotrie] Affectionately deprecating for *wench*, as in 1. 512.
1399. Gods pretious] Elliptical: *by God's* (*Christ's*) *precious blood*.
1403,
1404. deceived ... welcome] Cf. Tilley, G 338, L 424 and especially W 258 (*Welcome is the best cheer*). Apparently, the passage expresses a formula of etiquette found again in 11. 2479-80: to deprecate what one has to offer as a host and to assure one's guest that he is more welcome than the modesty of the food or lodging could indicate.
1406. concise roome] a pleasant room, "containing much in little space, small and compact" (*OED conj*.). The *OED* quotes this line as its only example of *concise* used in this inferred, conjectural sense (adj. 2).
1412. comely] seemly, decorous (connoting *graceful* here).

	salute] salutation (probably including both words and a gesture, such as bowing or touching one's hat, as in 11. 2275-6).
1414.	beare you out] carry you through.
1415, 1416.	set ... on't] carry it off well. Tilley (F 17), cites this line as an example.
1416.	that's flat] that's for sure. A proverbial expression of determination: see Tilley, F 345.
	and for] and as for, and as regards (see Abbott, 149).
1417, 1418.	here's ... better] As baker-legged was proverbial for deformed-looking legs, Bubble's assertion is a comically modest one (see OED, baker, 5), and Tilley, B 54 (He should be a baker by his bow legs).
1423, 1424.	Why ... selfe] Cf. Tilley, C 554 (Who commends himself berays himself).
1423.	for] about, on the subject of (= against here).
1426.	else] instead.
1428.	vilely] deprecatingly, degradingly.
1429.	collaud you] praise you highly, extol you(r virtues).
1430.	Let me alone] trust me, (or) leave it to me (as in 1. 2277).
1431.	arrantest] Var. of errantest: (1) most notorious; (2) most complete.
	Cockes-combe] Allusively, a fool, dolt.
1432.	Gipsies ... gerles] Described thus because they have been on an outdoor journey; a playful gibe, as being tanned or sunburned was not fashionable during the period. A Gipsy was often used as synonymous for a dark-skinned person.
1433.	utter] (1) reveal; (2) speak for; (3) give them currency.
	alone] by itself.
1438.	heere] i.e. kissing the older sister.
1439.	in conscience] = truly here.
1443.	set] formal and/or elaborate.
	shall] may.
1446, 1447.	this ... well] An implied stage direction: either Bubble has placed his hands on her and is adjusting her position in relationship to himself, or he is positioning himself before speaking (i.e. he feels he must "set" either his or her "attitude" before beginning his "set speech").
1465.	arranter] more complete, more thorough.
1471.	brother] Bubble and Scattergood have become "sworn brothers"; i.e. they have pledged to be close and lifelong friends (as in 11. 1507-09).
1472.	chose] Choose (Q1-3), is not listed as a variant of the present tense third person singular of the verb in OED. Dodsley's emendation to chose is accepted.
1474.	so] as long as, provided that.
1479.	so scurvily] as sorry, (or) unprepossessing, (or) unattractive. Bubble is carrying out Staines's advice to deprecate himself quite systematically.
1480.	frantique] lunatic, insane.
1484.	worse timberd] more badly framed (made).
1485.	pretty] proper, admirable.

	foure square Legge] having four equal sides.
1493.	bobd] gibed; here, = *scored a hit on,* "*got one up on.*"
1495.	out of] from, because of.
1498.	Augh!] = faugh! (here, an exclamation of mock-disgust.) comes to mee] scores, (or) has, me; = (*she's*) "*got me.*" Perhaps also = *is beginning to appreciate me.*
1499.	clownicall] farcical, clown-like. Only citation in *OED.* bald] graceless, dull.
1509.	goe] dress.
1520.	It ... sir] i.e. that you chose to react so charitably to the incident.
1522.	strange] distant (connoting *diffident* here). Ballance is hanging back as he is reluctant to bring the news about Spendall that he has apparently come to relate.
1531.	layd] marked, sought out.
1538.	have] be subjected to, bear.
	as] as to.
1539.	humors] whims.
1542.	Bewrayes] reveals.
	Generous kinde] well-born stock, gentle birth.
1545.	Guist] i.e. *guest*: *OED* gives *gist* and *giste* as old variants, so it is probable that this was another, perhaps reflecting a regional or dialectical pronunciation of the period.
1552.	strange] Here, connotes *far-off, seldom seen.* *Be not strange* is equivalent to "don't be a stranger."
1556.	*Asinus*] Latin for *ass*: addressed to Scattergood.
	Tu quoque] Here, *counterpart*: i.e. Bubble.
1557.	sweet-fac'd] benign, (or) complacent-looking.
	for] because of (see Abbott, 150).
1558.	countenances] expressions, aspects.
	Alexander and *Lodwicke*] A version of the medieval story of *Amis and Amiloun, Alexander and Lodowick* was the name of a ballad, the title of a play by Martin Slaughter mentioned in Henslowe's *Diary* (p. 79), and is alluded to in John Webster's *The Tragedy of the Duchess of Malfi* (1614, pub. 1623), I.i.572 (in *The Complete Works of John Webster*, Vol. II, ed. F.L. Lucas. Also see Lucas's note in Vol. II, pp. 142-3). The legend concerned two faithful friends who looked so much alike, they could not be told apart. Hence, Rash is saying that Bubble and Scattergood seem identical because of their appearance and attitude when seen together.
1559.	call Brothers] call each other brothers (i.e. become brothers-in-law).
1562.	S'fott] Var. of *'sfoot*: *by God's* (*Christ's*) *foot*.
1564.	couragious] (1) lusty; (2) eager (? *OED*'s last example of the word in this sense dates from the 15th c.).
1564,	
1565.	made ... Waxe] "as faultless as if modelled of wax" (*OED conj.*). Although there are several proverbs using *wax* to suggest pliability or inconstancy (as well as in Shakespeare, *Rom.*, III.iii.126), *a man of wax* (Tilley, D 453), is intended to suggest *a paradigm* or *model of excellence* (as, in this connection, is the intended meaning in Shakespeare, *Rom.*, I.iii.76). This, too, is almost certainly the sense that Rash intends though, characteristically, he is being ironic.

1573. Gloabe] The Globe Theatre (Bankside) was opened in 1599 for the Chamberlain's Men--Shakespeare's company--which became the King's Men in 1603. The Globe was burnt during a performance of Shakespeare's *H8* in 1613 and reopened in 1614. As there is evidence that *Greene's Tu Quoque* was performed at Court in 1611 (see Introduction), this is almost certainly a reference to the Globe before the fire of 1613.

1569-
1576. so ... looke] A *tour de force*, as Bubble's part was originally played by Thomas Greene, whose name ultimately appeared in the title of this play, and who was the leader and clown of Queen Anne's Men, the company that performed this play at the Red Bull Theatre in St. James, Clerkenwell (see Introduction). Hence 1. 1570 (For ... Foole), i.e. that Bubble would have no existence unless accompanied by a fool, could be taken to mean either (1) accompanied by Scattergood; (2) by himself (both because Greene is playing the part of a fool and because he is his company's clown).

1580. men before women] A possible quibble on the man's position in sexual intercourse (cf. "plac'd" in 1. 1581).

1584. busie] eager, importunate.
tutor] instruct.

1585,
1586. spie ... Spectacles] i.e. understand the situation at a glance.

1596. issue] outcome.

1597. streame] (1) direction; (2) force.

1598. buffet] contend. Cf. 1. 1598 and Tilley, W 431 (*To fight against the wind*).

1599. playes upon] blows against.
striv'd] striven (see Abbott, 343).

1601. slave] a submissive servant (a term of contempt).

1602. worse condition'd then] i.e. of a temperament and disposition beneath even those of.

1606. insurrection] revolt (connotes *disorder* or *confusion* here).
traind] led.

1607. bold spirits] (1) courage, resolution; (2) mind, faculties (i.e. the spirit[s] of my nature that made me determined and fearless).

1608. thoughts] feelings.

1610. retyres] withdraws, retreats (reinforces the military metaphor in ll. 1605-6; the subject-noun of the verb, *spirits* in l. 1607, may be considered as singular in thought. See Abbott, 333).
it] As the antecedent is *spirits* in l. 1607, this is an example of "confusion of proximity" (see Abbott, 412).

1611. Fight ... sides] i.e. strike her as hard (contend with her as violently) as you've struck me.

1612. hath] An example of third person plural in *-th*. See Abbott, 334.

1615. make to] approach.

1616. Curbes] Third person plural verb in *-s*, *-es*. See Abbott, 333.

1624. To ... kind] In modern idiom, "to give you a dose of your own medicine." A variant of the proverbial, *to pay one in his own coin* (Tilley, C 507), or *tit for tat* (Tilley, T 356).

1626. I ... vaine] i.e. I'm not in the mood (for it). Cf. Shakespeare,

	R3, IV.ii.116, 118.
1628.	quicke] alive.
1629.	Itro] i.e. I trow = *I think*, (or) *suppose* (used as an expletive, *OED*). Here has the neutral sense of "indeed."
1629-1633.	S'fott ... Charcoale] Cf. 11. 1319-22. These lines have been altered enough from the earlier prose passage they recall to be rendered as verse.
1638-1642.	Doe ... it] Cf. 11. 589-93.
1647.	yet] even now, finally.
1649, 1650.	Passion ... yee] Cf. 11. 648-50. Here, a prose passage has been altered from the verse passage it recalls.
1651.	troe] Elliptical for *I trow*; cf. 1. 1629.
1652.	Yes] Perhaps Dodsley's emendation to *yet* is a better reading, in which case, *yet* would be glossed as in 1. 1647 above. Still, *yes* can be defended, either as an expression of sarcasm, introducing an implied objection, and/or as an expression of impatience (*OED*, 3.c).
1653-1655.	Come ... twentie] Cf. 11. 661-3.
1656.	my ... spit] my spite is exhausted. Proverbial: see Tilley, V 28.
1659.	serve the turne] serve your purposes. though ... Coate] i.e. even if he's dressed as a servant (he's still a man). Cf. Tilley, M 243, M 244.
1664.	waxeth] wax, i.e. *burn* (in the sense of *wax out*, or *burn out* for lack of fuel, as a candle burns toward its extinction).

[SCENE XIII]

1666.	upon] according to my.
1667.	cheare] fare.
1671.	turne good husband] become a careful manager, (or) steward.
1675.	I had been] I would be. (The context suggests the subjunctive is intended. See Abbott, 361.)
1680.	Away, away] no more, enough.
1681.	busse] kiss.
1683.	Rascall] Intended playfully, especially when applied to a woman or girl (cf. in 1. 26).
1684.	fayle] miss, be absent at. Cf. Shakespeare, *Mac.*, III.i.27.
1688.	there's] there are. An example of the *-s* inflection preceding a plural subject (see Abbott, 335).
1693.	cashieard] dismissed from, barred from.
1694.	is turnd Banquerout] has become a bankrupt. ceaszd on] impounded.
1700.	prodigall] spendthrift.
1701.	hang him] = let him be hanged: an imprecation.
1704.	offer] try. fier him out] drive him out (with quibble on "infect with venereal disease." Cf. 1. 1800 and Shakespeare, *Son.*, 144, 1. 14).
1705.	With ... him] with a curse on him (an ironic imprecation coming from a prostitute who gave "the pox," i.e. syphilis).

1713. but] just, merely.
1717. ungratious] (1) unwelcome; (2) unlucky; (3) rude (hence, possibly, *presumptuous* here).
1719. belike] probably (as in l. 2164).
relieve] deliver, rescue.
1720. clap] shut.
1723. am] have. Subjunctive auxiliary form (see Abbott, 362).
1724. Even in the] within the very.
1726. thou Sees] Second person singular verb ending in -s rather than in -st, perhaps because of the influence of the northern inflection (Abbott, 340).
1729. Or] = *moreover* here.
1733. in good Sooth] truly.
1749. And if] if.
a would a] he would have (*OED*, have, v. and Abbott, 402).
tooke] taken. "Owing to the tendency to drop the inflection *en*, the Elizabethan authors frequently used curtailed forms of past participles" (Abbott, 343).
1753. But ... while] only for an instant (the time of a lightning-flash).
1756. locall] circumscribed.
1758. unlade] unload.
1763-
1765. Mayst ... Cart] Whipping was a common punishment for prostitutes; to be carried through the streets in a cart was the standard punishment for a bawd (*OED*, cart, v.).
1764. Beldame age] old age. (*Beldame* here has the additional meaning of *loathsome*, or *hag-like*.)
1766. Upholster] upholsterer.
Venerie] vice, licentiousness.
1769,
1770. Aqua ... withall] E.A.M. Colman notes in *The Dramatic Use of Bawdy in Shakespeare* that in John Marston's *Malcontent* (V.i.19), *aqua vitae* is referred to as a restorative for bawds (p. 183).
1771. at doore] outside a (stranger's) door; i.e. *in the street*.
1775. French Canniball] venereal disease (probably syphilis). *OED* cites this line as an example of one of the various epithets given to venereal disease, beginning with the adjective *French* (e.g. *French pox*, *French aches*, etc.).
1777. draw resort] i.e. induce them to repair to you (with the force of *making pilgrimage*).
1780. honest] chaste.
1787. profitable] useful, valuable.
1791. By *Dis*] An oath on the Roman name for *Hades* or *Pluto* (i.e. *Hell*).
Dis before] begin with, i.e. swear by Dis.

[SCENE XIV]

1794,
1795. Jupiter ... fingers] i.e. may Jupiter (Jove) send me good fortune. The line recalls the image of the Greek god Zeus sending down from his hand good and ill fortune indiscriminately from two urns.

1795,
1796.   ther's ... him] Cf. Tilley, L 505 (*Love has no respect of persons*).
1795.   estate] class, degree.
1796,
1797.   will ... minut] The *Isle of Man*, an island in the Irish Sea, is roughly equidistant from the coasts of England, Scotland, and Ireland. Sugden cites this line as an example of a *double-entendre*, the *Isle of Man* here used primarily in the sense of the microcosm man (p. 330).
1798.   *Middle-sex*] The county which includes London and Westminster (with a play on female genitalia [= "sex"], which are in the "middle" of the "Isle of [Wo]Man").
        keepes his Christmas] i.e. holds his Christmas (makes holiday).
1799.   mantion] mansion (i.e. residence, dwelling-place). Also an allusion to the human body as the "mansion of love," i.e., "the vehicle of love's physical activities" (Partridge, p. 145. Cf. Shakespeare, *Rom.*, III.ii.26-8).
1804.   fetch ... againe] gasp for breath afterwards.
1805,
1806.   O ... Starres!] A possible parody of a well-known passage from Thomas Kyd's *The Spanish Tragedy* (pub. c. 1592), which begins: "Oh eyes! no eyes, but fountains fraught with tears" (III.ii.1). At least the style represented by the passage is parodied here.
1808.   Keepe your station] Hold your position (the military metaphor being continued in "incounter" and "comming on" in l. 1809).
1810.   Base-vyoll] i.e. the *viola da gamba*.
        Consort] concert.
1811.   Sprightly ... Trebble] lively, (or) lighthearted, as the viol (i.e. the instrument of highest pitch, as contrasted with the "Base-vyoll," assigned to play the ground base or undersong).
1812.   play thy prize] i.e. engage in the contest with all your weapons. L. Stone in "English Sports and Recreations," explains that "playing a prize" is the process by which an aspirant became a "master of arms." The contestant "had to challenge all masters within a certain radius with a certain number of weapons for a prescribed length of time" (p. 12).
        Sciense] craft, art. (*Self-defense*, since at least the 16th c., was called *the noble science* or *art of defense*, similar to "honorable Sciense" here.)
1814.   wot off] know of.
1815.   disturbance] interference (perhaps connoting *distraction* here).
1816.   Silver Game] i.e. the prize, (or) quarry, of the hunt (?). This inference is made for three reasons: (1) *game*, during the 16th-17th c., could mean *sport derived from the chase* (e.g. Shakespeare, *LLL*, IV.ii.166), or *sexual quarry being hunted* (e.g. Shakespeare, *3H6*, III.ii.14); (2) some game could be described as "silver"--with the obvious analogy to a woman--such as the *hare* (see E.A.M. Colman, p. 197 and Partridge, p. 118), or the so-called *silver plover* or *snipe*; (3) ll. 1816-7 go on to use the metaphor of hitting the target in archery, thereby reinforcing the probability that "Silver Game" is the hunter's (i.e. wooer's) quarry.
1816.   give ayme] guide you (depending on the success of your courtship).

CRITICAL NOTES   147

1817.   hallow ... Clout] shout when (as a sign that) you've hit the
        target. (In archery, a *clout* was a piece of cloth serving to
        mark the center of the target. Cf. Shakespeare, *LLL*, IV.i.134
        and *Lr.*, IV.vi.92.)
1819.   opportunatly to] opportunely into.
1828.   a fooles Paradice] a false paradise (under the delusion of
        being "in heaven"). Proverbial: see Tilley, F 523.
1829.   for a draw-latch] i.e. instead of using a string, which hangs
        on the outside of a door by which a latch is drawn or raised.
        Only citation in this sense in *OED*.
1830.   thrumming of Caps] Literally, "to cover caps with thrums"
        (ornamental fringes). A proverbial phrase for *trifling*, (or)
        wasting work (or) *time*. See *The Oxford Dictionary of English
        Proverbs*, 3rd. ed., p. 820: *To thrum caps (buttons)*.
        for the matter] because of a matter (of this kind).
1834.   saw] An example of irregular sequence of tenses: see Abbott,
        370.
1835.   fit] answer fittingly.
1837.   subtile] sly, crafty.
        flouting] mocking, insulting.
        rogue] One of a mischievous disposition (*OED*, sb.3).
1837,
1838.   laugh ... countenance] disconcert or humiliate you with scorn.
1838,
1839.   talke ... her] i.e. talk to her for me, (or) for my part, on
        my account. "Me, thee, him, &c. are often used, in virtue of
        their representing the old dative, where we should use *for me*,
        by me, &c. ... This is especially common with *me*." (Abbott,
        220.)
1839.   wantonly] capriciously, frivolously.
        slightly] (1) carelessly; (2) slightingly.
1841.   carry ... wilt] Cf. Tilley, B 275 (*He bears away the bell*).
        Bully] Having the force of (*that's a*) *fine fellow*!
1845.   enquiring] inquisitive.
1846.   let] Has the force of *set*, *place*.
1847.   ceases on] seizes on.
1853.   has conspired] Third person plural verb ending in *-s* (see
        Abbott, 333).
1854.   play upon] make sport of, ridicule.
1859,
1860.   She ... motion] Cf. Tilley, M 1209 (*He scorns the motion*).
1860.   motion] proposal (connoting *overture* here).
        braying] crying out (connoting *whining*).
1865-
1874.   One ... doth] From the First Sestiad, ll. 255-64 of Marlowe's
        Hero and Leander. *One is no number* is proverbial: see Tilley,
        O 54.
1868.   Though] even if.
        never singling] i.e. who never separates ("neuer-singling"
        in Marlowe [1st. 4°, 1598, sig. C1]).
        couple] join (in wedlock).
1870.   Thinkes] Third person plural verb in *-s* (Abbott, 333).
        "Thinke" in Marlowe.
        all other things] In Marlowe, "all earthly things" (the *Q2*
        emendation to *things* is accepted; *Q1* has *thing*).

1875. have ... kind] i.e. I'll attempt to persuade you in another style of speech. *Have at you* was a formula to announce an attack.
1883,
1884. an other vaine] another vein; i.e. *another style.*
1889. to] for.
1890. choose but madde] help but madden (infuriate).
1892. guld] gulled.
1893. take libertie] be pleased to.
1894. Speake ... satisfied] Cf. Shakespeare, *Rom.*, II.i.9.
1895. but say but *Mum*] only say *mum*. *Mum* denotes an inarticulate sound made with closed lips. Variant of the proverbial *no word but mum* (Tilley, W 767).
1896. accent] syllable.
1897. direction] guidance, instruction.
1901,
1902. *Westminster* ... vacation] i.e. the London courts of justice during the long summer recess. Westminster Hall, the Great Hall of the Royal Palace of Westminster, housed the Courts of Common Law, Chancery, and the King's Bench (Sugden, p. 561; Stow's *Survay*, pp. 386-92).
1913,
1914. in my conscience] in reason, from all I can see.
1914. comfortable] comforting, soothing.
1917. worke] manifest.
1918. vent] unburden itself. (The most suitable sense, though the earliest example of this meaning of the verb given by *OED* dates from c. 1626.)
1920. Looke to your selfe] protect, (or) look out for, yourself; i.e. *you're on your own.*
1921. Brazen head] An allusion to the oracular head of brass, best known in England from the story of Friar Bacon, popularized in Robert Greene's *Friar Bacon and Friar Bungay* (pub. 1594).
1922. that] such.
        fly] run away.
1924. Just] squarely, right.
1925. What] who.
1927. fashion] sort, station.
1928. Brokers] Could be intended either as a plural or a possessive. A *broker* here is a dealer in second-hand goods, corresponding to the modern "jobber" in the wholesale trade.
1929. cast] cast-off; i.e. *discarded.*
1932. A ... you] i.e. A servant's coat and livery better become you.
1933. untrusse ... Poynts] unfasten your master's doublet from his hose; i.e. *help your master to undress* (as a valet).
1938. which] what.
1941. Oacker] Var. of *ochre*; i.e. *pigment.*
1942. Buckram] linen or cotton fabric.
1947. once] ever.
1951. cockerd with] (1) fostered by; (2) pampered by, indulging in. suggestion] prompting.
1952,
1953. meate ... Maister] i.e. a dish prepared for your master. Variant of the proverbial *she is meat for your master* (Tilley, M 837). Cf. Shakespeare, *2H4*, II.iv.125-6.

1956. for your Hatt] i.e. in return for your taking off your hat in salutation.
1957. as ... is] as the common (vulgar) trait (habit) is. Apparently, *trickes* is intended as singular in thought, similar to "manners" (see Abbott, 333). In addition, *trick* in the sense of *sexual stratagem* may be an intended meaning here (see Partridge, p. 205).
1958. sir reverence] An apologetic formula for introducing an offensive remark. Tilley cites this line as an example of this proverbial expression (R 93). In addition, *reverence* seems to carry the additional meaning here of *civility* or *courtesy* (*OED*, sb.2).
1961. Kindnesse] compassion, good will.
Lightnesse] wantonness.
1962. Favour] (1) a token of good will; (2) a mark of favor represented by some article or trinket.
1965-
1967. Men ... us] Cf. *Ram-Alley*, ll. 2182-6 (see Appendix), and cf. Tilley, V 68 (*To nourish a viper [snake] in one's bosom*).
1971. Furie] i.e. fury: a tormenting infernal spirit, often personified as a ferociously angry woman (*OED*, sb.6).
1982. Wild-cat] savagely ill-tempered woman. Cf. Shakespeare, *Shr.*, I.ii.196.
1983. carry ... away] thus carry the day.
1984. Champion] defender, (or) contender on your behalf (perhaps connoting *sponsor* here).
1985. Not] neither.
1995. Bandes] neck-bands (collars).
1996. Inn's a Court] Colloq. var. for *Inns of Court*: four sets of buildings in London (the Inner and Middle Temples, Lincoln's and Gray's Inns), belonging to the four legal societies which have the exclusive right to admit would-be lawyers to the bar and to maintain a law school; hence, the *Inns of Court* also represent the four societies themselves. See Stow's *Survay*, p. 327; Sugden, p. 268.
1996,
1997. faire ... Hangers] two handsome (matching?) loops or straps on a sword-belt, often richly ornamented.
2001,
2002. A ... selfe] Cf. Tilley, W 677 and W 678.
2005. pastime on] diversion of.
2013. try] test.
nimble footmanship] rapid agility. Only example in *OED* of *footmanship* in this figurative sense. Cf. *nimble-chappes* in 1. 503.
2014. SD *list*] choose, please. (The vagueness of this SD strongly suggests authorial provenance.)
2015. SP *Rash*.] The *Q1-3* speech-prefix *All speake.* seems clearly mistaken in view of the preceding SD *Rash speakes to Stayns*; nor do ll. 2015-16 lend themselves to more than one speaker. Because of the similarity in the wording of the following SD, it is possible that this SD represents an error in foul papers, or, what seems even more likely, a compositorial error.
2024. she ... Nuts] i.e. nothing has impaired her voice (?). Cf. Tilley, A 298 (*Apples, pears, and nuts spoil the voice*).

	Whatever its specific intended meaning, the phrase clearly comments on her loquacity.
2025.	Gentlemen] Emended from *Gent.* in *Q1-3, gent.* being a common abbreviation for *gentlemen*. Previous editors, from Dodsley through Hazlitt, emend to *gentle*, but the subsequent *Brothers I might say*, seems to make clear that the intended word is *Gentlemen*.
2026.	clap hands upon't] strike hands on it; i.e. *come to an agreement*, (or) *strike a bargain*. Cf. *clap it up*, 1. 2552.
2027.	Sister] i.e. sister-in-law to be (to Gartred).
2028.	collogue] confer.
2032.	be ... you] keep you in mind.
2035.	is] has. In passive verbs, particularly intransitive verbs of motion, *is* is often interchangeable with *has* (Abbott, 295).
2036.	warme] = exercised.
2037.	woulst] wouldst.
2037, 2038.	eate ... Lickorish] Var. of *liquorice*: i.e. for the purpose of conditioning my jaws and/or stimulating my tongue for such rapid talk (?).

[SCENE XV]

OSD.	*Hold-fast*, and 1. 2089 SD *Hold.*] The *Q3* emendations are accepted in lieu of *Q1 Lock-fast* and *Q2 Lock*. Speech-prefixes throughout the scene refer to the character as *Hold*. This is another indication of the authorial provenance of the MS from which *Q1* was printed.
2044.	fourtnights Commons] two weeks' rations (provisions).
2049.	say] says. Present subjunctive inflection (*OED*, v. A.4 and Abbott, 361).
2050.	plaine] blunt.
	Ward] Division or separate department of a prison. The prison was divided into areas segregated by the prisoners' ability to pay for food and other amenities (*OED*, sb. 17.a).
2054.	Philosophers Stones] The legendary *philosopher's stone*--one of three--was supposed to be able to turn baser metals into gold or silver. Possibly, a bitter quibble on *stones = testicles*. Cf. Shakespeare, *2H4*, III.ii.329-30, and *Tim.*, II.ii.110-11: " ... like a philosopher, / with two stones moe than 's artificial one."
2054, 2055.	clip Or coyne] clip the edges from coins or make counterfeit coin. Possibly, a play on *coyne = engender illicitly*: cf. E.A.M. Colman, p. 219, Partridge, p. 81, and Shakespeare, *Cym.*, II.v.5-6 ("Some coiner with his tools / Made me a counterfeit").
2056.	occasions] needs.
2058.	belike] apparently.
2061.	You're best] you had best, you had better (see Abbott, 230).
2062.	in] to, into.
	Two-pennie Ward] In his description of the *Counter* (or *Compter*), the London debtors' prison where Spendall is lodged, Sugden notes that: "The accommodation afforded to the prisoners depended on what they could pay. There seem to have been 4 grades: (1) the Master's side; (2) the Knights' Ward; (3) the

Two-penny Ward; and (4) the free Quarters, or the Hole" (p. 133).
2063. Is] which is, it is (see Abbott, 403).
2064. Hol1] The *hole* was "one of the worst apartments in the Counter prison in Wood Street, London" (*OED*). Also see Stow's *Survay*, p. 284.
2068. Such ... Carted] Procurers were publicly punished by being drawn through the streets in a cart and pelted by the crowd (cf. 11. 1764-5).
2072. Scrue] screw up your face to show your contempt.
contemptibly] contemptuously.
2073. surely] surly; i.e. *supercilious*.
groome] male attendant (connotes *lackey* or *underling* here).
2074. mallapertnes] impudence, sauciness.
2078. duetie] proper respect.
2079. slavish] vile, base (connoting *petty*).
2092. Stocke] blockhead. Cf. "like ... Stocke" (ll. 2091-2), with Shakespeare, *Shr.*, I.i.31: "Let's be no Stoics nor no stocks, I pray."
2096. this two yeare] for these last two years (*OED*, *this*, adj. II.1.f).
2099. faire estate] ample fortune, substantial means.
2112. SD *Prisoners*] Here, as in l. 2137, the plural is given in the SD, though apparently only one prisoner speaks during the scene. This is a possible indication of authorial provenance.
2113. Bread and Meate-man] one who distributes food. (For *Heer's ... come*, see Abbott, 295.)
2119. *Aqua fortis*] Nitric acid, or a similar corrosive.
2122. hold ... further] keep your jaws further away.
2125. powderd] salted, seasoned.
2130,
2131. it ... Victuals] i.e., even a dog would complain if it lacks its food. Cf. Tilley, D 533 (*Dogs must eat*), and Shakespeare, *Cor.*, I.i.205-6.
2135. give it] give it to (see Abbott, 201).
2135,
2136. seasond for] properly conditioned to be one of.
2145. full paunched] big-bellied.
2148. they're] Equivalent to *it's* (as *they're* and *are* modify *Sustenance* in l. 2147). An example of "confusion of proximity" (see Abbott, 412).
abusde] befouled.
2149. vild] vile.
2152. That] if that.
2153. impression] remembrance, effect.
2157,
2158. Experience ... sinke.] Cf. Tilley, D 324, G 27, W 329.
2158. Drabs] whores.
2168. able] wealthy and/or influential.
2173. For ... payment] i.e. for paying your debts on the day specified.
2175. Duties ... House] household bills.
to] for.
2183. That have] who have (the subject is *you* understood). *That* and *who* were often transposed during the period. See Abbott, 258

152   GREENE'S TU QUOQUE

         and 259, 1b.
2185.   a competent estate] comfortable or adequate means.
2189.   glad] am glad.

                        [SCENE XVI]

OSD.   gallanted] gaily or showily attired. OED cites this SD as the
         sole example of the word in this sense (OED, gallant, v. trans.
         I.2).
2192.   Jacke-alent] A puppet set up as a target for children to throw
         at (see Tilley, J 9).
2194.   becke] wave.
2195,
2196.   broken shinnes] i.e. the skin broken on my shins. Cf. Shake-
         speare, Rom., I.ii.52.
2201.   Que ... Coxcombie] Double-talk which would get a laugh at the
         still-recognizable final word.
2204-
2210.   I ... therein] If this is a gibe at Coryate's Crudities (pub.
         1611), we have a terminus a quo for the play. There is evi-
         dence that it was first performed at Court in 1611 (see
         Introduction).
2204.   perfect] fully accomplished, complete.
2209.   lowsie] miserable, unlucky.
2211.   are ... man] Cf. Tilley, I 88: You are Ipse (he, the man).
2216.   Exchange] i.e. The New Exchange, directly across from the
         Strand (see ll. 73, 850).
2218.   Genteell] (1) fashionable; (2) polished.
2218,
2219.   doe affect] (1) aspires to; (2) fancies. (An emphatic form
         of affects: see Abbott, 306.)
2219.   Genorositie] Here, probably nobility (with the connotation of
         high style).
         instituted] arranged according to, framed (OED, institute,
         v. 1.c).
2220.   nature ... habit] character, manners, and fashion.
         most exactest] most strictly correct, (or) most punctilious.
         Elizabethan double superlative (see Abbott, 11, and cf.
         Shakespeare, JC, III.ii.183).
2222.   neatest] most elegant, smart.
2225.   me] myself (ethical dative: see Abbott, 223).
2226.   but by qualitie] only by ability or by sheer ability.
         to ... build] to strive for and gain reputation.
         professing] teaching.
2227.   humane] gentle, courteous; hence, elegant, polite.
2228.   peculiar] exclusive, uncommon (as well as, with obvious irony,
         strange or queer).
2229,
2230.   has ... endes] Proverbial: See Tilley, F 245, T 413.
2233.   Bumbard] driveller.
         hee will ... burst] he will begin with swagger or bluster, but
         will be found insipid or empty at last.
2234.   smooth and loftie] polished and elevated (noble).
2235.   Cozen germane] cousin-german, first cousin.
2236.   salute] salutation.

CRITICAL NOTES   153

2238. infoldes ... sence] includes or contains two meanings.
       for] for in.
2240. imports] (1) implies; (2) denotes.
2243. the great Sophy] the Shah of Persia.
2245. Italianated] Italianized in appearance and behavior. The
       attitude of the audience toward the aping of Italian manners
       and dress can probably be inferred from the proverb *an English-
       man Italianate is a devil incarnate* (Tilley, E 154).
2248. opounctly] Reed glosses this word as *opportunely* (p. 94, n.
       35), but it seems to be derived--perhaps coined--from *punct*,
       i.e. *dot*, *point*, (or) *instant*. Hence, *opounctly* is equivalent
       to *on the dot*, (or) *punctually* (OED, *punct*, 1, 6).
2249. disrancke] disorder or put out of place.
       phisnomie] Var. of *physiognomy*.
2258. set ... matter] assume a bold yet dignified deportment in your
       business (courtship). *To set a good face on the matter* was
       proverbial: Tilley, F 17.
2259. Band] neckband, collar, ruff.
       to] fastened, pinned to.
2264. grosse, naught, inconvenient] crass, worthless, unseemly.
2265,
2266. stood ... Sargiants] was in peril of arrest (so that he jammed
       his hat over his eyes as a disguise).
2268,
2269. set ... so] set it on my head in the same way.
       Ellipsis of *it*: see Abbott, 404. (Possibly, the text is faulty
       and *set't* was intended, rather than *set on*.)
2270. remove] move, reposition.
2271,
2272. altogeather backward] entirely behind (the front of your face):
       Staines could be referring to a *hatband*, rather than to a
       shirt collar.
2275. condition you off] caution you of, alert you to.
       affront or salute] encounter and/or salutation (probably, a
       bow). Cf. *affront* and Shakespeare, *Ham.*, III.i.31.
2276. heere] Staines is illustrating either (1) a bow (?); (2) touch-
       ing the hat with a finger as in a salute (?).
       curtesie] (1) a bow (?); (2) gesture of greeting, salutation
       (?).
2278. carrie it away] carry the day; i.e. *execute it perfectly*.
       reach my] hand me my.
2284. Sa'y so?] Var. of *say ye so?* (?)
2287. eare] Var. of *ere*; i.e. *ever*.
2289. apparance] Var. of *appearance*. As *Q1* had *apparace*, the foul
       papers or MS from which *Q1* was printed might well have had
       apparăce.
2290. extasie] trance; i.e. *utter bewilderment*.
2295. I ... practise] I thought it up on my own initiative.
2305. rarely] unusually.
2309. rare] unusually acute, discerning.
2318,
2319. another ... pickle] someone else in the same boat. Cf. Tilley,
       B 365a, B 491, P 276.
2320. Hobby-horse] In the morris-dance or on stage, a simulated
       figure, fastened to which an actor imitated the movements of

2320, 2321.	a horse; hence, allusively, as here, a *buffoon*. is not forgotten] had not been left out. *The hobby-horse is forgot,* apparently a proverbial expression (*OED*), seems also to have been quoted from a ballad (e.g. Shakespeare, *LLL*, III.i.29, and *Ham.*, III.ii.135). Rash's meaning is that Scattergood and Bubble predictably imitate each other, even in outlandish ways.
2327.	tatterd-de-malian] Var. of *tatterdemalion*, i.e., *beggarly, ragged.* Earliest citation of this adjective in *OED*.
2332.	as Innocent ... borne] Proverbial: see Tilley, B 4.
2334.	Felts] Hats made of cloth, and/or of wool, fur, or hair.
2335.	Beaver] Hats made of beaver were fashionable, but relatively expensive.
2342.	blocke] mould; hence, *fashion* (of hat).
2348.	What] who, what manner of man.
2352, 2353.	Doe ... see] would ... should see; know ... see] would know ... should see. Conditional takes present tense form for vividness (see Abbott, 371).
2383.	earnest] pressing.
2391.	live ... limit] Cf. Tilley, C 577 (*Live within compass*).
2402, 2403.	the ... out] your palm indicates that your days as a single maid are over.
2409, 2410.	For ... *quoque*; to ... forefathers] Both phrases are euphemisms for consummating a marriage.
2413.	matter] news, information.
2414.	Matter] corrupt matter, purulence.
2415.	strike home] strike effectively, i.e. fatally.
2416.	blew Infection] disease, plague (possibly referring to the bluish appearance of the skin that accompanies some acute or morbid states of grave illness).
2419.	The ... doome] The Day of Judgement.
2420.	T'would ... us] Cf. Tilley, D 88: *It will be a black* (*bloody*) *day to somebody.*
2426, 2427.	lead ... Wildernesse] Cf. J. Webster, *The Tragedy of the Duchess of Malfi* (1614, pub. 1623), I.i.404-6 (in *The Complete Works of John Webster*, ed. F.L. Lucas, Vol. II).
2439.	trudge, trudge] Cf. Tilley, K 140: *Walk, knave, walk.*
2440.	With ... them] A bawdy quibble, apparently meaning that by turning "your backes" to me, I will not seem to be concerned while you "face" them.
2450, 2451.	brace Of Beagles] pair of constables (i.e. Sir Lionel could restrain the couples by force of law while forbidding the banns).
2451.	you shall ... to night] none of you shall be sent for tonight. (*Bid* was used to mean *invite* to a wedding, feast, etc.)
2454.	Eunuch in wit] witless, barren of invention.
2455.	Father ... Feast] originator or contriver of a joyous occasion. Weddings traditionally end with a "feast" or "banquet" as at the end of Scene XIX. There seems to be no persuasive reason

CRITICAL NOTES   155

         to emend *Feast*, which appears in *Q1-2*, to *jest*, as in *Q3* and
         all subsequent editions.
2457.   SD *strangely*] coldly, distantly.
2458.   How ... adversitie] Cf. Tilley, P 611, T 301.
2462.   A ... himselfe] Cf. Tilley, D 401, M 195.
2463.   once ... estate] waver only once in his prospects; hence,
         stumble only once in his fortunes.
2464-
2466.   Friendship ... my selfe] Cf. Tilley, R 61: *To lean upon (trust
         to) a broken reed*.
2465.   to] on.
2466.   Free of my selfe] entirely on my own.
2468.   thrust out] force, (or) make, my way.
2470.   argument] token, evidence.
2475.   Geneus] genius, (1) the attendant spirit allotted to every
         person at his birth to govern his fortunes, etc.; (2) dis-
         position, inclination.
2476.   active] sexually lively.
2477.   catch at] snatch at, try to lay hold of impulsively.
2477,
2478.   there's ... thought] See Tilley, W 673, W 674, W 698.

                          [SCENE XVII]

2480.   could] would.
2486.   As earnest of] as a pledge for.
2491.   send ... resurrection] have you wake up early (and safely).
         Cf. Tilley, G 187: *God grant your early rising do you no harm*.
2492.   God-night] good-night, God give you good-night (as in 1. 2490).
2500-
2658.   How ... day] Cf. ll. 2500-2658 in this scene and their source,
         L. Barry's *Ram-Alley* (1608, pub. 1611), ll. 2149-2253 (see
         Appendix). G. Langbaine in *An Account of the English Dramatick
         Poets* (1691), compares and contrasts these two scenes as follows:
         "The Plot of *Spendall's* gaining the Widow *Raysby*, has a near
         resemblance with that of *Will. Small-shanks* and Widow *Taffety*:
         [i.e. in *Ram-Alley*] tho' I think the Design is better wrought
         up in this Play, [i.e. *Greene's Tu Quoque*] because the Widow
         by a Counter-plot frees her self from *Spend-all*, and after having
         made a Tryal of the Sincerity of his Love, consents of her own
         accord to Marry him" (p. 72). A subsequent, though far more
         loosely-based imitation of the scene in *Ram-Alley* can be found
         in W. Rowley's [?] *A Match at Midnight* (c. 1622, pub. 1623),
         though here a widow is threatened with no more than a compromis-
         ing impropriety (in W.C. Hazlitt's ed. of R. Dodsley's series,
         A Select Collection of Old English Plays, 4th. ed., 1875, Vol.
         XIII, IV.i., pp. 77-81).
2505.   plyant] compliant, accommodating.
2513.   unthrift] spendthrift, or profligate.
         shame] propriety, decency.
2517.   Importund] urged, impelled. The *Q3* reading is substantively
         adopted (*Q3* has *Importun'd*), in lieu of *Importure* in *Q1-2*. It
         is probable that a compositorial misreading occurred of MS
         Importund: a misreading of final "d" as "e" was common in sec-
         retary hand (see McKerrow, *An Introduction to Bibliography*, pp.

	343, 346). Such a misreading would have been more likely had there been no apostrophe preceding the final "d" in MS, as with *moovd* in l. 2514. If, however, the *Q1* reading of *Importune* is correct, there is an irregular sequence of tenses here (see Abbott, 370).
2518.	Sirra] Here, used to express contempt and/or a reprimand.
2520.	attempt] (1) attack, assault; (2) attempted seduction.
2522.	hold your Clapdish] stop your mouth. First citation in *OED* of *clap-dish* used jocularly for *a talkative mouth*. Originally, it meant a wooden dish with a lid, carried by lepers and beggars to warn of their approach and to receive alms.
2529.	Totter] swing from the gallows.
2529, 2530.	to ... Lynings] to scratch out my life in dirty or scurvy clothing.
2533.	Lordships] domains, estates.
2534.	fayre] considerable.
2534, 2535.	have ... in] Cf. Tilley, H 520: *Not to have a hole to put one's head in*.
2535.	Coppy-hold] plot of land. Orginally, tenure of lands being parcel of a manor.
2538.	livelihood] liveliness (connoting *virility*).
2539.	quicken] stimulate, revive.
2540.	decayed] fallen off (connoting *dormant, untapped*).
2541.	lusty] vigorous.
2543.	Muscadine] In full, *muscadine-wine, muscatel.* Eggs] Raw egg in liquor was thought to be effective as an aphrodisiac (see E.A.M. Coleman, p. 192, and Shakespeare, *Wiv.*, III.v.30-32).
2547.	coffing ... forwards] coughing at both ends; i.e. *coughing and breaking wind*.
2550.	steam] noxious vapor, odor.
2552.	clap it up] agree on it, settle it.
2555.	Untrusse your Poynts] undress.
2572, 2575.	put up] put away, sheathe.
2579.	tak'st the course] Elliptical: *take the right way (to win a widow)*. Cf. Tilley, M 17, M 18.
2585.	Hymens] Hymen was god of marriage.
2588.	Heere ... provided] Spendall has apparently brought a *penner*, i.e. a *pen-case*, often carried together with an inkhorn (cf. l. 2848).
2590.	faire] clearly, neatly.
2591.	at large] (1) in full; (2) boldly (?).
2599.	naughty] wicked. (A stronger word of opprobrium than in modern usage.)
2601.	Adamant] loadstone, magnet. SD *Binde ... poast.*] Perhaps done as pantomime.
2620.	new fancied] newly-imagined.
2622.	guilded o're] covered over with a thin film of gold plating.
2624.	it] i.e. the gilding of delusion.
2632.	mischiefes] Here, *words of mischief* (*OED, mischief*, n.9.d); i.e. *abuse* and/or *wickedness*.
2644.	all] of all.

2647. divorc'd] (1) repudiated; (2) dispelled.
2658. drawes up] draws upon, overtakes. This sense of the verb is clearly the one intended, though the earliest example in OED dates from 1795 and was originally a term from racing (draws [up], v. 89.h).

[SCENE XVIII]

2662. if ... not] = I do.
with] by.
2664,
2665. It ... feare] Cf. Tilley, C 606, F 134, F 137.
2664. property] attribute, characteristic quality; hence, character, nature.
that passion] i.e. fear.
2667. Watch] night watchmen, sentinels.
2669. Interrogatories] questions. To examine upon interrogatories represented a formal charge or accusation of wrongdoing.
2679. another ... going] Ironical: another fine dish being cooked, (or) another fine plot being carried off. (Possibly a play on mutton = "woman regarded as food for the satisfaction of man's sexual appetite" [Partridge, p. 151, and see Shakespeare, MM, III.ii.181-4].)
2693. but] than. ("Negative and interrogative sentences containing a comparative [esp. more] were formerly followed by but; they now usually take than, or else the comparative is omitted and but retained ... " [OED, but, 5].)
2699. heere's] Third person plural in -s preceding a plural subject (see Abbott, 333 and 335).
2713. all's one] no matter.
2715,
2716. a generall ... particular] Proverbial: Tilley cites this passage as an example of P 600 (The profit of the commonwealth should be preferred to a private pleasure).

[SCENE XIX]

2722. unroosted] out of bed. First citation in OED of unroost used in the figurative sense.
2729. as] such as.
2731. mettall] mettle: spirit, "spunk" (with a play on mettle = natural ardor, or abundance [and vigor] of semen. See Partridge, p. 148).
2735. trussed] (1) have the "points" or laces tied with which the hose were fastened to the doublet; (2) dressed generally.
2740. SD within] offstage, behind the scenes (as in ll. 2555 SD and 2565 SP).
2742. SD Rash aloft.] i.e. on the upper stage or at a window.
2744. slowch] Here, a lazy, idle fellow.
2749. has out-slept themselves] See Abbott, 333, 335.
2750. Wilde poppy] the milky juice of the field poppy, whose narcotic properties induce sleep.
2753,
2754. Lettice ... sleepie] Wild lettuce contains a juice called lettuce-opium or lactucarium, which was used as a drug. OED

	cites this passage as an example of *lettuce* used in this sense.
2755.	heigh ho!] A yawn.
2758.	As ... oyster] Possibly proverbial.
2766.	respective] attentive, heedful.
2767.	outrageous] angry.
2768.	buckle our selves] gird, prepare ourselves (perhaps with an allusion to the humorous sense of *unite ourselves in marriage*).
2770.	Me ... fellowes] it did not seem to me that our shins (legs) were matched (i.e. *alike* or *paired*).
2771.	metamorphosed] transformed; i.e. *exchanged*. stockings] hose. want of splendor] lack of light.
2772.	what's that *Splendor*?] who is this fellow called Splendor?
2773.	'tis ... candle] A Christmas candle is particularly large, capable of giving off much "splendor" (= *brightness, shining*, from the Latin *splendere* = *to shine*).
2774.	love] flatter.
2778.	To ... circumstance] "to beat about the bush."
2782.	untoward] inept, awkward.
2786.	had ... them] had gotten there ahead of them. Cf. Tilley, S 828 (*He has gotten the start of him*).
2796.	we ... night] we shall tease them about this before nightfall.
2798.	marl'd] marvelled. that] why.
2799.	th'ad] they had. unwrapt] Here, *thrown off*.
2801.	Maides ... wife] Possibly proverbial.
2808.	quartane ... me] A *quartan ague* described a fever in which a fit (paroxysm) occurs every fourth (in modern reckoning, every third) day (*OED*). Rash describes his anxiety over the impending dénouement in terms of fever symptoms. He is saying the equivalent of "the jig is up."
2814.	knavery] trickery, deception. what are you?] who are you? (Probably addressed to Staines.)
2817.	Hoy day!] hey-day!, an exclamation of surprise.
2817, 2818.	Hoy ... married?] Cf. W. Rowley[?], *A Match at Midnight* (in Hazlitt's ed. of Dodsley, *A Select Collection of Old English Plays*, Vol. XIII, V.i., p. 90): "Heyday, we are cheated by the rule, i' faith. / Now, sirrah, they day you are to be married too."
2821.	anone] straightway, directly (connoting *soon, from now on* here).
2822.	eene] Var. of *even*, used intensively or emphatically here, equivalent to *straight, directly*.
2826.	turne stinckard] become a stinker (someone to be avoided).
2828.	Ecce signum] Latin for *here is the sign*. A proverbial expression: Tilley, S 443. t'affirme] to confirm.
2830.	pleasant] merry, jocular. God morrow] God give you good morrow (cf. *God-night* in l. 2492).
2832.	geare] business.
2834.	Take ... nap] go back to bed for a second nap.
2837, 2838.	goes ... stomacke] Cf. Tilley, S 874: *To go against one's stomach*.

2839,
2840. Wood-cocke] Similar to a *snipe*, and "much esteemed for food" (*OED*). Also used to describe a "fool," like "cockscomb."
2848. Hee's ... Inck-horne] he's the author of this script, instigator of this plot (cf. note on 1. 2588). There seems to be no need to emend *penner*, appearing in *Q1-3*, to *pen*, as in Dodsley and all subsequent editions.
2850,
2852,
2854,
2858,
2862,
2873. SP *Sta.*] First emended by Dodsley from *Scat*. Most probably, the *Q1* readings are due to compositorial error, merely followed in *Q2-3*.
2858. flourishing] boastful, ostentatious (possibly connoting *manifest* here).
2862. duty] deference, respect due from.
2864. gracious] (1) acceptable; (2) prosperous.
2869. hote in expence] feverish or raging with extravagance.
2874. sufferance] sanction, consent.
2885. knave] Applied here to a male servant or menial in general, similar to *sirrah*.
2892. Sergeant] Emended from *Q1-H Sergeants* (cf. 2850 SD and 11. 2858, 2883).
2899. Tenter-hooke] A metal hook used in stretching cloth on a frame; here, figurative for *an arresting officer* (one who racks or tortures).
2901,
2902. colour ... knavery] excuse for his roguery (trickery). Cf. Tilley, C 419: *He has a cloak for his knavery*.
2905. Conny-catch ... wife] cheat or dupe a man out of his wife. Originally, a *cony-catcher* was one who snared rabbits.
2906. put it up] submit to it, tolerate it (as in 1. 2909).
2913. *vale*] Latin for *farewell*.
2916. all ... guests] i.e. the audience.
2917. well-temper'd bloods] well-balanced or well-tempered dispositions (connoting *reconciled minds* here).
Bacchus] The Roman god of wine and revelry. Cf. Tilley, W 461: *Good wine makes good blood*.
2919. these, Gentlemen,] Emended from *these Gentlemen* in *Q1-H*, as *these* here = *the characters in the play who are about to speak*, whereas *Gentlemen* = *the members of the audience*.
2922. kind enamouret] fond lover.
2925. doe best] perform my part in the best way.
2930. riot] recklessness, profligacy.
2931. civil] sober, seemly.
2933. clappe] applause (with a play on *gonorrhoea*). Cf. Tilley, C 404.
2935. please ... of] deign to be pleased by.

APPENDIX

From Lording Barry, *Ram-Alley or Merrie-Trickes* (1st. 4°, 1611), ed. Claude E. Jones, Materials for the Study of the Old English Drama, new series, 23 (Louvain: Librarie Universitaire, 1952), pp. 60-62, 11. 2149-2253. Speakers: Taffeta, William Smallshanks, Adriana (Taffeta's maid).

Taf. What would you sir with vs,
That on the suddaine, and so late you come.   2150
W.S. I haue some secrets to acquaint you with,
Please you to let the chamber maide shake off,
And stand as Centinel. *Taf.* It shall not need,
I hope I haue not brought her vp so ill,
But that she knowes how to containe your secrets,   2155
As well as I her Mistresse: Therefore on.
W.S. It is not fit forsooth that I should on,
Before she leaue the roome. *Adr.* Tis not indeed.
Therefore Ile waite in the with-drawing roome
Vntill you call. *Taf.* Now sir, what's your will?   2160
W.S. Deere widdow, pitty the state of a young,
Poore, yet propper Gentleman, by *Venus* pap
Vpon my knees I'de creepe vnto your lap
For one small drop of fauour, and though this face
Is not the finest face, yet t'as beene praisd   2165
By Ladies of good iudgment in faces.
Taf. Are these your secrets? *W.S.* You shall haue
    secrets
More pleasing, nay heere sweet widdow,
Some wantons doe delight to see men creepe,
And on their knees to woe them. *Taf.* I am none of those,   2170
Stand vp, I more desire a man should stand,
Then cringe and creepe that meanes to winne my loue,
I say stand vp, and let me goe ye'ad best.
W.S. For euer let me creepe vpon the ground,
Vnlesse you heere my sute. *Taf.* How now sir sawce.   2175
Would you be capring in your fathers saddle,
Away you casheerd yonger brother, begon,
Doe not I know the fashions of you all,
When a poore woman has laide open all
Her thoughts to you, then you grow proud and coy,   2180
But when wise maides dissemble and keepe close,
Then you poore snakes come creeping on your bellyes,
And with all oyled lookes prostrate your selues,
Before our beauties sunne, where once but warme,
Like hatefull snakes you strike vs with your stings,   2185
And then forsake vs, I know your tricks begon.
W.S. Foote Ile first be hang'd, nay if you go
You shall leaue your smock behinde you widdow,

Keepe close your womanish weapon, hold your tongue,
Nor speake, cough, sneeze or stampe, for if you doe,   2190
By this good blade Ile cut your throte directly,
Peace, stirre not, by Heauen Ile cut your throate
If you but stirre: speake not, stand still, go to,
Ile teach coy widdowes a new way to woe,
Come you shall kisse, why so, Ile stab by Heauen   2195
If you but stirre, now heere, first kisse againe,
Why so, stirre not, Now come I to the point,
My hopes are past, not can my present state,
Affoord a single halfe-penny, my father
Hates me deadly; to beg, my birth forbids,   2200
To steale, the law, the hang man, and the Rope
With one consent deny; to go a trust,
The Citty common-councell has forbad it,
Therefore my state is desperate, stirre not,
And I by much will rather choose to hang,   2205
Then in a ditch or prison-hole to starue,
Resolue, wed me, and take mee to your bed,
Or by my soule Ile straite cut off your head,
Then kill my selfe, for I had rather dye,
Then in a street liue poore and lowsily: 2210
Doe not I know you cannot loue my father.
A widdow that has knowne the *quid* of things,
To doate vpon an old and crased man,
That stinkes at both ends, worsse then an elder pype,
Who when his bloud and spirit are at the height,   2215
Hath not a member to his palsie body,
But is more limber then a Kings head pudding,
Tooke from the pot halfe sod doe I not know this?
Haue you not wealth enough, to serue vs both?
And am not I a pritty handsome fellow,   2220
To doe your drudgery, come, come, resolue.
For by my bloud, if you deny your bed,
Ile cut your throat, without equiuocation,
If you be pleased hold vp your finger, if not
By heauen Ile gar my whyniard through your weombe,   2225
Ist a match. *Taf.* Here me but speake. *W.S.* Youle prate
to loud.
Ta. No. *W.S.* Nor speake one word against my honest
sute.
Ta. No by my worth[.] *W.S.* Kisse vpon that and speake,
Ta. I dare not wed, men say yare naught youle cheate.
And you do keepe a whore. *W*[.]*S.* That is a lie,   2230
She keepes her selfe and me, yet I protest,
Shees not dishonest. *Ta.* How could she then maintaine you,
W.S. Why by her commings in, a little thing,
Her friends haue left her which with putting to best vse.
And often turning yeelds her a poore liuing,   2235
But what of that; shes now shooke off, to thee
Ile onely cleaue, Ile be thy marchant.
And to this welthy fayre, Ile bring my ware,
And here set vp my standing: therefore resolue,
Nought but my sword is left ift be a match,   2240
Clap hands, contract and straite to bed,

If not, pray, forgiue and straight goes off your head.
Ta. I take thy loue. *W.S.* Then straite lets both to bed.
Ta. Ile wed to morrow. *W.S.* You shall not sleepe vpont.
An honest contract is as good as marriadge.   2245
A bird in hand you know the prouerbe widdow,
Ta. To let me tell thee, Ile loue thee while I liue,
For this attempt giue me that lusty lad,
That winnes his widdow with his well drawne blade,
And not with oaths and words: a widdows woing,   2250
Not in bare words but should consist in doing,
I take thee to my husband. *W.S.* I thee to wife,
Now to thy bed and there weele end this strife.

BIBLIOGRAPHY: INTRODUCTION AND CRITICAL NOTES

Primary Sources

Barry, Lording. *Ram-Alley or Merrie-Trickes*. Ed. Claude E. Jones. Materials for the Study of the Old English Drama. New Series. Gen. ed. H. De Vocht. Vol. 23. Louvain: Librarie Universitaire, 1952.

Beaumont, Francis, and John Fletcher. *The Knight of the Burning Pestle*. Ed. Andrew Gurr. Fountainwell Drama Texts. Edinburgh: Oliver & Boyd, 1968.

Cooke, Jo[hn]. *Epigrames. Served Out in 52. Severall Dishes for Every Man To Tast without Surfeiting*. London: G. Elde, 1604.

----------. *Greene's Tu Quoque, or, The Cittie Gallant*. London: Pr. for John Trundle, 1614.

----------. *Greenes Tu Quoque, or The Cittie Gallant*. London: Pr. for Thomas Dewe, 1622.

----------. *Greenes Tu Quoque, or, The Cittie Gallant*. London: M. Flesher, n.d.

----------. *Green's Tu Quoque: or, The City Gallant*. Ed. R. Dodsley. A Select Collection of Old Plays. 1st. ed. London: R. Dodsley, 1744. Vol. III, 1-85.

----------. *Green's Tu Quoque: or, The City Gallant*. Ed. I. Reed. A Select Collection of Old Plays. 2nd. ed. London: J. Nichols, 1780. Vol. VII, 3-120.

----------. *Green's Tu Quoque: or, The City Gallant*. Ed. W. Scott [?]. The Ancient British Drama. London: James Ballantyne, 1810. Vol. II, 538-73.

----------. *Green's Tu Quoque: or, The City Gallant*. Ed. J.P. Collier. A Select Collection of Old Plays. 3rd. ed. Vol. VII, 1-99. London: S. Prowett, 1825.

----------. *The City Gallant*. Ed. W.C. Hazlitt. A Select Collection of Old English Plays. 4th. ed. Vol. XI, 173-289. London: Reeves & Turner, 1875.

----------[Thomas Heywood?]. *How a Man May Chuse a Good Wife from a Bad*. Ed. A.E.H. Swaen. Materialien zur Kunde des älteren englischen Dramas. Gen. ed. W. Bang. Band XXXV. Louvain: A. Uystpruyst, 1912.

Coryate, Thomas. *Coryats Crudities, Hastily Gobbled up in Five Months' Travels.* 2 vols. London: W. Stansby, 1611.

Dekker, Thomas, and Thomas Middleton. *1 The Honest Whore.* Ed. F. Bowers. *The Dramatic Works of Thomas Dekker.* Vol. II, 1-132. 1955; rev. ed. Cambridge, England: Cambridge Univ. Press, 1964.

Dekker, Thomas. *The Shoemaker's Holiday.* Ed. F. Bowers. *The Dramatic Works of Thomas Dekker.* Vol. I, 7-104. 1953; rpt. Cambridge, England: Cambridge Univ. Press, 1970.

Greene, Robert. *Friar Bacon and Friar Bungay.* Vol. XIV of The Malone Society Reprints. London: J. Johnson at the Oxford Univ. Press, 1926.

Harrison, William. *The Description of England*, Bk. II, ch. xi. In *The Renaissance in England.* Ed. H.E. Rollins and H. Baker. Boston: D.C. Heath, 1954, pp. 36-9.

Heywood, Thomas. *An Apology for Actors.* London: N. Okes, 1612.

Kyd, Thomas. *The Spanish Tragedy.* Ed. Thomas W. Ross. Fountainwell Drama Texts. Berkeley: Univ. of California Press, 1968.

Langbaine, Gerard. *An Account of the English Dramatick Poets.* Oxford: G. West & H. Clements, 1691.

Marlowe, Christopher. *Hero and Leander.* London: A. Islip, 1598.

----------. *1 and 2 Tamburlaine the Great.* Ed. John D. Jump. Regents Renaissance Drama Series. Lincoln: Univ. of Nebraska Press, 1967.

Massinger, Philip. *A New Way to Pay Old Debts.* Ed. M. St. Clare Byrne. London: Univ. of London, Athlone Press, 1956.

Matthew. The King James Version of The Holy Bible. New York: The American Bible Society, n.d.

Middleton, Thomas. *Michaelmas Term.* Ed. Richard Levin. Regents Renaissance Drama Series. Lincoln: Univ. of Nebraska Press, 1966.

----------. *Your Five Gallants.* London: G. Elde, 1608.

Rowley, William[?]. *A Match at Midnight.* In *A Select Collection of Old English Plays.* 4th. ed. Ed. W.C. Hazlitt. Vol. XIII, 1-98. London: Reeves & Turner, 1875.

----------. *A Merrie and Pleasant Comedy: Never Before Printed, Called A Shoo-maker a Gentleman.* London: I. Okes, 1638.

Shakespeare, William. *The Riverside Shakespeare.* Ed. G.B. Evans et. al. Boston: Houghton Mifflin, 1974.

Stow, John. *A Survay of London.* London: John Wolfe, 1598.

Stubbes, Philip. *The Anatomie of Abuses*. London: Richard Iohnes [Jones], 1595.

Webster, John. *The Tragedy of the Duchess of Malfi*. Ed. F.L. Lucas. *The Complete Works of John Webster*. Boston: Houghton Mifflin; New York: Chatto & Windus, 1928. Vol. II, 3-210.

----------. *The White Divel, or The Tragedy of Paulo Giordano Ursini, Duke of Brachiano, with The Life and Death of Vittoria Corombona the Famous Venetian Courtesan*. Ed. F.L. Lucas. *The Complete Works of John Webster*. Boston: Houghton Mifflin; New York: Chatto & Windus, 1928. Vol. I, 67-288.

Secondary Sources

Abbott, E.A. *A Shakespearian Grammar*. 3rd. rev. ed. 1870; rpt. New York: Dover Publications, 1966.

Baskervill, Charles R. *The Elizabethan Jig and Related Song Drama*. Chicago: The Univ. of Chicago Press, 1929.

The Cambridge History of English Literature. Ed. Sir A.W. Ward and A.R. Waller. 1917; rpt. Cambridge, England: Cambridge Univ. Press; New York: Macmillan, 1933. Vol. VI. *The Drama to 1642*: Part Two.

Chambers, E.K. *The Elizabethan Stage*. 4 vols. Oxford: Clarendon Press, 1923.

Colman, E.A.M. *The Dramatic Use of Bawdy in Shakespeare*. London: Longman Group Ltd., 1974.

The Dictionary of National Biography. Ed. Sir L. Stephen and Sir S. Lee. 1917; rpt. London: Oxford Univ. Press, 1959-60. Vols. XVIII and XIX.

Gibbons, Brian. *Jacobean City Comedy: A Study of Satiric Plays by Jonson, Marston and Middleton*. Cambridge, Mass.: Harvard Univ. Press, 1968.

Greg, W.W. *A Bibliography of the English Printed Drama to the Restoration*. 1891; rpt. London: Oxford Univ. Press, 1939. Vol. I.

----------. *Dramatic Documents from the Elizabethan Playhouses*. 1931; rpt. Oxford: Clarendon Press, 1969. Vol. I.

Harbage, Alfred. *Shakespeare and the Rival Traditions*. New York: Macmillan, 1952.

Leggatt, Alexander. *Citizen Comedy in the Age of Shakespeare*. Toronto and Buffalo: Univ. of Toronto Press, 1973.

McKerrow, Ronald B. *An Introduction to Bibliography for Literary Students*. 1927; 2nd. impression 1928; rpt. Oxford: Clarendon Press, 1964.

----------. "Edward Allde as a Typical Trade Printer." *The Library.*
4th. ser. *Transactions of the Bibliographical Society*, X, No. 2
(Sept. 1929), 121-62.

McTear, J.S. "Gleek: A Forgotten Old Game." *The Gentleman's Magazine.*
Ed. S. Urban. London: Chatto & Windus. Vol. 287 (Oct. 1899),
358-67.

Miller, C. William. "A London Ornament Stock: 1598-1683." *Studies
in Bibliography*: Papers of the Bibliographical Society of the
University of Virginia. Ed. F. Bowers. Charlottesville: The
Univ. Press of Virginia. Vol. VII (1955), 125-51.

Nungezer, Edwin. *A Dictionary of Actors and Other Persons Associated
with the Public Representation of Plays in England before 1642.*
New Haven: Yale Univ. Press, 1929.

Onions, C.T. *A Shakespeare Glossary.* 1911; 2nd. rev. ed. London:
Clarendon Press of Oxford Univ. Press, 1953.

The Oxford Dictionary of English Proverbs. 3rd. ed. Comp. W.G. Smith.
Ed. F.P. Wilson. London: Oxford Univ. Press, 1970.

The Oxford English Dictionary. 13 vols. Ed. J.A.H. Murray, H. Bradley
et. al. 1933; rpt. Oxford: Clarendon Press, 1961.

Partridge, Eric. *Shakespeare's Bawdy.* 1947; rev. and enl. ed.
London: Routledge & Kegan Paul, 1968.

Pollard, A.W., and G.R. Redgrave. *A Short-Title Catalogue of Books
Printed in England, Scotland, and Ireland, and of English Books
Printed Abroad, 1475-1640.* London: The Bibliographical Society,
1926.

Reynolds, George F. *The Staging of Elizabethan Plays at the Red Bull
Theater, 1605-1625.* The Modern Language Association of America.
General Series IX. New York: MLA; London: Oxford Univ. Press,
1940.

Schelling, F.E. *Elizabethan Playwrights.* 1925; rpt. New York:
Benjamin Blom, 1965.

Spevack, Marvin. *The Harvard Concordance to Shakespeare.* 1973; rpt.
Cambridge, Mass.: Belknap Press of Harvard Univ. Press, 1974.

Stone, Lilly C. "English Sports and Recreations." Folger Booklets
on Tudor and Stuart Civilization. Washington: The Folger
Shakespeare Library, 1960.

Sugden, E.H. *A Topographical Dictionary to the Works of Shakespeare
and His Fellow Dramatists.* Manchester: Manchester Univ. Press,
1925.

Tilley, Morris Palmer. *A Dictionary of the Proverbs in England in
the Sixteenth and Seventeenth Centuries.* Ann Arbor: Univ. of
Michigan Press, 1950.

Wright, Louis B. *Middle-Class Culture in Elizabethan England.*
1935; rpt. Ithaca: Cornell Univ. Press, 1958.

For Product Safety Concerns and Information please contact our EU
representative GPSR@taylorandfrancis.com
Taylor & Francis Verlag GmbH, Kaufingerstraße 24, 80331 München, Germany

www.ingramcontent.com/pod-product-compliance
Lightning Source LLC
Chambersburg PA
CBHW052120300426
44116CB00010B/1738